ESCAPE IN AMERICA

Escape in America

The British Convention Prisoners
1777–1783

RICHARD SAMPSON

Picton Publishing, 1995

© Richard Sampson

First published in 1995
by
Picton Publishing (Chippenham) Limited

ISBN 0 948251 77 8

Set in Monotype Bembo by
Carnegie Publishing Ltd, 18 Maynard St, Preston
Printed and bound in the United Kingdom by
Picton Publishing (Chippenham) Limited
Queensbridge Cottages
Patterdown, Chippenham
Wiltshire SN15 2NS
Telephone (01249) 443430

Other Works by Richard Sampson

They Came to Northern Rhodesia
A record of 875 Europeans who entered Northern Rhodesia
(now Zambia) by 1902.
Library of Congress RL S 015515

So This Was Lusaakas
A history of the capital of Northern Rhodesia
(now Zambia) to 1936. 1st edn Library of Congress 77–247949
2nd edn Library of Congress 75–316830

The Man with a Toothbrush in his Hat
The story of George Copp Westbeech, the first permanent European
settler in the territory later known as North-West Rhodesia
(now Zambia)
Library of Congress 75–320576

Contents

Illustrations

A secret message from Clinton to Burgoyne. A seemingly innocuous letter turns into a military opinion.

Clinton Papers, William L. Clements Library

The Americans
    Major General George Washington
    Major General Philip Schuyler
    Major General Horatio Gates
    Major General William Heath

The British
    Lieutenant General John Burgoyne
    General William Howe
    Lord George Germain
    All from the William L. Clements Library

Major General William Phillips, R.A.
    National Army Museum
Described by George Washington as "a dangerous man"

Major General Clinton
    National Army Museum
Always a friend of the Convention Prisoners

Lieutenant James Moody rescuing Private Robert Maxwell from Newton, Sussex County, New Jersey Jail.
    National Army Museum
From a 1785 painting.

Maps

Introduction

D URING the War of American Independence and following the British defeat at Saratoga in 1777, Lieutenant General Burgoyne's army laid down their arms under a treaty which became known as the Convention of Saratoga. The terms of that treaty allowed Burgoyne's surviving Canadian and Loyalist soldiers to march back to Canada, while the British and German troops were to go to Boston and wait there for vessels to take them back to Europe. Before the British and Germans could sail, American politicians suspended the treaty and this led to the incarceration of Burgoyne's army for more than five years.

Sir Edward Creasy, quite correctly, and despite the comparatively small numbers involved, included the Battle of Saratoga in his Fifteen Decisive Battles of the World. The battle transformed what had been a British civil war, into a conflict between the leading maritime nations for the domination of the seas. Its historical importance has been recognised by historians of both sides and they have researched in depth, Burgoyne's strategy, the battle itself, and the related political wrangling. What has not been given adequate attention is the impact of the battle and the subsequent politics on the surviving ordinary British soldiers. This book is an attempt to meet that deficiency.

When, Sir John Fortescue in his monumental History of the British Army, referred to the prisoners, he wrote,

> . . . although there were a few men who purchased comfort at the price of desertion, the majority stuck faithfully to their officers, or escaped and made their way to the British Army at New York. Finally in 1781, the men, by direct infringement of the capitulation, were seperated from their officers, and vanished no man knows whither.

Since Fortescue wrote those words some 80 years ago, much additional information has been uncovered, which has assisted in reaching a better understanding of what happened to a large number of these men. Curiously, it has been American historians who have shown the most interest in their story. Two doctoral dissertations, George W. Knepper's, "The Convention Army, 1777–1783", and "After Saratoga; The Story of the Convention Army" by William M. Dabney, both written in 1954, showed that the story of the experiences of the prisoners needed to be told. These have been followed by other valuable American studies on different aspects of the subject. On the other hand, apart from passing references, most British military historians appear to have been satisfied to "write off" these men, with only a limited interest exhibited in their story.

All British soldiers made prisoners in America appear to have escaped in large numbers, but the Convention Prisoners are of particular interest. From being a privileged group, with rights to be repatriated home, their fortunes steadily declined until they became hostages to the political aims of the American Congress. Most other prisoners of war who had not escaped were eventually exchanged, but apart from invalids and officers' servants, the Convention Prisoners had to remain captive until the war was over. The price set for their freedom was that Britain had to recognise Congress as a sovereign government, which she refused to do until her final defeat was brought about by the intervention of the French army and navy.

During their incarceration, the other ranks suffered great hardships, including semi-starvation and lack of adequate shelter in winter conditions. Many died from a variety of causes. The American army cannot be blamed for that. Their own men were not much better off. It is only when we come to the demands and attitude of the politicians, can any criticism be levelled. After suspending on spurious grounds the treaty negotiated by their victorious general, Congress foisted the prisoners on individual states who had neither the organisation or food supplies to make provision for their subsistence. This had a calamitous impact on both the prisoners and the communities in which they were forced to live. The only relief available to the prisoners was to escape or desert.

Discipline in the eighteenth-century British army was undoubtedly savage, and many officers, up to the time of, and including, Wellington, have spoken very disparagingly about the character of their men. This was not so in Burgoyne's army. A remarkable degree of affection and mutual respect existed between the regimental officers and the soldiers. On many occasions, the officers broke the terms of their parole in helping their men to escape. In the eighteenth century, a breach of parole in this way, was considered highly dishonourable on the part of an officer. In other instances, we find them giving the soldiers money from their own pockets to buy food and clothing. This attitude may have been due to Burgoyne training his officers in the management of their men. In that respect Burgoyne was far ahead of his times. On the other hand, I have come to suspect that, despite the oft-repeated adverse comments made by officers, such relationships probably existed in many British regiments. The small British army could not have achieved what it did in the eighteenth and nineteenth centuries, if it were otherwise.

The escape incidents described have been selected from four British intelligence books, papers of the British Adjutant General, miscellaneous American sources, and from a Board of Enquiry minutes. During the latter enquiry, the men would have been subjected to cross examination by the Judge Advocate. In several cases the stories are supported with independent evidence.

One of the reasons little attention has been given to the conduct of the prisoners, has been the word "desertion". There was no such word as escape in the eighteenth-century British army. If a man left his regiment for any reason without permission, it was termed desertion. If he was trying to regain an active British army to continue the fight, it was still termed desertion. To meet the unusual situation of the mass escapes which took place, Burgoyne, in a speech made to Parliament, had to resort to the term "honourable deserters". Where evidence shows a man leaving with the intention of regaining active service I have called it escape and not desertion.

The high level of succesful escapes is surprising. While getting away from camps and marching columns was comparatively easy, obtaining assistance from the local population was always a matter of chance. Although perhaps as many as a third of the American population supported the British cause, Congress, its army, state committees and governments were ruthless towards any of their people caught helping escaped prisoners. The retribution meted out to them, was frequently equal in ferocity to that which existed in occupied Europe in the twentieth century. There was no appeal from the sentences levied by the various American courts martial, committees and local courts.

Two individuals stand-out in this story. The first is George Washington. Recognising the unique methods of escape some of the British soldiers were using, it was only his personal intervention that stopped the number of escapes escalating still further. He had great difficulty in making his officers understand what the British soldiers were up to. His correspondence on the subject is illuminating! The second person of special note is Major General William Phillips, who during the campaign was second-in-command under Burgoyne. After the defeat and when Burgoyne was paroled, Phillips took command of the prisoners. In spite of official British policy for the men to stay put, he appears to have encouraged "desertion", or at the very least, he certainly did nothing to stop it. At the same time he was telling British headquarters that the men were well behaved. To the Americans he was pleading his inability to stop the men escaping.

This work can only be considered a start on the subject of the escape of the British Convention Prisoners. We still do not know how many prisoners there were in the first place; how many died; how many were exchanged; how many truly deserted and how many escaped. The few surviving muster rolls and strength returns prepared for various purposes, frequently contradict each other. However, what I have tried to show is that many of the men who in the past have been considered to be deserters, were nothing of the sort.

Very little is contained herein concerning the German prisoners. Their attitude to the war was much different to that of the British soldiers. Large numbers of Germans did desert, although there were remarkable exceptions, including some who trekked hundreds of miles to Canada to join up with Loyalist "commando" units. To do their story justice, a German-speaking researcher needs to discover and translate German language documents. Likewise there is very little in this work concerning the British officers. Their story is well documented and because of eighteenth-century protocol of parole and exchange, their experiences in the main, were much different from that of their men.

To make it quite clear who is being referred to, I have used the word Loyalist for Americans who supported the British. At the time, they, (and sometimes their opponents), were often referred to in the British army, as Provincials. Likewise, the opponents of the British, were often referred to as rebels, which was much disliked by them. I have called them Americans. I have also avoided the use of slang terms prevalent at the time when Loyalists were "Cow Boys" and the Americans were "Skinners".

When showing quotations, I have changed capital letters to lower case and vice versa, so as to make them conform with modern practice and at the same time, easier to read. Spelling, grammar and punctuation in the quotations, have been left as originally written.

In appendix 5, I have listed by name several hundred of the men who escaped, or who were caught after attempting to escape. A few who are specially identified, were not strictly Convention Prisoners, because they were first captured shortly before the signing of the Convention. They have been included because they are part of the main story. Others who turned up in New York, have been omitted as they may have arrived as exchanged officers' servants, rather than by escape. The list is by no means complete. In many surviving records, both successful escapees and those who were recaptured, are often recorded by count rather than by name. Furthermore the spelling of family names in the eighteenth century had not been completely standardised and this has caused some confusion. Often, the names of men referred to, were spelled in several ways. In these cases, for the purposes of the list, I have selected the form in most common use today. At the same time, so as to avoid duplication as far as possible, I have omitted some names found, where there is an impression that a man may already be listed under a variation of the same name.

1995

Richard Sampson
Salem, South Carolina.

Appreciation

THIS book could never have been adequately researched and completed without the active support and interest of G. Kenneth Yates, formerly of Westford, Massachusetts, and now a near neighbour. Not only is Ken Yates a descendant of one of the Convention Prisoners, but he is also an authority on the men of the British 47th Foot during the War of American Independence. That regiment was one of those subjected to the Convention of Saratoga. Apart from giving much advice on the subject, he frequently directed me towards records and documents which proved invaluable to my research.

Likewise I am indebted to John M Houlding, a notable authority on the British army, who on more than one occasion pointed me in the right direction. In addition his prizewinning book Fit for Service provided much additional back-ground material on the eighteenth-century British army.

The services of the following Government and Educational Institutions all played essential parts in the preparation of this work; The Canadian Archives and National Library in Ottawa, Canada; the William L Clements Library and Graduate Library at the University of Michigan in Ann Arbor; the New York Public Library and the New York Historical Association in New York; the University of Virginia Library and the Albermarle County Historical Society in Charlottesville; the Pennsylvania Historical Society, Philadelphia; the Sussex County Historical Society, Newton, New Jersey; the Newberry Library in Chicago; the libraries at Clemson University, Clemson and the University of South Carolina, Columbia; the Library of Congress, Washington DC; special mention must also be made of the help of the National Army Museum and Public Records Office in London.

I also want to thank the Librarians and their staffs of the Vernon Area Public Library in Illinois and the Oconee County Library in South Carolina, who ably assisted me over a period of several years in obtaining through the inter-library loan service, long out of print books and articles.

Others who provided assistance included the numerous municipalities and historical societies of the towns and villages on the routes taken by the Convention Prisoners when being marched through the various states. Their patience in answering my questions is very much appreciated.

I would like to thank Brian Follack and Brian Hubner for permission to use their map of Burgoyne's campaign, which first appeared in the Journal of the Society for Army Historical Research.

While the structure of the book and opinions expressed by me are solely my own, I must also mention the names of friends and neighbours who were "conscripted" by me to read the various drafts and who made numerous valuable suggestions. They were Major General James M. Bunting (US Army Retired), Cyril H. Ford, William F. Kelly, Robert W. Lindgren and Keith A. E. Sacre. Each in their various ways contributed thoughts and ideas which were very helpful.

Finally I must express my appreciation to my family and friends, who over the years have had to bear with patience my enthusiasm about the subject.

Richard Sampson

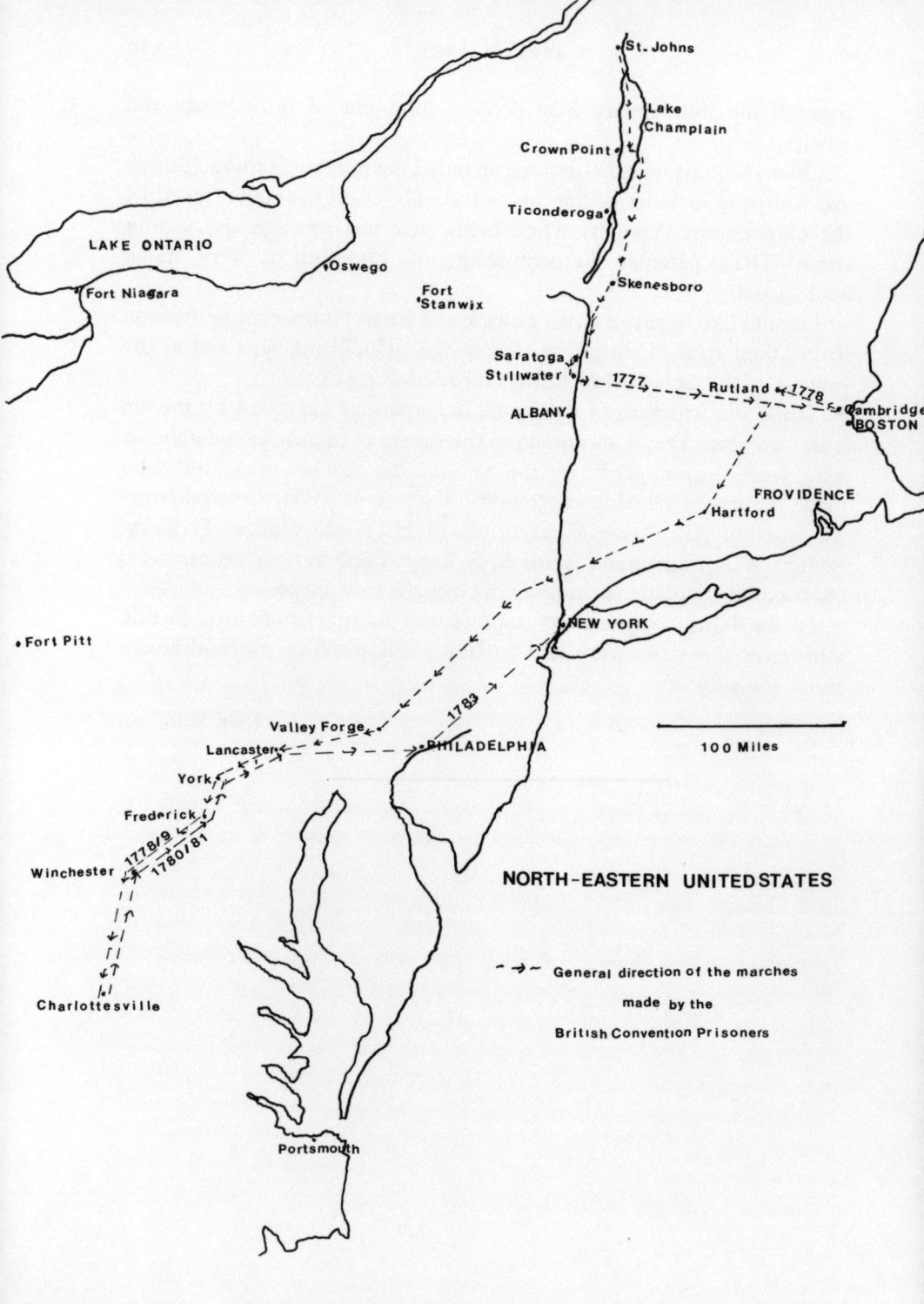

St. Johns

Lake
Champlain

Crown Point

Ticonderoga

Skenesboro

LAKE ONTARIO

Oswego

Fort Niagara

Fort
Stanwix

Saratoga
Stillwater _ 1777 _ Rutland _ 1778 _ Cambridge
BOSTON

ALBANY

PROVIDENCE

Hartford

Fort Pitt

NEW YORK

Valley Forge _ 1783

Lancaster

PHILADELPHIA

York

100 Miles

Frederick

Winchester _ 1778/9 _ 1780/81

NORTH-EASTERN UNITED STATES

Charlottesville

- - ► General direction of the marches

made by the

British Convention Prisoners

Portsmouth

CHAPTER I

The March to Disaster

L IEUTENANT General John Burgoyne, leading his polyglot force of British, Germans, Canadians, Loyalists and Indians, was elated with a string of minor victories and the ease with which he had pushed the Americans aside. At Skenesboro (now Whitehall) on Sunday 13th July 1777, he ordered services of thanksgiving for the army; to be followed in the evening by a 'Feu du Joie' using both cannon and muskets. When news of the advance arrived some five weeks later, London also celebrated. Betting odds on whether American Independence would be recognised, moved from even money before receipt of the news, to a subsequent five to one against. Some of the American Loyalists who had taken refuge in England began booking their passages back to New York, so as to be on hand when Royal Authority was re-established. The King expressed his satisfaction by rushing into his wife's room exclaiming, "that he had beaten all the Americans."[1]

Even while Burgoyne was celebrating, the British strategy was already impossible to achieve and destined for defeat.

The intentions were simple enough—on paper. Partly initiated by Burgoyne himself when in London the year before, it called for an army to drive southwards from Canada, by way of Lakes Champlain and George, and thence down the Hudson River to Albany. To add weight, a small force of Loyalists and Indians under Colonel Barry St. Leger would also move south by way of Lake Ontario and the Mohawk River, linking up with the main force where that river joins the Hudson. The prime object of the strategy was to join the army from Canada with that under General Sir William Howe in New York City. Thus would be established a chain of military posts along the 300 miles of wilderness and isolated farm lands lying between the Canadian settlements and New York. In this way the belligerent New England colonies would be separated from those, supposedly less intractable, further south. While the strategy dictated no additional mandatory objectives, it did recognise that a successful joining of forces would open up more than one opportunity of bringing an end to the rebellion.[2]

From the very beginning, the whole strategy was marred by poor planning and administrative confusion. The Minister in London responsible for directing the American War was Lord George Germain, the Secretary of State for the American Colonies. Germain had changed his name from Sackville in order to benefit under a will. It was in his former name that after commanding the cavalry at Minden in 1759, he was court martialled for disobeying orders. He was adjudged "unfit to serve his Majesty in any military capacity whatever." Despite that sentence, politics, influence, George III and perhaps, on occasion, some real ability on his own part, Germain had since risen to the de facto position of commander of all the troops in America. Whether or not his court martial sentence was justified, he demonstrated both at Minden and during the early years of the American War, a casual approach to matters and a lack of a sense of urgency. Not only was he ignorant of operational conditions in America, he ignored the difficulty in trying to direct a war 3,000 miles away. At that time, a communication between America and London took an average of six weeks in either direction, which meant a three month wait for a reply to be received on any matter. A good share of the blame for the disaster must be laid at his door, in attempting to direct a war in such a manner.[3]

Germain issued firm instructions to Burgoyne to proceed with his advance to Albany. This order was issued despite that Howe, showing a complete disregard for the difficult task proposed for Burgoyne, had already informed London he intended to move south to attack Philadelphia, (then the second largest city in the British Empire); he would leave only a limited garrison under the command of Major General Sir Henry Clinton in New York City. In his correspondence with Howe, Germain gave him discretion as to what course to take. It seems that both Germain and Howe ignored problems which would arise should Burgoyne need assistance.

Burgoyne however, also cannot be absolved from blame as to what happened. Three months before he left Canada, he knew of Howe's intentions, but nothing would stop him. He held that his orders were firm. Although his correspondence shows some doubts he did nothing to have them changed. To the time of his final defeat he demonstrated a blind over-confidence in the numbers he would require to carry out his purpose.

Notwithstanding the poor planning and lack of cohesion, the forces available to Great Britain were quite insufficient to achieve the objects of the strategy. Even if a link-up of the Northern and the New York armies had been accomplished, it is extremely doubtful whether a series of military posts along the Hudson River could have survived for long. Even before the defeat at Saratoga, the Americans, taking advantage of one foggy morning, captured the British camp outside Ticonderoga and other isolated groups of soldiers at Lake George. The British Command had still not appreciated the difficulties in fighting a large scale guerilla war. It has been estimated that the colony of Massachusetts alone, could have put into the field for short periods of time, some 30,000 militia. Although these were no match for the trained British and German soldiers in a set-piece battle, the sheer weight of their numbers would have overwhelmed the small British forces available for garrison purposes along the river.

Burgoyne himself, received at least one view that the strategy would not work. John Wilkes, an American meeting with him in Bath, England in the winter of 1776/7, learning he was intending to carry out his advance to Albany, said to him, "Why, then, you will as certainly be taken a prisoner by Arnold; pray accept a letter from me to Hancock." But Burgoyne would have none of it.

Burgoyne, born in 1723, is believed to have joined the army at the age of 15. After selling his commission in 1741, he re-joined the army as a cornet in the Royal Dragoons in 1744. Transferring to the 11th Dragoons, he saw his first active service in the Seven Years War, when he took part in two short-lived landings on the French coast in 1758. In the following year he took the financial risk of forming a new regiment, the 16th Light Dragoons. As a Brigadier General, he commanded a successful campaign in Portugal against the Spanish in 1761 and following this he was elected a Member of Parliament. In his leadership of the 16th he was probably a hundred years ahead of his times with regard to the treatment of other ranks. Starting with the proposition that "English soldiers are to be treated as thinking beings," he gave his officers detailed instructions on their relationship with the men, impressing on them the manner in which to impose discipline and stressing the importance of the men's welfare. This attention to their well-being made him very popular with his soldiers and there was no doubt that he was a "soldiers' general."

Germaine had detailed the regiments which were to form Burgoyne's invasion force. They were:

British Infantry

9th Foot	24th Foot	53rd Foot
20th Foot	47th Foot	62nd Foot
21st Foot		

In addition, he ordered that the flank companies, (i.e. the Grenadier and Light Companies) of certain British regiments stationed in Canada, were to be added to the force. These were from the 29th, 31st and 34th Foot. Despite being parts of British regiments, in Burgoyne's army these companies were usually referred to as the "Canadian Companies." Later the two flank companies of the 53rd also came under the same designation when the remaining companies of that regiment by chance escaped the defeat when left on the lines of communication and were able to retreat into Canada. The strength of a British infantry regiment at the time consisted of 477 men of all ranks. This figure included three "contingent" men for each company, i.e. fictitious men allowed to cover the Colonels' recruiting expenses. In America, very few regiments were able to maintain the authorised strength.

British Artillery
    One battalion of Royal Artillery

German Troops (mostly from Brunswick and Hesse-Hanau)
    5 Infantry regiments
    1 Regiment of Dragoons (mostly unmounted)
    1 Regiment of Artillery

The Brunswick Dragoons having few horses proved to be of little value. Dressed in leather pantaloons, high boots, gauntlets and carrying heavy swords and short carbines, they were obliged to march and drill the same as infantry. One description claims their hats weighed as much as the equipment of a light infantryman. The quality of the Brunswick troops was very mixed. When inspected before leaving Europe, one observer said, "far from making a fine body of men, having a great number of small and ill-looking and many old people among them." In addition their uniforms were old and tattered.

Burgoyne experienced man-power difficulties even before he left Canada. Major General Sir Guy Carleton, who commanded there, found great difficulty in bringing the units up to strength. He had his own problems in defending a line of forts protecting Canada, stretching from Maine to Fort Detroit. Although he had been disappointed in not being given the command of the invasion, he had loyally supported Burgoyne in finding as many men as he could muster. By chance, Lieutenant Nutt (33rd), had arrived in Canada with 154 young recruits destined for the 33rd Foot and other regiments forming part of Howe's army. Instead of sending them around to New York by sea, Carleton tacked them on to Burgoyne's army. Later, while the latter moved southwards, additional companies, amounting to some 300 recruits for Burgoyne's regiments arrived from Europe and again Carleton hurried them on to join the force.

In addition, 148 French-speaking Canadian light infantry (the Voltigeurs) and small detachments of the King's Loyal Americans, the Queens Loyal Rangers and the Loyal Volunteers were included. Burgoyne refused to take with him The Royal Highland Emigrants on the grounds of their unreliability. A more likely explanation was his prejuidice against their commander and many of the men who had Jacobite leanings and had been with Bonnie Prince Charlie in the Netherlands after 1745.

The problem with numbers was compounded by the huge artillery train that Burgoyne took with him. He thought the guns would be needed to reduce the fort at Ticonderoga. There would also be other defensive works which, it was assumed, the Americans would erect to bar his advance. The 257 artillerymen he had with him, were quite insufficient to handle the number of guns. These already included 40 infantrymen who had been drafted from the 24th Foot, his most valuable infantry regiment due to its training in light infantry work. He had no option but to hurriedly train as gunners, Lieutenant Nutt's raw infantry recruits. This further reduced his already meagre infantry. As it happened, most of the artillery proved of little use. Burgoyne left Canada with less than 10,000 men, of whom 1,100 were Canadian civilians

employed by contractors. These were wagon drivers together with
bateaux men led by a small group of Royal Navy personnel. He took
with him 500 wagons for supplies, with additional wagons to portage
the boats where rapids prevented their use. His transport train was
"many miles in length."

The wagons also caused him difficulties. They were two wheeled
"Canadian Carts" and no less than 1,000 horses were needed to pull
them. An additional 400 horses were required for the artillery train.
Burgoyne was late in requisitioning the carts, and this tardiness caused
them to be constructed of unseasoned wood, resulting in repeated delays
due to maintenance. In addition there never were enough horses, this
shortage being the main reason for him subsequently ordering the
ill-fated foray to Bennington, which was to cost him almost 20 percent
of his infantry.

Following his celebration at Skenesboro, Burgoyne now made the
first of a series of tactical errors, which compounded the difficulties
inherent in the British strategy. Instead of moving back to Ticonderoga
and floating his army down Lake George, he decided that only his
artillery and stores would take that direction; his infantry would march
overland from Skenesboro to Fort Edward, the very route he had
rejected earlier when planning the strategy. While there appeared little
difference between the two alternatives, and although the marching
route between the two places was only 23 miles, this decision gave the
American General Philip Schuyler, the opportunity of delaying
Burgoyne by putting to work a thousand men. They destroyed bridges
over the streams, at the same time felling trees every 10 or 12 yards
to block the road. These tactics, together with the transport problems,
so delayed the British Army that they did not reach Fort Edward until
29th July. Further delays were experienced in gathering a sufficient
supply of food needed for the onward march.[4]

Philip Schuyler, a wealthy estate owner of Dutch descent, had fought
a defensive campaign, dropping back before the British, keeping his
small force intact. While he had intended to maintain his position at
Ticonderoga, his subordinate, Brigadier General Arthur St. Clair had
allowed the British to place their artillery in a position making the
defence of the historic fort impossible. The subsequent evacuation led
to the series of battles and skirmishes, extending as far south as Fort

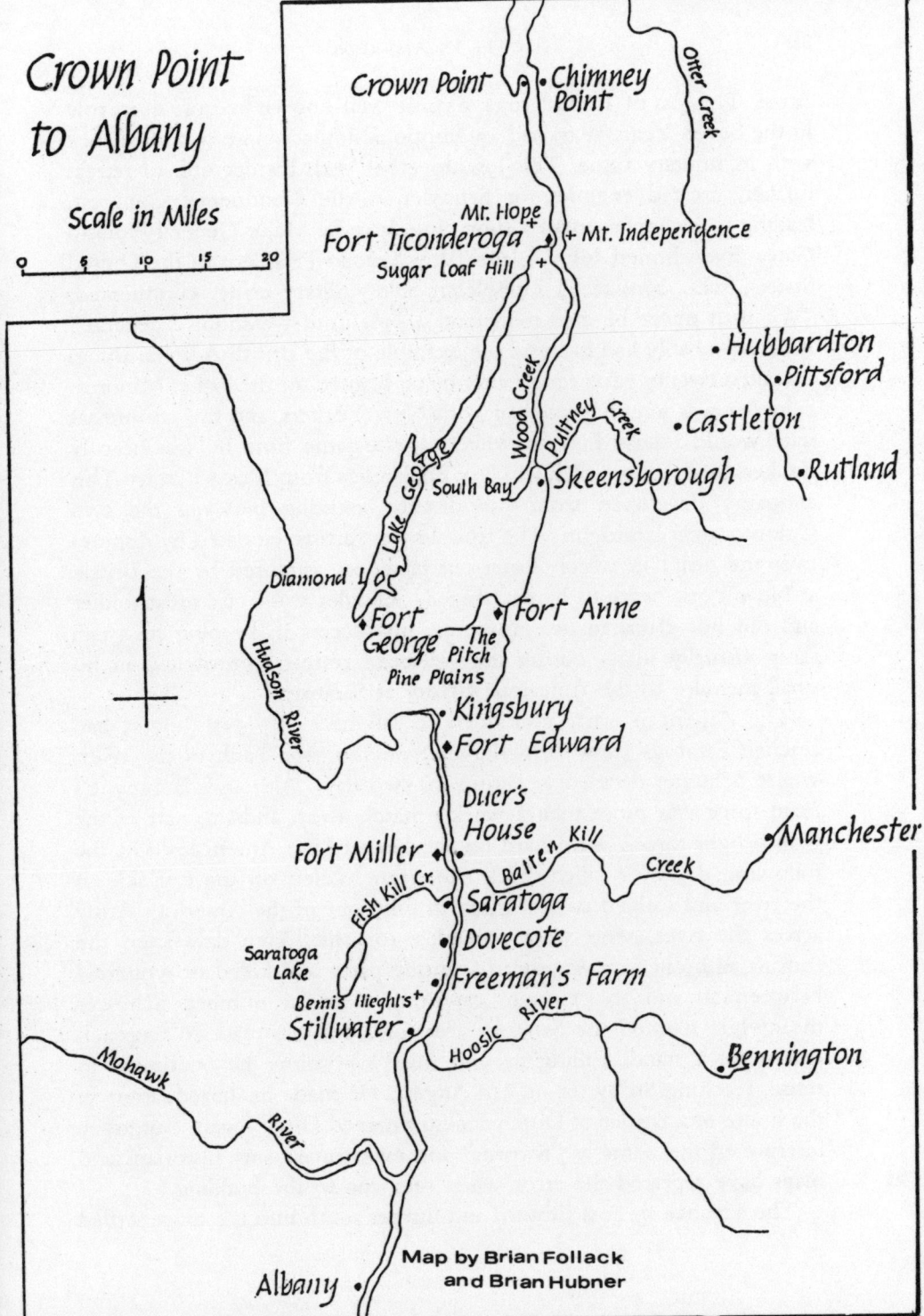

Crown Point
to Albany

Scale in Miles

0   5   10   15   20

Crown Point • • Chimney Point

Otter Creek

Mt. Hope +
Fort Ticonderoga   + Mt. Independence
Sugar Loaf Hill   +

• Hubbardton
• Pittsford
• Castleton
• Rutland

Wood Creek

Putney Creek

Lake George

South Bay   • Skeensborough

Diamond I.

Hudson River

• Fort Anne
Fort George   The Pitch
Pine Plains

• Kingsbury
♦ Fort Edward

Duer's House

Fort Miller ♦   ♦   Batten Kill   Creek   • Manchester

Fish Kill Cr.
• Saratoga
Saratoga Lake   • Dovecote
Bemis Hieghts +   • Freeman's Farm
Stillwater   Hoosic River

Mohawk River   • Bennington

Albany •   Map by Brian Follack
and Brian Hubner

Anne. The loss of Ticonderoga, a name well-known because of its role in the Seven Years War, had an emotional impact quite out of balance with its military value. This loss, together with his decision to retreat further, created enemies for Schuyler in the Continental Congress, leading to his replacement a short time later by Major General Horatio Gates. Even honest John Adams (later Second President of the United States), who considered himself an able military critic, commented, "We shall never be able to defend a post until we shoot a general." Adams probably had in mind the example of the British Admiral Byng, executed twenty years earlier after being blamed for the loss of Minorca. Schuyler was intensely popular with New Yorkers, and men from that state would follow him anywhere; at the same time he was heartily disliked by the more plebian New Englanders from Massachusetts. This antipathy developed from the disputes existing between the two Colonies over landrights. The trouble was further escalated by disputes over the order in which American prisoners, captured by the British at New York, were to be exchanged. Schuyler was not a great soldier and did not claim to be. However, his success in keeping his small army virtually intact during the weeks of retreat, contributed in no small measure to the American victory at Saratoga.[5]

The American army continued to fall back. By 31st July it had reached Saratoga (now Schuylerville) on the west bank of the river, where Schuyler decided to lay up for two days. Although Burgoyne's main force was more than a week's march away, Indians, part of the British light forces, were hard on the heels of the Americans. On the following day they killed three American soldiers on the east side of the river and scalped two of them in full sight of the American Army across the river, who were powerless to assist. Two days later, the Indians ambushed an American scouting party and killed or wounded between 20 and 30 of them, capturing a similar number. Schuyler meanwhile scouted the Saratoga area for a suitable place to entrench and make a stand. Failing to find such a position, he continued to retire, reaching Stillwater on 3rd August. He made his headquarters in the house of a farmer of Dutch ancestry named Dirck Swart. Burgoyne interpreted the name as "Swords" and ever since many historians and maps have repeated the error when referring to the building.[6]

The advance to Fort Edward and further south into the more settled areas, put the whole of the upper Hudson Valley into widespread panic, largely due to the use of Indians as forward scouts. They took every opportunity to attack settlers. Both sides had tried to recruit Indians to their cause; the Americans mustering not more than 150 of the Oneida tribe; the British more successful in having more than 700 recruited from the remainder of the tribes of the Six Nations. Despite appeals from Burgoyne to follow European eighteenth-century standards of warfare, he was able to exercise little control over the Indians. The resulting carnage was a major cause of the number of American militia who eventually rallied to oppose him. Now, however, settlers supporting the American cause, often left their belongings behind them, fleeing either down the Hudson to Albany or eastwards to Manchester (in the present State of Vermont). One young boy caught up in the general uproar, described how his parents released their pigs into the forest saying the British would have to catch them if they were going to enjoy them. He added they also buried their household utensils in the road and were fortunate in recovering them after the British defeat. He went on to recount the long line of wagons stretched along the road filled with all kinds of furniture, not often selected by the owners with reference to their use or value. While there were exceptions, in their fear the refugees generally forgot the claims of humanity, paying no heed to others needing help, and it was, "Everyone for himself, and the devil take the hindmost."[7]

Inevitably, the situation gave rise to rumours and exaggeration. Sergeant Lamb, serving with the 9th Foot, saw one local paper which stated that 700 settlers had been scalped by Burgoyne's Indians in an area where there were not more than 10 dwellings. General Gates placed the number killed at "upwards of one hundred men, women and children." He, and many others, quoted the Jane McCrea incident where she, the fiancee of a Loyalist named Jones, serving with Burgoyne, was killed and scalped while on her way to join him. The facts are in dispute, but whatever the truth, the damage caused by such stories gave rise to much anger among the settlers, and was another reason feeding the determination of the Americans to resist British intentions.[8]

It should not be thought that during this period Burgoyne was getting matters all his own way. Desertion, always a problem with eighteenth-century armies, was increasing. Carrying equipment weighing 60 pounds on their backs; short rations; hot and humid weather; and the never-ending physical labour in man-handling wagons, artillery and supplies over destroyed tracks and replacing bridges, took its toll among the men. The drop in morale was particularly marked among the German conscripts of the Brunswick and Hesse-Hanau regiments. They had no interest in the war and the temptations offered to them by the comparatively high standard of living enjoyed by the settlers, were often too much for them. The British regiments did not escape the disaffection entirely. Here again, it was Germans in those regiments, said to constitute up to ten percent of their strength, who were more liable to desert than were the British soldiers. These Germans came mainly from Hanover and had only one year's service in the British army. German deserters, regardless of regiment, appear to have been treated, when apprehended, more harshly than their British counterparts.

By 6th August, Burgoyne informed the army that there had been several deserters from the regimental companies of the 53rd (who by now had been left behind to garrison Ticonderoga and Fort George); he believed they had been scalped by Indians. He gave orders that any report of an absent man was to be sent to headquarters within one hour after each rollcalling, in order that Indians who had been given orders to scalp all deserters, could be sent immediately in pursuit. A few days later a man from the Riedesel Regiment named Taffelebend was executed in front of his regiment. Before the end of August, a German recruit in the 9th Foot named Hundertmark suffered the same fate. Patrick McDonald (47th Foot) was sentenced to 1,000 lashes for desertion. Walter Harris of the Light Company (53rd) was court martialled for advising two men to desert with him to the Americans. By early September, an officer had to be arrested for deserting his post when seeing to his own affairs.[9]

Relationships between the various nationalities making up the army was also deteriorating. Achieving harmony among a force consisting of Brunswickers, Hessians, French and English-speaking Canadians, Loyalists and British, would have been difficult under any circumstances. Even before the march had started, friction was caused by the Germans being more adept with their artillery, much to the chagrin of the British. The more rapid march pace used by the British, upset the Germans who found difficulty in keeping up with them. As the army proceeded, conditions grew worse; with rations reduced, animosity increased. A riot broke out between some British and German soldiers, for which Burgoyne blamed the British for being drunk and insulting a German guard. While liquor played a part in this incident, the inborn sense of superiority over foreigners held through the ages by the British soldier, (which is both his strength and his weakness), has often been the cause of friction in allied armies. As the Americans were to find, these same characteristics would make many British soldiers very difficult prisoners to handle.[10]

While the settlers supporting the American cause were fleeing, another problem for Burgoyne was the number of Loyalists coming into the British camp with requests and complaints. So great was the pressure, that he ordered the establishment of a Board which would meet at the end of each day's march to determine "complaints, abuses, and irregularities" and to administer Oaths of Allegiance, and regulate enlistments and supplies. One of the earliest consequences of this was the sentencing of William Sheen and John Deering (both 47th Foot), to 1,000 lashes each for robbing a Loyalist settler. Years later, Deering applied for arrears of pay while an escaper, and the Board of Enquiry examining his claim, seems to have ignored this sentence. They recommended, because of his escape record, he be given compassionate consideration.[11]

Meanwhile the commander of the opposing force, General Schuyler, was growing increasingly despondent. He wrote to Congress at length on 4th August, stating that his Massachusetts militia were insisting on going home and that his Continental troops did not exceed 4,000, adding "if men, one third of which are negroes, boys, and men too aged for field, or indeed any other service, can, with propriety be called troops." He went on to estimate accurately that Burgoyne still had about 8,000 men, (this number included the Canadian wagon drivers and boatmen). Although his recently arrived new second-in-command, Brigadier General Glover wrote in a similar vein, the Massachusetts politicians were, within a week, able to use Schuyler's letter to obtain support for his removal. Congress then asked George Washington to nominate a replacement. He refused to get mixed up in the inter-colonial politics and declined to name an officer. Thereupon, Congress appointed General Gates, who earlier had refused to serve under

Schuyler when offered the command at Ticonderoga. Gates took command of the Northern Department at Van Schaicks Island at the mouth of the Mohawk on 19th August. Schuyler's bitter dismissal was accompanied with false accusations of being a traitor to the American cause and receiving pay from the British.[12]

Horatio Gates, a Godson of Horace Walpole and said to be the son of the Duke of Leeds's housekeeper, was a very "political" general, who enjoyed considerable support from his friends in Congress. At one point, he came very close to replacing George Washington as the supreme commander. A former British Officer, Gates had come to America as part of the army which defeated the French in the Seven Years War. He was so taken with the country that he returned after the war and in the meantime, had become much-favoured by the New Englanders. By coincidence, he had started his military career in the 20th Foot, now one of the British regiments opposing him. Former British officers and men in the American forces were by no means unusual. Of the first thirteen Major Generals appointed by Congress, no less than twelve had held British commissions, and three of them had served in British Regiments. Their presence emphasises the conflict was more in the nature of a civil war rather than a revolution, as that term is usually viewed. Sergeant Lamb estimated that one third of the American force had seen service with the British in former days. On the other hand another British officer, Major Skene, retired on half-pay, whose mansion and settlement gave their name to Skenesboro, and who had also settled in America after the Seven Years War, was an enthusiastic supporter of the British cause. Skene, who was attached to Burgoyne's force as an advisor on local matters has often been blamed for part of the latter's tactical errors. Although technically a Loyalist settler and no longer a serving officer, he held the distinction of having been the only such person classed as a Convention Prisoner. In one listing he described himself as "a poor follower of the British Army."[13]

There now occurred a series of events which showed that Burgoyne was running into serious trouble. St Leger having moved down the Mohawk, also experienced delays caused by the Americans laying waste to the roads and bridges. He had to employ many men in clearing obstacles. He then found he was unable to take Fort Stanwix (later Fort Schuyler). The best he could do was to lay a weak siege to the

Fort. When 350 Americans made a brief sortie from the fort, they succeeded in raiding his camp. Having lost their belongings, his Indians, who constituted a large part of his force, became much disaffected and most went home. The siege was interrupted on 6th August by the arrival at nearby Oriskaney, of an American force of militia under Colonel Nicholas Herkimer. The British were successful in ambushing and defeating the Americans, but like so many of the battles during the war, while the British remained in possession of the ground they had by now eroded much of their strength. By 11th August, St Leger succeeded in getting a messenger through to Burgoyne reporting that American Brigadier General Benedict Arnold was on his way with 3,000 men and that he intended withdrawing to Oswego to obtain heavier guns. Arnold had used a ruse-de-guerre to create this impression and Burgoyne replied that Arnold did not have 3,000 men and gave St. Leger four alternatives i.e. storm the fort; maintain the siege until Burgoyne could reinforce him; leave the fort and march to the Hudson; or return to Montreal and join Burgoyne by way of Ticonderoga. St Leger chose the latter and started for Canada. In a message dated 27th August he wrote saying he intended, after reaching Canada, to use Burgoyne's own route to overtake him. This never occurred. Firstly, men were taken from him to man the forts in Upper Canada. Then, reaching Ticonderoga on 29th September his way was blocked by Americans who, as the British army moved down the river, had re-occupied several places behind them. A further message to Burgoyne asking for instructions fell into the hands of the Americans and was never delivered.[14]

A more immediate and serious loss occurred on 16th August when Burgoyne detached a force consisting mostly of German troops, with a few British light infantry and Provincials. Their object was to raid Bennington to secure horses and food. Apart from the horses, obtaining additional provisions was crucial. As the supply line lengthened, the difficulty in obtaining rations increased. At Bennington, the force was ambushed, with most being killed or captured. Only a handful escaped. Worse, when a German relief force, attempted to go to their aid, they in turn, were only extricated with difficulty and further ill-affordable losses were incurred. The debacle cost 1,220 irreplaceable men.

An additional set-back arose from the need to leave troops at

Ticonderoga, Fort George and Fort Edward to protect communications with Canada. What had happened was that by mid-1777 the relationship between Carleton in Canada and Germain in London was almost at breaking point. Germaine, unfairly, was critical of Carleton for not moving south during the previous year. In retaliation, Germaine had not only stipulated which units were to remain in Canada, but also where each unit was to be posted. In the direction of New York, none were to be further south than the Isle aux Noix. This took any discretion and effective command away from Carleton, virtually reducing him to an administrative capacity. When refusing to provide Burgoyne with garrison troops, Carleton replied,

> Whatever I may think of His Lordship as an officer or a statesman, I must respect his office and . . . he must be obeyed. I am ready to acknowledge that I think the whole of our Minister's measures, civil and military, very strange; indeed to me they appear incomprehensible, unless they turn upon private enmity and resentment.

When Carleton, always outspoken, reported to Germaine his refusal, he referred to "the evil caused by [your] arrangements." He later told Germaine in no uncertain terms that, "[You] should employ an efficient man and let him act unhindered."

These garrisons, added to the casualties at Bennington and those incurred in winning his earlier minor battles, reduced the number of fighting soldiers available to Burgoyne to less than 4,500. Even before news of these set-backs had reached either of the adversaries, John Adams had written to James Warren that, "Burgoine is treading on dangerous ground and proper exertions will ruin him." When the news of the defeat at Bennington and the raising of the siege at Fort Stanwix spread among the settler population, they began rallying to the American cause in even greater numbers.[15]

Bennington produced a spate of recriminations between the enemies and within the British expedition. Two survivors of Bennington told how the Americans turned on their Loyalist prisoners and treated them, "with the utmost cruelty." Burgoyne wrote to Gates protesting that some Germans had been refused quarter. Gates replied, "nothing had happened but what is common when works are carried by assault," and went on to refer to Burgoyne hiring savages to scalp, resulting in the deaths of men, women and children. In turn, Burgoyne protested that he had never encouraged the Indians. British officers also added to the debate by criticising the German conduct at Bennington, although under the circumstances in which the battle was fought, it is difficult to see how British regiments could have done better.[16]

Burgoyne's difficulties increased. He had moved down the river on the east or left bank, while most of the Americans were now on the west side. Further progress on the east bank would be difficult due to marshy country and defensible hills. His intended destination, Albany, was also on the west side. He therefore decided to construct a bridge, consisting of logs, across the Hudson. The work was completed on the same day as the battle at Bennington. The next morning, he had another set-back when the bridge was swept away by rapidly rising water, leaving part of the British force in a precarious position on the west bank. These were fortunate not to be attacked, and were extricated and returned across to the east bank only with great difficulty. The loss of the bridge caused further delay owing to the need, first to salvage the materials and then to re-commence construction at a more favorable place down-stream. This second bridge was some 425 feet long, constructed with bateaux used as pontoons. For nearly a month, the army remained strung out along 12 miles of the river bank between Fort Edward and the Battenkill, while the new construction took place, with the river continually rising and falling, due to periodical torrential rain.[17]

At the same time, the weather did not contribute to good campaigning. It was stiflingly hot with intermittent thunder storms. Troops dropping out on the march had already been reported, and British officers had been heard to comment that the weather was, "hotter than Madras."[18]

The set-backs, together with the conditions under which the troops laboured, caused the rate of desertion to increase. Burgoyne reported that another four German recruits in different British regiments had deserted and parties of Indians had been sent in pursuit. He expressed the opinion that emissaries of the enemy had penetrated the camp to entice soldiers to desert by making, "spurious promises and false representations and perhaps by a readiness in the German language." A further loss occurred when most of the Indians left. On 23rd August it was reported that Brigadier Fraser was left with "hardly more than 50," although other reports give 180 as the number remaining. While most described the Indians' conduct as desertion, at least one British soldier was of the opinion that they had to leave to do their hunting before winter.[19]

There is even less certainty as to the number of Loyalists who remained with the expedition after the set-backs described. Du Roi reported that on 20th August, more fugitives were arriving from Albany, fearing the cruelties of the Americans. The thirty or forty recruits a day led him to the hope that another regiment of Loyalists might be formed. On the other hand, Channing has recorded that by 1st September the larger part of the Loyalists had abandoned the expedition. The only definite favourable development was the arrival of 300 additional British recruits from Canada, who had caught up with the column.[20]

The series of set-backs began to show. Lieutenant Digby commented on the bad news, "which might easily be perceived on the faces of some of our great men, who I believe began to think our affairs had not taken so fortunate a turn as might have been expected." Burgoyne, still in an unruffled manner, did not hesitate to continue his advance. His second effort to cross the river began on 13th September after continuous rain had caused further delays. The crossing was not completed until the 15th and even then, the 20th Foot forded the river so as to avoid further congestion.

When the crossing was completed, Burgoyne ordered the bridge demolished. If it remained, he would not only need to keep men on the east bank to deny its use by the enemy; more importantly, he needed the boats with which it was constructed, to continue transporting his supplies. The end of the bridge also meant that his communication with Canada was cut and there was now no easy escape route, should it be required. The die was cast. There was no alternative but to press on.

On the 15th, the army moved forward about 3 miles with bands playing, reaching that evening Dovegat (now Coveville) on the heights of Saratoga, where it camped. Now that the Americans had apparently stopped their retreat, those required on picket duty increased, with many small alarms caused by patrols of the enemy coming very near the British camp. In every case, these were soon put to flight, but with one officer complaining "duty turned very severe."[21]

Since Bennington, militia had flocked to the American colours. There was one exception. When Stark came in with his brigade of New Hampshire militia, they, despite their victory at Bennington, insisted their time was up and they left for home. Gates retained Stark by creating another brigade from newcomers. Literally thousands were arriving from New England and elsewhere, encouraged by the victories at Fort Stanwix and Bennington, plus their anger fermented by the circulation of the stories of the McCrea killing. In addition, Benedict Arnold, after the success in putting St. Leger to flight, had also returned. Most important of all, was the arrival on 30th August of "Old Wagoner," Colonel Morgan, with 500 marksmen using the so-called Kentucky rifle. They had been selected from regiments of the regular Continental Army around New York and sent by George Washington to reinforce Gates. On their arrival, this contingent was supplemented by an additional 300 men chosen in the same manner from Gates's regiments. The combined rifle force was considered the elite of Gates's force; so much so, that Gates ordered Morgan to report directly to him and not through his brigadiers. Some 16,000 American soldiers and militia were now ranged against Burgoyne's 4,500 fighting soldiers.[22]

Gates had inherited Schuyler's headquarters at Stillwater, but with his strength now augmented, he considered he could challenge the British further north, at a site selected by Arnold and the Polish engineer Thadeus Kosciusko. This was at Bemis Heights, where the hills closed in on the west bank of the river. The British were largely dependent on water-borne transport for their supplies and they could not go far from the river's edge. Making a stand at this point, where the road led directly beneath the heights, would be the best place to stop the British. An entrenched camp was constructed on the heights with added protection provided by a deep natural ravine in front.[23]

The British did not know exactly where the Americans were. On 16th September, 2,000 men with six guns made a reconaissance-in-force but made no contact. On the 17th, the army advanced about another 3 miles, arriving at Dirck Swart's house which earlier had been occupied by Schuyler. The army was now within 5 miles of the American fortified position.[24]

On that same day, although neither side at Saratoga were aware of it at the time, American troops were demonstrating the flawed British strategy, when 600 men under Colonel Brown captured the various parties of soldiers at landing sites north of Fort George, while others regained possession of Mount Defiance. Another detachment under Johnson captured additional troops close to Ticonderoga. 318 British were taken prisoner and at the same time 118 American prisoners were released. All this was the result of Germaine's incredible attempt to plan the tactical disposition of Canadian-based troops from 3,000 miles away despite a three month turn-around in communication time. Germaine's interference in Carleton's command and his failure to delegate responsibility, is only matched by Adolf Hitler, who, in World War II, tried to direct his armies in the same way, with similar disastrous results.[25]

At least one of the men captured at Bennington was able to escape. He was Private William Dyers (9th) but he did not succeed until 1779. He had been taken to a prison in Rutland, Massachusetts and from there he took three months to get into New York. Other captives were more fortunate and succeeded much earlier. Four men of the 53rd captured at Lake George, all named John, made their escape almost immediately. They were Privates Wishart, Drury, Duncan and Smith. They were successful in reaching Halifax, Nova Scotia, during the following January, after passing themselves off as sailors.

Another group escaped from Lake George. They were Private Daniel Driskill (24th) and five others. Three months later they were recaptured and sent to Albany jail, where they spent twelve months in irons. As soon as the irons were removed they escaped again. After several adventures, Driskill spent another fifteen weeks in jail at West Point. On agreeing to work he was released from jail and employed at various places. He deserted his last employer finally reaching freedom in New York on 8th August 1781.[26]

On the 18th September some 3,000 Americans moved out from Bemis Heights, seeking to attack the British in the flank. In the thickly wooded country, they failed to make contact, but continued their aggressive patrolling and succeeded in killing or wounding 30 men and some women foraging for potatoes. This caused a British officer to complain of their bloodthirstiness, saying they could easily have captured them rather than killing and wounding. This incident caused Burgoyne to issue orders that any allied soldier caught foraging beyond the advanced sentries of the Army, would be instantly hanged.[27]

For some days, the weather had been growing noticeably colder and the morning of the 19th was cool and bracing, the grass white with hoarfrost. The sun rose bright and clear but it was not until about 10 o'clock that the army started to move out to come to grips with the enemy. Gates was already forwarned of this movement; since dawn a small scouting party had posted themselves in the trees across the river from Swart's house. They were able to count no less than 800 tents. They then noticed movement which clearly presaged a major development. On receiving a message containing this news, Gates immediately ordered his army to stand to. At the same time, he demonstrated his timid nature which, several years later, ruined him at the Battle of Camden. He gave orders for his own tents to be struck and to prepare teams for a rapid retreat. It appears this order was repeated on each of the next five days.[28]

By ironic chance Burgoyne's Adjutant General had chosen as the password for the day "St. Eustacia" and the countersign as "Holland." Although he was probably not aware of it, the Dutch West Indian island of St Eustacia had been the place where, on 16th November 1776, the American flag had received from a foreign nation its first official recognition and salute.[29]

In conformity with common military practice of the time, Burgoyne had formed composite battalions from the grenadier and light companies of all the Regiments under his command. Also included were the six similar "Canadian Companies." In the British army these companies were considered the elite of each battalion; the grenadiers selected for their height and physique and the light companies for their intelligence and ability to work independently. The two composite battalions were brigaded with the 24th Foot, which as an experiment, had been trained as light infantry. Also included in this brigade were the 148 Canadian Voltigeurs, some detachments of Loyalists together with the Indians. In all, it consisted of 2,000 men, under the command of Brigadier General Fraser.

Burgoyne had decided to advance in three columns. He placed Fraser's brigade on the right. The center column under himself, consisted of about 1,100 men of the regimental companies of the 20th, 21st and 62nd Regiments, with those of the 9th Foot in reserve. The left column, numbering about 1,100 men was under command of the German Commander, Major General Von Riedesel. These were mostly German troops, but they did include the regimental companies of the 47th Foot made responsible for guarding the hospital and boats at the riverside. The British artillery, led by Major General William Phillips, also remained on the left.[30]

When the enemy position was located, the plan was for the right and center columns to make a junction and from there, attempt to turn the American left. Meanwhile the left column were to follow the river road to within a half-mile of the American positions. After hearing three minute-guns, they were to threaten the American right until Burgoyne had executed his flanking movement. The advance was very slow and laborious, as numerous obstructions had to be demolished and bridges repaired.[31]

The two right columns were in a precarious position, advancing through heavily wooded and broken country intersected with ravines. A determined attack by the Americans on these columns at that place would have ended the British invasion then and there. However, at this stage, Gates could not bring himself to order the Americans to attack, preferring the shelter of his defensive works, much to the chagrin of his subordinate, Benedict Arnold. Arnold was a totally different personality to Gates and the ill-feeling between them can be gauged by Arnold's references to "Granny Gates" and "that damned old midwife in buff and blue." Much of Arnold's role at both Freemans Farm and Bemis Heights is in dispute. One version says he recognised the opportunity rapidly being lost, together with the increasing danger of the British gaining even higher ground on the left of the American position, and is reputed to have, "urged, begged and entreated" Gates to move. Whether or not in response to Arnold's urging, or whether Arnold finally moved without orders, is unclear. One version claimed Arnold "borrowed" some 3,000 men, but whatever the case, Morgan went forward with his riflemen, with Dearborn's light infantry covering in turn his left.[32]

About one o'clock, the first clash of the battle took place in a ravine, when Morgan's troops came upon a picket of Fraser's under the command of Major Forbes, consisting of Canadians, Indians and Loyalists. Every officer of the picket and many of its men fell on the first firing. Morgan continued his advance, but Major Forbes immediately counter-attacked with a strong detachment of Loyalists and the American riflemen broke and ran. Morgan is said to have been reduced to tears at this rebuff and it was some minutes before he could rally them again to play an important part in the battle.[33]

By this time, Burgoyne's column had reached Freemans Farm, a clearing about 350 yards long, consisting of 15 or 20 acres around a log house. It was this farm which gave its name to the first of the two Battles of Saratoga. Burgoyne posted his artillery along the northern edge of this open ground, with three regiments behind them; the 21st on the right; the 62nd in the center; the 20th on the left. The 9th continued in reserve.

Fraser on the far right of the British line, hearing the sounds of Morgan's skirmish with Forbes, immediately swung his force left in order to join up with Burgoyne's column. In the meantime, Arnold, with the balance of his "borrowed" men, tried to move in between Fraser and Burgoyne. There was an immediate clash between Arnold's and Fraser's forces and for a time, is was touch and go whether Fraser would have to retreat. However, the German grenadiers forming part of his column came up just in time and it was Arnold who was forced to retire. His set-back did not last long. As the sublime opportunist, and with others of the American left coming to his assistance, Arnold "contermarched" his men and immediately attacked Burgoyne's troops, drawn up in their lines.

The conflict had now moved from a series of ambushes and sudden clashes into a battle which raged to and fro over the tiny clearing of Freemans Farm. First the British were forced back into the woods on the north side. Here they rallied and with a bayonet charge, forced the Americans back into the trees on the south side. Again, the Americans charged only to be stopped once more. The 21st Foot, so as to avoid being outflanked were forced to swing back so they were facing west. This left the 62nd on the corner of the line and it was they who suffered the most severe casualties. All along the whole British line, officer casualties were increasing out of proportion to those of other ranks, as Americans with rifles posted in the trees, deliberately picked off the distinctively dressed officers. It seems the British officers had taken no notice of the order issued in March 1776, given to officers when leaving for America, that they were to wear the same uniform and have their hair dressed in the same manner as their men, so that they would be indistinguishable from their soldiers.

Each time the Americans advanced, they took possession of the British artillery, the surviving gunners moving back to the protection of the infantry, carrying with them their lighted linstocks. Having neither horses available to move the guns or linstocks to ignite them, the Americans, in turn, had to abandon the guns each time the British advanced. Of the 48 British artillerymen who took part, 36 became casualties. On one occasion, the 62nd, despite its losses, moved forward in a desperate bayonet charge. They went too far, and left their flanks exposed. After losing 25 men as prisoners, the rapidly diminishing group of survivors were saved only by a charge of the 20th Foot, led by artilleryman Major General Phillips, who had come across from the river road to assess the situation.

Arnold now believed he could, with reinforcements from the American right, defeat the British, despite it was they who remained in possession of the field. The sheer weight of numbers were beginning to tell, and he asked Gates to give the left some assistance. Gates, who never ventured on to the field at any time during the battle, refused. He stated later that he, "deemed it prudent not to weaken" his lines. When it was too late, he did send another brigade, but these contributed little to the battle as they were quickly brushed aside by Fraser.

Riedesel, in command of the British left on the river road, ordered his force to move as soon as he heard of the precarious position the other two columns were in. Not waiting for all his regiments to come up, he personally led two companies of the Rhetz regiment in a charge deep into the flank of the Americans, driving them back into the woods. Meanwhile two 6 pounder guns that Riedesel had brought with him, were able to reach the part of the line occupied by the 21st and 9th. Survivors from these regiments, including officers, dragged the guns into position opening up on the Americans with grape "within good pistol shot distance." After twelve or fourteen rounds, the guns were moved forward some 60 paces, at which point another twelve or fifteen shots were fired, causing the Americans to make a hurried withdrawal. This brought an end to the battle. It was growing dark, the Americans withdrew into their defensive works and the British bivouaked on the field. Not another shot was heard all night.[34]

Although no further firing was to be heard, there were other sounds. As with all eighteenth-century battles, there were no battlefield medical services. Most of the 300 wounded British lay all that freezing night, groaning and sighing where they had fallen. In relation to the numbers involved in the fighting the total casualties were heavy. While Burgoyne had probably 2,500 men on the field, only about 800 of the 20th, 21st, and 62nd were deeply and continuously engaged; of a total of 556 killed, wounded and missing, no less than 350 came from these three regiments. The 62nd started the battle with about 350 men; by evening, they had scarcely 60 remaining effective.[35]

Some 35 Commissioned officers and 26 non commissioned officers were among the casualties. Of these, ten regular officers were killed. The auxiliary forces also did not escape the carnage. One of the Canadian voltigeurs, Captain Monin, who had his eleven year old son fighting by his side, was also among the dead. This seems to deny to some extent, the subsequent criticism by Anburey, that the Canadians could not be depended upon.[36]

The Americans did not come off lightly in the vicious fighting, which at times, included hand to hand combat. Although proportionately much lower, they had 8 officers and 57 others killed, 21 officers and 197 others wounded, with 36 reported missing.[37]

In tactical terms, the day was probably a draw. As with many of the set-piece battles during the American war, the British finished unbroken and holding the ground. In strategic terms however, due to the ratio of casualties and without a ready source of reinforcements, they were now in a most hazardous position. Despite this, over-estimating the enemy losses, and convinced by the evidence they could not stand-up to artillery fire, Burgoyne, as always optimistic, immediately planned a second attempt at breaking through the American position.

Burgoyne expressed an opinion that in the close fighting, the British had relied too much on individual musket fire and not sufficiently on the bayonet. He stated that the men acted impetuously and fired at will, not waiting for orders from their officers. He expressed his conviction that now they had experienced a battle this would be corrected in the next engagement.[38]

On the day following the battle, orders were issued for the whole army to march at 3 o'clock, the late hour due to the need for a heavy mist to disperse. General Fraser, however, convinced Burgoyne that his grenadiers and light troops were too fatigued from their efforts on the previous day. It was agreed that the intended attack would be postponed for a further day. If the planned renewed attack had taken place when Burgoyne had wanted it, there could have possibly been a quite different outcome. Gates's Adjutant General, Colonel James Wilkinson, expressed the opinion that without reinforcements "[we] must anticipate the consequences of defeat." Whether or not this would have been the case, the opportunity was missed.[39]

A truce was called to enable each side to collect their wounded and bury their dead. The British wounded had to be transported in wagons for nearly a mile over broken ground to a tented hospital which had been placed near the river. About 20 of them died on each of the following days. Among the captured there was found a wounded British officer, sixteen years old, expiring. He had been wounded in a leg and while he lay, unable to regain his own lines, an American camp follower, described by Wilkinson as "a murderous villain," had shot him through the body. Despite everything which was done for him, the youth died the following day. Those killed in action were buried where they fell. Ensign Anburey left a graphic description of his duty in charge of one of the burying parties. The only distinction given to officers was being placed in graves separate from the men. He reported that three subalterns of the 20th were buried together, the eldest not exceeding the age of seventeen. Despite searches made in more recent times, their grave sites have never been located. Anburey gives a clue as to the reason, complaining that the superficial burying by parties other than his own, resulted in the bodies being uncovered by animals. Other records mention that for years, human bones were continually being ploughed up when the land was farmed.[40]

The resumption of the attack, planned for the 21st, was then postponed indefinitely. Burgoyne had received a message from Sir Henry Clinton, in command of the reduced garrison in New York, saying he was going to advance north and endeavour to take Albany. Cancelling the attack did not mean that Burgoyne had given up his intention to continue his advance southwards. He now planned to wait until he could mount a joint effort with Clinton and attack the enemy from both directions. He issued orders that 20 Loyalists, "of tried bravery and fidelity," were to be drafted to each of the six British regiments to supplement their reduced numbers.[41]

Some of the messages sent between Burgoyne and Clinton in New York never reached their destination. Although much of the heavily wooded country provided cover for messengers, the numbers of American troops on the ground were considerable. Not only had Gates's army to be avoided, but there were other garrisons spread along the 150 mile route to New York, all of which had to be evaded. The risky nature of being a courier behind enemy lines during a civil war, is revealed by the several versions of the fate of Sergeant Daniel Taylor (9th), one of the messengers moving between the British commanders. On approaching Fort Montgomery, and misled on meeting some American soldiers wearing captured scarlet uniforms, he enquired for General Clinton and was taken to the American General George Clinton. On realising his mistake he swallowed a silver ball containing the message, but he was given an emetic and the Americans, on recovering the message, executed him.[42]

On the day he cancelled the second attempt to breach the American lines, Burgoyne ordered the construction of still another bridge, the third one across the Hudson. A much flimsier affair than the previous two he had made upstream, it was quickly completed by the 23rd. It was constructed to enable the army to forage on the east bank of the river. At this point of time he certainly had no thoughts about retreat, and indeed when that did become necessary, the bridge does not seem to have entered into his calculations.[43]

During the next two weeks, Burgoyne, still assuming that Clinton was coming to his aid, occupied most of his troops in building defense works which included two redoubts near the site of the battle. A third redoubt, named the Great Redoubt, was constructed near the camp by the river. All three were to play a role in future events. Meanwhile there was aggressive patrolling by both sides, resulting in both casualties and desertions. In one incident a post was attacked by Americans in strength, the Germans losing one man as prisoner and two wounded.

The Americans in this attack lost seven wounded and four prisoners. The remaining Indians on both sides were also active, and succeeded in bringing in prisoners, deserters, and scalps.[44]

With the supply line from Canada cut, together with the failure of the Bennington raid, food supplies were dwindling rapidly. If the army was to survive until the two British forces could make a joint attack, it was necessary to cut rations. Orders were issued to reduce them by one third. Both General Riedesel and Sergeant Lamb commented that the reduction was received with no complaint or murmur. At the same time, it seemed that someone in camp had obtained a small supply of fresh meat and Burgoyne was forced to instruct the Provost to try and obtain evidence as to who was trafficking in the food and find where they had obtained it! [45]

Cutting rations provided no long term solution. As the days dragged by with no news from Clinton, it was clear that the impass could not continue much longer. Not only were further ration cuts needed, but in addition, horses and cattle were beginning to die of starvation. It became clear that the tactics of the Americans were to starve the British into surrender. On 4th October Burgoyne met with Phillips, Riedesel and Fraser. He proposed leaving the camp with its supplies and the wounded, guarded by 800 men. He would then attack the enemy's left flank with the remainder of the army. Due to continuing lack of intelligence concerning the exact position of that flank and its approach roads, it was decided to meet again on the following day to determine the course to be taken.[46]

On meeting again, Burgoyne was fully committed to take some action to bring matters to a head. Failing this there would be no alternative, but to retreat to the north of the Battenkill, re-cross the Hudson to re-open a supply route from Fort George, then wait for Clinton's force. Both Riedesel and Fraser supported the proposal to attack, with Phillips ambivalent. Burgoyne decided to lead a reconnaissance in force against the enemy's left wing to detemine whether it could be attacked successfully. If such was possible, an attack would be made; if not, he would order the retreat to take place.[47]

During all this time, the Americans continued with nuisance artillery fire, which caused little damage and no casualties. 6th October was spent on administrative duties. These included making arrangements for Germans serving with the British regiments to attend Lutheran Church services with the German regiments and an issue of rum to all troops. At the same time, four days reduced rations were issued.[48]

At 10 am on the morning of 7th October, 1,500 men, selected from every unit in the army, marched out towards the enemy line on Bemis Heights, which was to give its name to the second of the Saratoga battles. The remainder of the force stayed in the camp, hoping to keep the American's attention on the river road. Those moving off, together with 10 cannon, were formed in three columns. As in the action at Freemans Farm, Brigadier Fraser's Light companies with the 24th Foot, Canadians, Loyalists and the remaining Indians were on the British right. Riedesel was in the center with the German Grenadiers, while on the left, were the British Grenadiers. Burgoyne, as before, placed himself in the center. By noon, the movement had been detected by the enemy, and the sound of drums beating-to-arms was heard. The 1,500 men were then deployed into a wheat field, situated on sloping ground near, but not in sight of, the American defensive positions. Here they were formed up into two ranks and were ordered to sit down while officers endeavoured to see where the American lines were located. Both flanks rested against heavily wooded country.[49]

This time, there was no delay on the part of the Americans to take countermeasures. Morgan and his riflemen were given immediate per-mision to circle round the British right, under cover of the trees and be ready to attack down the slope when firing was heard on the British left. Before Morgan was in position, more Americans attacked the British left. One version of events states that Arnold, in defiance of being removed by Gates from active command, led others against the center. Morgan was not far behind. He, with his men, came pouring out of the woods attacking both the right front and flank. As the British tried to change their front to meet the onslaught on their flanks, additional Americans attacked, causing the Light Troops to break their line. Their commander, the Earl of Balcarras, succeeded in rallying them and reformed behind a fence at the rear of their original position.[50]

The fighting now raged all along the British line. It has been estimated that no less than 9,200 men poured out of the American position against the 1,500 soldiers in the allied force. It was a repeat of the fighting at Freeman's Farm. The battle raged forwards and backwards across the

wheat field with the guns being captured and recaptured several times.
Finally after an estimated 52 minutes, the Anglo-German line, under
sheer weight of numbers, broke and retreated, leaving the guns to the
Americans. Who broke first is a matter of dispute. The British blamed
the Germans. The Germans blamed the Canadians. In view of the
numbers of enemy on the field, there is really no blame to be laid
against anyone. The British retreated in orderly groups to one of the
redoubts accompanied by most Germans. Other Germans went into a
second redoubt where, after their Colonel had been killed, they were
overcome.[51]

The losses were crippling. 17 officers and 144 men were killed; 26
officers and 485 men wounded; 5 officers and 45 men were prisoners
and 118 men were missing; all this from an original force of 1,500.
The officer casualties included many of senior rank; Brigadier Fraser
mortally wounded by an Irish American named Tom Murphy; Major
Acland, the Grenadier commander severely wounded, captured and
just escaped death by the timely intervention of Colonel Wilkinson
stopping a boy from killing him where he lay; Sir Francis Clerke,
aide-de-camp to Burgoyne, killed; Major Williams, one of the oldest
men in the expedition, commanding the British battery was captured
along with his 12 pounders. Once again, the casualties were concentrated in a comparatively small area. One memoir described that in one
place of not more than 15 square yards, 18 Grenadiers lay dead or
dying with three officers propped up against trees, two of them mortally
wounded and almost speechless.[52]

Fortescue summed up the conduct of the British troops in the two
battles of Saratoga thus,

> In the whole history of the Army I have encountered no grander display
> of steadfastness and fortitude than the heroic stand of the Twentieth,
> Twenty-first, and Sixty-second, with their little handful of gunners, on
> the 19th September; and it is surely a marvellous instance of gallantry
> and discipline that fifteen hundred men should have moved out cheerfully
> and confidently as they did on the 7th of October, in spite of much
> hard-ship and heavy losses, to attack an enemy of five times their
> number; that when forced back they should have retired with perfect
> order and coherence; and that though fighting all day and marching or
> entrenching all night, they should never have lost heart.[53]

Finally realising the impossibility of his situation, Burgoyne gave orders to give up the forward redoubt and for the whole force to withdraw to the river. His only hope now, would be to retreat behind the Battenkill and try to develop a supply route from the north, until assistance could reach them from the south.

Although some desultory shooting continued into the evening, night once again brought hostilities to an end. It was 11 pm before all the Americans camped for the night. Again, Gates had not ventured himself onto the field of battle, and the success of American arms was mostly due to the dash and elan of Morgan and Benedict Arnold, despite the latter being wounded. Arnold's detractors claim he was drunk. Whether or not this was so, despite their losses, including 150 killed, there was great elation among the American officers and men. It was the first time in the north that they had fought and won a pitched battle against British troops, causing them to retreat.[54]

CHAPTER 2

The Convention

THE day after the battle, Burgoyne abandoned the camp. He brought everyone into the Great Redoubt by the river. The day was spent re-organising the army, making ready for a retreat that evening. While this was taking place, the Americans quickly over-ran the camp. They brought up their artillery and kept up a continuous bombardment which did not do a great deal of damage. At eight that morning, Brigadier General Fraser died and his funeral was set for six in the evening. In accordance with Fraser's own request, he was buried in the Great Redoubt. Seeing the number of officers gathered on the prominence, American artillery fire was directed at them. The firing caused no casualties, although the service was conducted with difficulty, with cannon balls flying among the mourners. As soon as the funeral was over, the British artillery quickly silenced that of the Americans. Later General Gates said that if he had known it was a funeral taking place, he would have ensured that the fire was directed elsewhere.

That evening, immediately after the funeral, the army began to move northwards. However, lack of adequate transport dictated abandoning the wounded and sick where they lay; the men in tents and the officers in Swart's house. At least one, Major Harnage, who had been shot through the abdomen at Freeman's Farm and was still "miserably ill," struggled to his feet and marched with the army. The senior British surgeon, John Macnamara Hayes, described as a "facetious, amiable Hibernian" stayed with the wounded. He surrendered his charges to Colonel Wilkinson, indicating there was great fear among the men for their personal safety. They feared what the riflemen and Indians serving with the Americans might do. On this account the American gave them his assurances of protection. The sick and wounded who went into captivity at this time were looked after as well as could be expected, in view of the limited facilities available to both sides. There were insufficient carts to move all of them at once and those that were not transported immediately, were by the 15th, without provisions. It took two weeks to move the survivors. They were taken down-river to Schenectady and Albany, where a number of buildings were converted into temporary hospitals.

There is some doubt as to the number of hospital cases reaching their destination. Sergeant Lamb, who served as a surgeons mate, put the number of casualties at 460 British and Germans. Many records, including Wilkinson, say 300; another estimate put it as high as 800; American surgeon Dr. Thacher recorded 1,000 British, German and American casualties being treated two weeks later at Albany, but these probably included those from other actions. A return signed by Dr. Hayes and dated 9th October, shows the British patients consisted of 9 officers, 240 men attended by 5 medical staff. Taking into account the deaths occurring since the battle, his figure would bring the total back to about 300. Of these, 197 were still alive according to a return prepared by Hayes on 14th November and by which time the British had been separated into their own hospital, designated by Hayes as His Majesty's Hospital.

In the best medical tradition, the American Surgeon-General Potts ordered there was to be no difference in the treatment accorded between prisoners or American casualties and these orders were carried out to the letter. With a total of more than a thousand patients from both armies to be attended to, they were for some days all mixed together and were treated by 30 British, German and American surgeons and mates, without distinction. Despite some horrendous wounds, several remarkable recoveries were achieved and recorded. An American surgeon paid tribute to their British colleagues who performed "with skill and dexterity," but observed that the Germans with a few exceptions, "do no credit to their profession; some of them are the most uncouth and clumsy operators I ever witnessed, and appear to be destitute of all sympathy and tenderness towards the suffering patient."[55]

There are traces of what happened to some of these men. Private John Saddler (20th) wounded, was captured when the hospital was over-run during the retreat. He was taken to Albany where he was hospitalised until the following April. Treated as a Prisoner of War, he was given a pass to go farming near Johnstown which he did for five months. He then absconded and started for Canada, but was recaptured and put in jail at Albany. After a second escape and re-capture, he enlisted in an American unit from which he deserted three months later. Working for a year to support himself, he was caught again and given a hundred lashes by the Americans for desertion, which kept him quiet for another year. Deserting still again in New Jersey, he was caught the next day and put into Morristown jail. There he was tried as a deserter and sentenced to be hanged. Sub-sequently pardoned, he escaped again and finally entered New York on 10th June 1782.

Thomas Symester (47th), escaped when released from hospital and was recaptured. He spent one day in Hartford Jail, when he was bailed out to do work. He deserted his employer, and ignoring the proximity of New York, headed for Philadelphia, then occupied by the British. He reached there on 8th March 1778, and was drafted immediately into the 17th Foot.

Other hospitalised prisoners have left record of their trail. These included Private Jonathon Clews (24th), who after an escape, spent three years in Hartford Jail. He was able to get away again and arrived in New York during October 1781.[56]

Meanwhile, as the evacuation of the Great Redoubt continued, the bridge across the Hudson was set on fire. Digby complained that the bridge should have been used to cross to the east side of the river and commented "our retreat was not conducted so well as it might have been." The British rear-guard did not clear the area until late at night. The wet weather interfered with the burning of the bridge and when the Americans advanced, they were able to salvage the bateaux used in its construction and use them for the transport of supplies. All next day (9th October), in continuous pouring rain, the retreat went on, described by one German officer as a "minuet-retreat" showing the enemy "our teeth and claws" and inflicting casualties with the cannon. He complained that they marched at the fast "English step" until Dovecot, 2 miles south of Saratoga, was reached. Bad roads and the wretched weather, put more cannon and baggage into enemy hands. In addition, a picket of some 50 or 60 Germans deserted to the Americans. There must also have been some confusion. Baroness Riedesel the wife of the German commander, who never missed an opportunity to criticise either the private life or military prowess of

Burgoyne, complained that the retreat was slowed by his ordering a halt for the guns to be counted.[57]

The Americans had already surmised that the defeated army would make for Saratoga, in order to cross to the east side of the river. Gates sent a message of warning to Brigadier General Fellows. He had been despatched with 1300 men to occupy that place on the day before the Bemis Heights battle had taken place. Fellows had a narrow escape because Lieutenant Colonel Sutherland, the new commander of the 47th Regiment, had been sent out to reconnoitre Saratoga. He found the camp of the Americans quite unguarded. On his return, he asked Burgoyne for permission to advance with the 47th and attack, but was refused. By next morning, when Burgoyne ordered the army to continue their march, a message pointing out the danger he was in had reached Fellows. The Americans crossed over to the east bank of the Hudson and consequently Burgoyne's opportunity to make up for part of the defeat was missed.[58]

The morning of 10th October saw the pouring rain return. Since the Americans had by now been rationed, they set out in pursuit of the allied army, reaching the vicinity of Saratoga about four in the afternoon. Here they found Burgoyne ensconced in the old French defensive works on a hill beyond the Fishkill. The bateaux were being unloaded and the supplies carried up from the river. The Americans quickly brought the carrying party under artillery fire, killing several of the British. However, a heavy and rapid response from the allied artillery quickly silenced the American guns. A few Americans crossed to a small island in the river, but a detachment soon drove them off. The next morning, Gates had determined to continue his advance, assuming that the British had continued their retreat. A desperate game of hide and seek now took place in the thick morning fog, causing casualties to both sides. This convinced Gates to remain put. For the next two days there were patrol clashes and exchange of artillery fire. This skirmishing caused Burgoyne to abandon the house, owned by General Schuyler, which he was then occupying. To clear a field of fire, the house and other buildings were then burnt down, although the Church was saved by some American transport riders frightening off the soldier detailed for that task.[59]

Burgoyne now realised that the Saratoga crossing was held in force by the Americans and crossing the river to the east bank at that point would be impossible. He, therefore, despatched a party of engineers, with Loyalists troops, the 47th Foot and some of Fraser's marksmen, to move northwards up the west bank of the river to arrive opposite Fort Edward. Their object was to repair bridges as they went and cross the river at that point. After covering 19 miles and within an hour of the crossing to Fort Edward, they were about to repair the remaining bridge, when a courier overtook them with orders for the 47th to return to Saratoga. While there was an American force with artillery holding the area, it was doubtful whether they could have denied the passage of the British army. This was evident from an attack they made, as soon as the 47th started to retrace their steps. The Americans were very quickly repulsed, with one soldier of the 47th claiming they took from the river 44 American bodies, together with some wounded. As soon as the men of the 47th had left, the Loyalists who were supposed to remain protecting the engineers, also disappeared. This left the engineers to escape as best they could.[60]

The reason for the recall order was that the Americans had brought up a further three brigades of troops and there were now 16,000 Americans present at Saratoga. These, apart from the garrisons up-river, were sufficient in strength to virtually surround the allied army. On the morning of the 11th, after a brief skirmish, the Americans were repulsed, but only after the bateaux with most of the remaining bulk supplies had been lost. Barely six days of reduced rations now remained, with the prospect of total starvation looming. Corporal Fox (47th) recalled that they had lived for the past ten days on four biscuits per man and then only received a small quantity of flour. Five years later, Private Michael Tiffin of the same regiment made application for two months ration money in lieu of rations reduced or not issued during the retreat. In one of their rare instances of munificence, the British army actually paid up.

From information given by the German deserters, the Americans were well aware of the army's desperate straits and they made matters more uncomfortable by maintaining a steady artillery and musket fire into the fortified position.[61]

A meeting was called that evening by Burgoyne, attended by Phillips and Riedesel. It was proposed that there was still an opportunity to make a retreat to Canada. The plan was to abandon the baggage, let the army carry their rations on their back and go north on the west bank since that road still appeared open. Then, to avoid a clash at Fort Edward, they would ford the river 4 miles below and strike north to Fort George. Riedesel maintained in his memoirs that it was he that suggested this desperate plan, but Phillips, in a letter written two weeks after the event, said he made the suggestion that he take to the woods and get to Ticonderoga, "but I was not allowed to attempt it." For his part, Major Skene advised Burgoyne to scatter the stores and the American militia would stay to collect them and the troops would have the opportunity of getting clear away. Nothing was decided except to hold a further meeting on the following day.[62]

Would such an effort have succeeded? An officer of the 47th thought in retrospect,

> that at least half of our little Army being cut to pieces, and the remainder perhaps prisoners of war, as from the then situation of the Enemy, I believe few would have reached Canada. But the attempt would have been glorious, the failure to be attributed to the natural chances of war, could not have been but honourable.

He was probably right. British Brigadier Orde Wingate experienced a somewhat similar situation towards the end of his first incursion into Burma during World War II. In the midst of strong Japanese forces, he divided his Chindits, withdrawing towards India in small parties. In doing so they suffered heavy casualties, but Wingate saved his reputation.[63]

The meeting resumed the next afternoon, with Brigadiers Gall and Hamilton also attending. The minutes of the meeting show that five alternatives were discussed:

— Wait for an attack.
— Attack the enemy.
— Retreat, repairing the bridges as they went to save the artillery.
— Retreat by night, leaving the artillery and baggage, and forcing their way with musketry.
— If the enemy left a gap, march rapidly for Albany.

After a review had been made of their own situation and the numbers and location of the enemy, it was decided that the night retreat, abandoning both the artillery and baggage, held the only likelihood of success. Various routes were discussed and it was agreed to make for the ford at Fort Edward. Having taken the decision to implement the desperate plan, it was then found that the remaining meagre rations had not been issued to the men. The move would have to be delayed until this had been done. When at 10 pm that night Riedesel reported everything was ready, he found that Burgoyne's apparent luke-warm acceptance of the plan had evaporated. Burgoyne stated it was now too late and the army should remain where it was.[64]

On the 13th October, yet another Council of War was called, this time enlarged to include all officers down to the rank of captains commanding corps. The army was now virtually surrounded with only five days of reduced rations remaining. Artillery and musket fire continued to rain down on them. Despite this, the spirits of the British troops remained remarkably high, although as usual, and perhaps in some cases unfairly, they retained a low opinion of their German allies. Burgoyne made it clear to the assembled officers that no one but himself, could be blamed for the situation they now found themselves in. He then put the following questions to them:

— Whether military history furnished any examples of an army having capitulated under similar circumstances:

— Whether the capitulation of an army placed in such a situation would be disgraceful:

— Whether the army was actually in such a situation as to be obliged to capitulate.

The answer he received to the first question was, that among other examples, the situation of the Saxon army which capitulated at Pirna, and that of General Fink at Maxan, were not as bad and helpless as that in which the army found itself placed at this moment and no one could have censured those generals. The fact that General Fink was cashiered by the King of Prussia was chiefly due to personal dislike.

The unanimous response to the second question was that the capitulation of the army could not be disgraceful for the reasons cited in answer to the first question.

To the third question, it was unanimous that all present were ready to fight if Burgoyne thought anything could be gained by such a sacrifice, but capitulation would follow when the last of the rations were consumed, or worse, they would be attacked and scattered by the enemy and separately destroyed; therefore a thoroughly honorable capitulation was preferable.

On receiving these unanimous declarations, Burgoyne produced a draft of a capitulation document which was approved immediately without dissent.[65]

The next day, many of the remaining Canadians, with some Indians, were sent out of the camp to try to make for Canada. They must have gone in a very pleased state of mind as, by mistake, they had been paid twice. One record states that they took with them the military chest, so that the gold would not fall into the hands of the Americans. Burgoyne then sent by drummer, a letter to Gates stating that he wished to send a field officer to him, to discuss a matter of "high moment" to both armies. Gates agreed to meet the emissary at 10 o'clock the following morning. When Gates's aide, the twenty two year-old Colonel Wilkinson, learned of the exchange, he asked Gates whether he had "not condescended improperly in agreeing to receive the deputy of his adversary." After some reflection Gates replied "You are right, young man; I was hasty; but what's to be done." Next morning, with his superior's agreement, Wilkinson tried to intercept Burgoyne's adjutant general, Major Kingston, and take the message from him so as to maintain protocol. Kingston refused and Wilkinson was obliged to conduct him to Gates, but not before Kingston, after protesting, agreed to be "hood-winked" with his own handkerchief. On their walk of a mile to the American headquarters they chatted about the beautiful scenery of the Hudson river at that time of the year.[66]

Kingston, in fact, carried two messages. The first was a reply to a letter which Gates had sent, protesting the burning of General Schuyler's house and other buildings. Burgoyne pointed out that the buildings were protected until the American troops had approached and that the burning was done to make a field of fire and not in any vindictive spirit. Other complaints contained in the letter were also responded to.[67]

Kingston then read from notes, which Wilkinson summarised as follows:

> I am directed to represent to you from General Burgoyne, that after having fought you twice, he has waited some days in his present position determined to try a third conflict against any force you could bring to attack him.
>
> He is apprised of the superiority of your numbers, and the disposition of your troops to impede his supplies and render his retreat a scene of carnage on both sides. In this situation he is impelled by humanity, and thinks himself justified by established principles and precedents of state and of war, to spare the lives of brave men upon honourable terms; should Major-general Gates be inclined to treat upon that idea, General Burgoyne would propose a cessation of arms, during the time necessary to communicate the preliminary terms, by which in any extremity he and army mean to abide.[68]

To Wilkinson's utter astonishment, Gates put his hand in his pocket and pulled out a piece of paper, saying these are the terms on which the army must surrender. Kingston read the note and was startled. The note consisted of little more than a demand for unconditional surrender. Gates surveyed him attentively through his spectacles, while Kingston appeared exceedingly upset. He asked to be relieved of the responsibility of taking such a note to Burgoyne saying, "although I cannot presume to speak for him, I think the propositions it contains cannot be submitted to." On Gates insisting the note be taken, Kingston requested it might be sent by one of his own officers. This Gates declined to do, remarking, "that as he had brought the message, he ought to take back the answer." Kingston then reluctantly left with the note, once more blind-folded, and conducted by Wilkinson to the American advanced post. This time, his conversation was very different. He talked of the pride and spirit of the British army, and recalled the feats performed by six British regiments at the battle of Minden. All this mystified Wilkinson because at that point, he was still ignorant of what the note had contained.[69]

When he returned to the headquarters and learned of what had been written, Wilkinson expressed his opinion that Burgoyne had been given an advantage, by Gates presenting his own terms and not waiting to receive the British overtures. Wilkinson pointed out that in the capitulations of Cape Breton, Quebec, Montreal, and other places, the propositions were made by the besieged and modified or refused by the besiegers at their discretion. Wilkinson recalled that Gates clapped him on the shoulder and exclaimed with much complacency and affection, "Wilky, you are right again; but it is done, and we must make the most of it; I shall be content to get the arms out of their hands."[70]

Burgoyne recalled his Council of War to consider the six articles in Gates's letter. There was a unanimous declaration from the officers, that they would rather die of hunger than to agree to such disgraceful articles. By sunset of that day, Kingston was back in the American lines, delivering the total rejection of the American document and presenting Burgoyne's own proposals. Much to the surprise of the British officers, Gates, with only minor modifications, accepted them promptly. In a further letter from Burgoyne, only the demand that the capitulation be completed by two p.m. on the same day (15th October) was objected to, on the grounds that secondary articles needed to be prepared. The delay requested was acceded to.[71]

Having now an agreement ready for signature, Burgoyne turned his attention to the safety of his Loyalist officers and men. Since the commencement of hostilities, Americans on both sides had ill-treated their American adversaries when they fell into each other's hands. He was anxious that there should be no instances of this behaviour. He, therefore, gave the Loyalists orders to leave the camp and make their way through the American lines to Canada. Because of the criticism that had been levelled against other Loyalist detachments for abandoning the engineers near Fort Edward a few days before, Lieutenant Colonel John Peters, the senior Loyalist officer refused to accept such an order verbally. He went to Major General Phillips, who in turn spoke with Burgoyne and Peters was given written instructions to leave. He, with his remaining 34 men, then left and most reached Canada safely.[72]

At the same time, Burgoyne was having some second thoughts. Lieutenant Colonel Sutherland and Captain Craig of the 47th had been appointed to negotiate the secondary articles and sign the final documents. After working all day with the Americans and signing draft agreements, Captain Craig at ten thirty that night, on the instructions of his superiors, wrote to Colonel Wilkinson, who had been appointed as one of the American negotiators, stating that General Burgoyne had approved every article except the title. With Burgoyne's political skills coming to the fore, he had asked Craig to say "Capitulation" was misleading while a treaty of "Convention" was intended. With the single alteration of this word a fair copy signed by General Burgoyne would be handed over the following day. By midnight, Wilkinson had obtained Gates's approval for the change. The treaty was now clearly a Convention and not a Capitulation.[73]

Appendix 1 sets out the full document. Summarised and paraphrased, its most important points were: (Article 1), arms and artillery were to be given up: (Article 2), the troops to be withdrawn to Europe by way of Boston on the condition of not serving in the war again: (Article 3), exchange would expunge the foregoing article: (Article 4), the army to be quartered in or near Boston while waiting for shipping: (Article 5), provisions to be supplied on same scale as issued to the American army: (Article 6), no baggage to be searched by Americans on assurance no public stores were contained therein: (Article 7), officers and men not to be separated as far as circumstances permit: (Article 8), the treaty to apply to all corps and camp followers in the army regardless of nationality: (Article 9), Canadians to be allowed to return to Canada by the shortest route to the British post on Lake George: (Article 10), three officers to be allowed to take despatches to Canada, New York and Britain: (Article 11), officers to be admitted to parole and wear side arms during their stay in Massachusetts while waiting transport to Europe: (Article 12), clothing and baggage from Canada to be allowed transit.

A cease fire had been in effect since the start of the negotiations. This led to some fraternisation taking place between the British and American soldiers. Both were using the Fishkill for bathing, and Sergeant Lamb recorded that Private Maguire (9th) suddenly recognised his brother on the other side of the river, who was serving in the American army. The reunion in mid-river, must have been an emotional experience for both participants and onlookers, bearing in mind the circumstances under which the meeting took place. Stone relates several other instances where brothers, or fathers and sons, from both sides, met on battlefields, although not with such a happy outcome.[74]

Burgoyne, when he returned to England, made a speech in Parliament referring to the attitude of his men at this point,

Whatever fate may attend the general who led the army to Saratoga, their behaviour at that memorable spot must entitle them to the thanks of their country—Sir, it was calamitous, it was an awful, but it was an honourable hour—during the suspence of the answer from the general of the enemy, to the refusal made by me of complying with the ignominious conditions he had proposed, the countenance of the troops beggars description—a patient fortitude; a sort of stern resignation, that no pencil or language can reach, sat on every brow. I am confident every breast was prepared to devote its last drop of blood rather than suffer a precedent to stand upon the British annals of an ignoble surrender.[75]

The Convention was still not ready for complete acceptance by the British. Another element of doubt had entered into their minds. An American deserter had come into the British lines that evening, (Wilkinson describes him as a British spy—probably incorrectly), and stated he had heard "third hand" that the British General Clinton, in a drive north, had taken possession of the entrenchments of the Highlands and in all probability had arrived by this time at Albany. Immediately, there was a great desire among the officers to break-off the negotiations and Burgoyne called another Council of War. In his usual manner, he asked a series of questions to be answered:

— Whether a treaty which had been definitely settled by fully empowered commissioners could be broken with honor:

— Whether the intelligence just received was sufficiently reliable to allow the breaking of a so advantageous agreement:

— Whether the army had sufficient reliant spirit to defend their present position to the last man.

When a vote was taken on the first question, 14 officers to 8 were of the opinion that where the enemy had granted all of the demands, the treaty could not be broken with honor; there was also divided opinion on the second question, that the evidence of Clinton's achievement was hearsay and the distances still to be covered so great, that he would still be unable to assist the beleagered troops; on the third question the officers of the units near the river said yes, but those further inland were doubtful whether their low ground was defendable.[76]

The mixed reaction left Burgoyne in a quandary. He decided to play for time. He had information that several hundred of the New York militia's terms of service had expired and had marched off, (according to Wilkinson, without permission). On the morning of the 16th, he wrote to Gates claiming that as a considerable force had been detached from the American army, he required two of his officers be permitted to see the strength remaining, so as to ensure the principles of superiority on which the treaty was based still existed. Receipt of this letter filled the American general with indignation. Wilkinson was again sent off to tell Burgoyne in no uncertain terms to either ratify or dissolve the treaty and that he expected a decisive reply. A young observer professed he heard Gates call after Wilkinson, "Tell Burgoyne if you are not back in an hour and a quarter, I'll open every battery I have upon him."[77]

Wilkinson passed on Gates's comments, and received the response, "General Gates has no idea of the principle and spirit which animates the army I command; there is not a man in it, I assure you Colonel Wilkinson, who does not pant for action." It was then agreed that the truce would end in one hour and Wilkinson left saying "After what has passed, there can be no treaty; your fate must be decided by arms, and General Gates washes his hands of the blood which may be spilled." Burgoyne replied, "Be it so." Wilkinson himself had used some bluff, because at that stage, the American units were scattered in trying to keep the British army surrounded and he recalled that, "the men had got the treaty into their heads, and had lost their passion for combat." However, Wilkinson had only gone a short distance, when Major Kingston came running after him and asked him to return. Burgoyne then requested time to consult with his officers and it was agreed they would meet in two hours. Wilkinson did not return to the American camp but waited at an American forward post on the perimeter of the British defences.

While there, he saw Lieutenant Colonel Sutherland across the creek and called him over. He showed him Captain Craig's letter written the night before, assuring Gates that with a change in the title the treaty would be accepted. Sutherland stated he had not been privy to the letter and would Wilkinson give it to him for a period of fifteen minutes. Wilkinson, apparently willing to do so, loaned it to him. Sutherland then hurried with it to the British headquarters. Meanwhile,

Gates, now losing his patience, sent a peremptory message to Wilkinson instructing him to break off the treaty. To this, Wilkinson replied by the messenger, that he was doing the best he could and would see him in half an hour. As promised, Sutherland returned promptly accompanied by Captain Craig. They brought with them the Convention signed by General Burgoyne. When Gates received the document from Wilkinson, he added and signed an additional paragraph, stating, that although Burgoyne was not mentioned, he fully understood the document.[78]

It is not difficult to understand the reasons why Gates gave the liberal terms described in the Convention. He too, was getting information regarding the success and progress of Sir Henry Clinton's force below Albany. He had received a letter from the American Major General George Clinton dated 9th October, informing him that two messengers from Sir Henry Clinton to Burgoyne had been intercepted. They carried with them the news that Fort Montgomery on the River Hudson had been captured on the 6th October. This was a direct threat to Albany, making him anxious that Saratoga be brought to an end before he, in turn, might be forced to flee. Neither party to the Convention knew that Clinton's strength was already spent and within a few days had begun to move back down the river.[79]

A week after the Convention had been signed, Phillips, expressing a view probably shared by all the officers, wrote to Clinton explaining that the latter's movement north was too late and that they had no alternative but to capitulate or starve because, "attack we could not, and attack they would not."[80]

In the explanation to Congress by Colonel Wilkinson, made on the instructions of Gates, it was stated that with the enemy entrenched with 12 days' provisions, the loss of Fort Montgomery endangering the Arsenal at Albany, there was no time to contest the convention. The alternatives were to hazard a "disadvantageous attack" or to retire from their position.

> . . . had an attack been carried against Lt. Genl Burgoyne, the dismemberment of our Army must necessarily have been such as would have incapacitated it for further action.[81]

While Congress and other American politicians were immediately critical of the terms contained in the Convention of Saratoga, Gates was never criticised personally for the liberal terms he had granted the British. Soon after, based on his Saratoga victory, his friends in Congress started their first moves to try and have him replace Washington as the supreme commander of the army. While nothing came of this, within a matter of weeks, he was appointed President of the Board of War, the equivalent of present-day Chiefs of Staff and to whom Washington reported.

American public opinion, when they heard of the terms granted was divided. Shrewd observer, Abigail Adams, wrote to her husband John Adams reporting,

> Many people find fault with them but perhaps do not consider sufficiently the circumstances of General Gates, who [perhaps] by delaying and exacting more might have lost all.

The British were also surprised by the terms granted. Captain, the Earl of Harrington of the 29th Foot, said at the subsequent Parliamentary enquiry into the defeat, "Few persons in the army expected so good terms as those which were granted."[82]

The American success at Saratoga led to France joining in the struggle against Britain, which proved to be the turning point in the War of American Independence. The action taken by France was soon followed by Spain and the Dutch. What had started as a skirmish outside of Boston two years earlier, now quickly escalated into a contest between the major maritime powers for the domination of the World.

CHAPTER 3

The March to Cambridge

ON the morning of 17th October 1777, Burgoyne, escorted by Wilkinson, forded the Fishkill creek and presented himself to Gates at his marquee. Burgoyne, "in a rich royal uniform and Gates in a plain blue frock," raised his hat saying "The fortune of war, General Gates, has made me your prisoner." To which Gates replied, "I shall always be ready to bear testimony that it has not been through any fault of your excellency." After introducing their senior officers, the two groups retired inside the marquee for a meal. What they ate is on record, as were the toasts to the King and George Washington, but nothing has survived as to what they talked about while eating.

The Americans on the south side of the Fishkill were kept within their own lines. The bridge having been destroyed during the retreat, the survivors of the allied army had to ford the stream, led by a band, and followed by the Light troops "dressed in their clean white Kersey-meres." (Appendix 2 lists the regiments). Lieutenant Digby left a graphic impression of his emotions:

> About 10 o'clock we marched out, according to treaty, with drums beating and the honours of war, but the drums seemed to have lost their former inspiriting sounds, and though we beat the Grenadiers' march, which not long before was so animating, yet then it seemed by its last feeble effort as if almost ashamed to be heard on such an occasion. Thus was Burgoyne's Army sacrificed to either the absurd opinions of a blundering ministerial power, the stupid inaction of a general who, from his lethargic disposition, neglected every step he might have taken to assist their operations, or lastly, perhaps, his own misconduct in penetrating so far as to be unable to return.

The bitterness felt by the soldiers was made apparent, when one of the British officers gave his sword to an American transport rider saying, "You damned rebel, take this, I have no more use for it." Phillips directed his rage at Germaine. Writing to Clinton he said he pitied "poor Burgoyne," but he had his orders and it was to such orders "we owe our present situation." He continued, "I must not write on the subject or I shall grow wild."

The American Light Horse paraded near the marquee to receive the British force, were dressed in blue coats with white facings, their heads covered with bear skin caps and "long white hair streaming in the wind." The regiment was well dressed and well mounted. But all was not well within the American army. General Schuyler had come north to see the surrender and was seen by some of the New England troops. One was heard to say that if he showed his face, he would put a brace of balls through him. While nothing came of the threat, it is indicative of the extent of the ill-feeling that existed between the units of the American army, which the victory had not assuaged.[83]

As the British troops entered the American camp, the two generals emerged from the marquee and a band struck up Yankee Doodle. The tune was well known to the British because they had, for over 130 years, often marched to it. To them, it was Lydia Fisher's Jig, taken to England by British mercenaries after service with the Dutch. Since Bunker Hill, the New Englanders had adopted it for their own and at the same time, turned the insulting word of Yankee, bestowed on them by Virginians, to a proud title. This led Anbury to comment, that to hear them play this tune on such an occasion was a "little mortifying."[84]

Burgoyne was described as large, stoutly formed with a rough and hard countenance, but had a "handsome figure and noble air". Gates was smaller, much less of manner, destitute of that air which distinguished Burgoyne. Apparently, by a previous understanding between the two, General Burgoyne stepped back, drew his sword, and before the two armies, presented it to General Gates, who received it and then instantly returned it in a courteous manner. The two stood for a few minutes silently gazing as the British army stacked their arms and marched away; then, without a word, the two retired again into the marquee.

Great tribute was paid to the appearance of the British soldiers by American observers. The light infantry, still in advance, ". . . were extraordinary men. Finer and better looking troops I never saw," despite, "they were not seen to much advantage, however, for their small-clothes and gaiters having been wet in the creek, the dust adhered more readily to them in consequence." On the other hand the Germans were observed in less complimentary terms, "The Hessians came lumbering in the rear. When were they ever in advance? Indeed, their equipments prevented such an anomaly. Their heavy caps were almost equal to the weight of the whole equipment of a light infantry soldier. I looked at these men with commiseration." And again, "The Hessians were extremely dirty in their persons, and had a collection of wild animals in their train, the only thing American they had captured." Listed was a black bear, a tamed deer, young foxes and a young racoon. "There were a good many women accompanying the Germans, and a miserable looking set of oddly dressed, Gipsy featured females they were."[85]

When Burgoyne's army had left Europe, he had stipulated in accordance with standing orders, only three wives for each company could travel with their menfolk. In return for their rations, but without pay, they had to sew, cook and nurse all the men of their company. For them to stand-up to the rigours of a miltary campaign, carrying heavy loads, marching for long distances, often being under musket or artillery fire, they had to be particularly single-minded and perhaps physically more like a man than a woman. During their march through Canada and later through the colonies, Burgoyne seems to have relaxed his limitation on the number of women accompanying the men. While the few muster rolls which have survived reflect only the official number of women, most accounts indicate there must have been substantially more, particularly among the Germans. The men seem to have had no difficulty in attracting female company and this led in turn to an increasing number of children following the army.

American regiments were detailed to line each side of the road as far as the exit from the American camp, under strict orders to make no demonstration against the captives. As far as the American soldiers were concerned, the orders were obeyed. However at the edge of the camp as they marched away, the British rank and file gave vent to their feelings by hurling abuse at the Americans and the American camp followers replied in kind. The British soldiers were preserving their usual attitude of superiority and contempt for the Americans; later it was to be the cause of more serious trouble.[86]

Of the allied soldiers who laid down their arms that day, approximately

3,000 were British (see appendix 3). It seems that no sooner had they left the camp, when some of them began to slip away from the columns. A few were true deserters. Others, wishing to continue the fight, were only the first of many to start out for Canada, Rhode Island, New York and other places, with the object of rejoining an active British army. Some of the adventures experienced by these escapees are described in later chapters.

Because of the anger felt by the militia, and for their own protection, the remaining Indians were separated and kept at a farm across the river, quartered under a strong guard in the farmer's kitchen. Three were described as being "between six and seven feet in height, perfect giants in form, and possessing the most ferocious countenances I ever saw." A few days later, after promising never to take up arms again, they were allowed to go north. With them went Canadians, Captains Boucheville and Beambier with their 8 officers and 99 men. Both these, and the Canadian civilians who had left earlier, appear to have made it safely back home. By November Burgoyne was authorising payment to contractors for the services of the bateauxmen.

Meanwhile, 500 Americans were detailed as guards and on that day the prisoners were marched to Freemans Farm, where they camped for the night. The Americans now sent in liberal supplies of food and for the first time in several weeks the men had more than enough to eat. The following day, some officers visited General Fraser's grave and were outraged when they found that it had been opened by American troops, probably suspicious that British guns or gold had been buried with the corpse. The army then marched as far as Stillwater where they were ferried across the river to commence their journey eastwards to Boston. Meanwhile, Burgoyne, Phillips and Riedesel, together with Riedesel's family, continued south to Albany with an escort of 20 Americans. There, despite having burned down his Saratoga house, they were lodged, entertained and well looked after by General Schuyler. After a few days they too moved eastwards, overtaking the army on their way to Boston.[87]

As soon as the British army had left, detachments of the Americans were sent southwards to ensure that any further advance north by Sir Henry Clinton would be stopped. The American camp then began to break up. The New England militia explored the field for plunder and immense quantities of camp furniture and fragments of every description were taken. With the ending of hostilities discipline, also broke down and cases occurred of plundering local farmers for anything of value, demonstrating once more, the antipathy existing between the New England militia and the New Yorkers.[88]

Due to a shortage of rafts it took two days for the prisoners to be ferried across the Hudson. Once across, in order to ease problems of accommodation and supply, the Germans were separated from the British and were marched on a more southerly route by way of Kinderhook. The British officers and men, with an escort, took a more northerly route by way of Williamstown.

Since the 7th October, rain had been almost continuous; the weather now turned much colder, and it began to snow. As the march progressed, conditions grew steadily worse. It took two days to cross the Green Mountains on roads which were almost impassable. Anburey who, on the second day, was in command of the baggage guard, described conditions thus:

> It is impossible to describe the confusion that ensued; carts breaking down, others sticking fast, some oversetting, horses tumbling with their loads of baggage, men cursing, women shrieking, and children squalling! It should seem that I was to encounter every unpleasant duty that can fall to the lot of an officer, for this very day I had the baggage guard; exclusive of being covered with snow, and riding about after the bat-men, to keep them together, and to assist each other, my attention was directed to a scene, which I did not think it possible human nature could have supported, for in the midst of the heavy snow-storm, upon a baggage-cart, and nothing to shelter her from the inclemency of the weather but a bit of an old oil-cloth, a soldier's wife was delivered of a child, she and the infant are both well, and are now at this place. It may be said, that women who follow a camp are of such a masculine nature, they are able to bear all hardships; this woman was quite the reverse, being small, and of a very delicate constitution.[89]

During the course of that terrible march, 12 men died, and by the time the column had reached Williamstown, many had to fall out. An Army strength return, indicates between the date of capitulation (17th October) and 31st October, 160 men absented themselves. Some of these may not even have started out from Saratoga, but had been gathered up by the Americans and treated as prisoners of war rather than as Convention Prisoners. Others left sick at Williamstown, recovered later and tried to catch up with the army. A few of these were picked up on the road by Americans and treated as escapees. One of those left behind, Private James Maguire (47th), spent some years on the run but finally made it into New York several years later. Others took the opportunity to slip away when the Americans, to ease problems of food supplies and accommodation, divided the British column into two groups, one taking a course through Greenfield to Northfield, while the other went through Pittsfield.[90]

In general, the Americans took the view that where a Convention Prisoner escaped and was then recaptured, he lost his privileges under the Convention and was classed as an ordinary prisoner of war. Until the Americans suspended the Convention, this change in status was important. A Convention Prisoner was entitled to receive full rations; a prisoner of war qualified only for a reduced scale of food. Probably equally important to most of the men, the Convention Prisoners were, under a signed agreement, on their way to Europe; a prisoner of war could only hope that an exchange of prisoners would be made some time in the future. Before long, there was to be a dramatic reversal in repatriation prospects, but at this point in time, the Convention Prisoners were receiving the same rations as their escort and were on their way home.

Despite the terrible conditions in which the march took place, there were some amusing incidents. Officers were billeted in houses on the route of march and Anburey describes how he first encountered the New England custom of "bundling," being invited to sleep in the same bed with the daughter of the house. He goes on at length to assure his readers that he was able to avoid this temptation. In another incident, he describes how a British officer complained to the American Brigadier General commanding the escort, that he was very uncomfortable in the terrible weather, having lost his boots. The General immediately offered to sell him his own for a guinea and dismounted to complete the sale there and then. He had to be convinced to leave the sale until they reached their destination that evening.

The conditions in the countryside through which they passed brought home to the British, the sacrifices which the New England population had made during the struggle. Although the area had not been fought over, the inhabitants had stripped their farms bare to support their army. One report referred to inhabitants having only two blankets, but willingly gave up one to their soldiers.

It was during this march that the British officers also first learnt of the impact war has on the currency of a country. Congress had fixed the official exchange rate for the dollar at four and one half to a gold guinea. The published rate was of little consequence since the American population already understood that the paper currency issued by the new American states was worth much less than its stated value. A black market had already developed. The officers obtained nine dollars for each guinea. For the Americans, this was probably still very much a bargain, because the rate rapidly went to above 20 dollars. Later in the war, in return for gold, dollars went to astronomical levels. At Williamstown the local population were bidding against each other, so keen were they to secure gold.

As the men trudged on towards the coast, they were oblivious to the political storm which was brewing over their fate. The unofficial news of the defeat spread rapidly within the 13 colonies and Canada, but disbelieved by the British officers of the New York garrison and the army at Philadelphia. One man was arrested for spreading the news. By 22nd October, General Howe in Philadelphia, heard about it and in writing to Germaine added, "I mention it with my opinion, that it is totally false." Article 10 of the Convention allowed three officers to take the despatches containing news of what had happened; one to London via New York with the original copy of the Convention; another went to General Carleton in Quebec, who immediately sent the officer on to London; the third went to General Howe in Philadelphia, who received it on 31st October, the same day as the news reached Congress.[91]

Carleton, who made no secret of his opinion of Germain, either directly to him or to others, wrote to Burgoyne,

> This unfortunate event, it is to be hoped, will in future prevent ministers from pretending to direct operations of war, in a country at three thousand miles distance, of which they have so little knowledge as not to be able to distinguish between good, bad or interested, advices, or to give positive orders in matters, which, from their nature, are ever

upon the change; so that the expedience or propriety of a measure, at one moment, may be totally inexpedient or improper in the next.[92]

Gates never sent the news of the victory to his commanding officer, George Washington, who worried that the rumours were not true. He asked Congress if they had any authentic information, but they were unable to help him. Washington finally learned officially from Major General Putnam, who passed to him a copy of the Convention he had received directly from Gates. Wilkinson, apparently to make amends for the conduct of his chief, wrote to Washington on 24th October, "being uncertain whether you are apprised of the fact", told him what had happened. This public slight by Gates, naturally upset Washington and he chided him for his failure to inform his superior officer.[93t]

Colonel Wilkinson presented the official news to Congress, then sitting in York, Pennsylvania, on 31st October. The delay on his part was the result of his stopping off in New Jersey, to see the lady who was to become his wife. He claimed that he had suffered a "convulsive colic". Never missing the opportunity of making a point, the ever-caustic Congressman Samuel Adams proposed to John Hancock that in appreciation of his services, Wilkinson should be given a gift of a horse whip and a pair of silver spurs. Congress, however, promoted him to Brigadier General for bringing the good news and declared Thursday, 18th November as a day of thanksgiving.[94]

The British post in Rhode Island heard of the British defeat very quickly. A Jewish trader brought in the news. Rumours of Burgoyne's increasing difficulties, as he moved south, had already reached London via Canada. As early as 26th October, Horace Walpole wrote, "Burgoyne is said to be beaten"; and on 3rd November, he claimed the news was definite. By mid-November, the rumours were wide-spread. Germain was criticised by Lord Shelburne as,

> a man who has so great a confidence in his military talents as to think he can command an army and ensure victory in his closet at three thousand miles distance from the scene of the action.

The Duke of Richmond joined in criticising the strategy of the campaign, stating,

> Supposing, which is most improbable, that Mr. Burgoyne has got to New York, what has he effected? He has lost several thousand men

and he might have arrived at New York two years ago by sea from England without any loss at all.[95]

Although the official despatches did not reach Whitehall until 15th December, the news via Canada reached London on 2nd December, causing an uproar in the House of Commons. Speaker after speaker attacked both the strategy and the lack of planning and co-ordination of Burgoyne's and Howe's armies. Edmund Burke made the point saying,

> The intended measure was a conjunction between Howe and Burgoyne, it was to be produced in the strangest way he had ever heard of; the armies were to meet yes: Howe was travelling southward, and Burgoyne in the same direction.

Fox joined in by saying

> An army of 10,000 men destroyed through the ignorance, the obstinate, wilful ignorance and incapacity of the noble Lord, called loudly for vengeance.

Despite the uproar in Parliament, there was no despondency in Britain. Manchester and Liverpool led in giving funds to raise new regiments, and Scotland provided many men. 15,000 recruits were raised from such private means.[96]

When the news reached the German Principalities, there was an immediate reaction and concern on the financial implications. The Duke of Brunswick's minister wrote to Colonel Faucitt, the British commissioner responsible for German recruiting, stating that the German troops subjected to the terms of the Convention prohibiting their employment during the war, should not be allowed to return to Brunswick and discourage others from enlisting. He suggested they be sent to, "one of your islands in America." The Duke's real concern was that he continued to be paid so long as his soldiers remained in the service of the British, and if they could not take part in the American War, then they should be employed elsewhere.[97]

The American Agents in France learned of the defeat of the British on 4th December from the Secretary of the Massachusetts Board of War. The message had arrived on a vessel making a very fast thirty-one day passage across the Atlantic. Receipt of the news was the final factor to convince France to join in the fight against England, with Spain and the Dutch following shortly afterwards.[98]

The immediate military impact of Burgoyne's defeat caused the small garrisons he had left at Ticonderoga and Fort George to be dangerously exposed. Their commander, Brigadier General H. Watson Powell, asked Carleton in Quebec for instructions as to what to do. Carleton was unable to help him. As Germaine had removed him from all command outside of Canada, he told Powell he would have to make his own decisions. Powell called his officers to a Council of War, following which, the order was given to evacuate the forts and fall back to St John's and other places in Canada. As soon as they had gone, the Americans quickly occupied the posts. It would be more than two years before the British could muster the strength to evict them.[99]

On the 6th November 1777, after a three week march of nearly 200 miles under appalling conditions, the Convention Prisoners arrived in Cambridge, just outside Boston. In ignorance of all the turmoil developing, they assumed their stay would be only for a matter of days or weeks until transports arrived to take them home. They never realised that it would be over five years before many would enjoy that happy day.

CHAPTER 4

Cambridge

As the Convention Prisoners marched into Cambridge, the British seem to have caused less comment than the Germans. An eyewitness, Mrs. Winthrop, described the scene thus:

> Last Thursday, which was a very stormy day, a large number of British troops came softly through the town via Watertown to Prospect Hill. On Friday we heard the Hessians were to make a procession in the same route. We thought we should have nothing to do but view them as they passed. To be sure the sight was truly astonishing. I never had the least idea that the creation produced such a sordid set of creatures in human figure—poor, dirty, emaciated men. Great numbers of women, who seemed to be the beasts of burden, having bushel-baskets on their backs, by which they were bent double. The contents seemed to be pots and kettles, various sorts of furniture, children peeping through gridirons and other utensils—some very young infants, who were born on the road—the women barefoot, clothed in dirty rags. Such effluvia filled the air while they were passing, that had they not been smoking all the time, I should have been apprehensive of being contaminated. After a noble-looking advanced-guard, General Burgoyne headed this terrible group on horseback. The other generals also clothed in blue cloaks—Hessians, Waldeckers, Anspackers, Brunswickers, etc., etc., followed on. The Hessian generals gave us a polite bow as they passed. Not so the British. Their baggage-wagons drawn by poor, half-starved horses.[100]

In preparation for the arrival of the British and Germans, a thousand militia had been called out from the surrounding area. They were put to work constructing a guard house on Bunker Hill for the use of the camp guards. After the arrival of the prisoners, the militia was increased to 1,200 men. Later, when relationships between the British and Americans deteriorated, the number was again increased to 1,500.[101]

The British prisoners were allocated to barracks on Prospect Hill and the Germans to similar accommodation on Winter Hill. If the

prisoners did not look attractive to the residents, likewise, the location
and accommodation did not look attractive to the prisoners. Cambridge
had been used to house the American militia in 1775 when investing
British-held Boston. The little village had suffered at the hands of the
Americans, and Burgoyne wrote,

> The once thriving village, famed for its beauty, with its common "like
> a bowling green" was almost unrecognisable. Spared . . . from the
> actual ravages of the enemy . . . it had endured the almost equally
> severe handling of a year's occupation by an ill-disciplined militia.

The whole neighbourhood between Cambridge and Boston was
filled with bare and barren hilltops, covered in part with barracks. These
were erected without foundations, with bare boards, through which
entered, from above, below, and all around, the wind, the rain and
snow. They had no windows, only holes. As Corporal George Fox
later recalled, "good usage but very cold barracks."[102]

Since the lifting of the Boston siege, the buildings had fallen into
disrepair, and some had since been used as a hospital for innoculations
against small-pox. In many cases, thirty or forty persons, men, women,
and children, were indiscriminately crowded together in one hut. Lamb
described the conditions,

> in the night time, those that could lie down, and the many who sat
> up from the cold, were obliged frequently to rise and shake from them
> the snow which the wind drifted in at the openings.[103]

The junior officers were not much better off. While the terms of
the Convention, promised "quartered according to his rank," nothing
was provided for them and they mostly found themselves in the same
accommodation as the men, although only six to eight to a hut. Ensign
Anburey confirmed Lamb's description of the conditions thus;

> We reached the barracks on Prospect Hill very late in the evening,
> which were unfortunately in the worst condition imaginable for the
> reception of troops, being so much out of repair that we suffered
> severely from the inclemency of the weather; the barracks were in fact
> bare of everything; no wood, and a prodigious scarcity of fuel, insomuch
> that we were obliged to cut down the rafters of our room to dry
> ourselves. The method of quartering was dreadfully inconvenient, six
> officers in a room not twelve feet square.[104]

Colonel Lee, commanding the guards, felt it necessary to express his fears of what might arise from the conditions in the camp;

> This morning rode round the lines and found the Field Officers and some others walking by their barracks to keep themselves from perishing with cold; not one stick of wood to put into the Fire, and if some other method cannot be found to supply them they must either perish or burn all the public buildings.

In a later reports, he complained of their pulling off barn doors; carrying away fence rails for fuel; demolishing an empty bakery and house in their need to find fuel.[105]

Even before the war started, the population of the Boston area had increased to the extent that fire wood had to be brought in from Maine. The American army's consumption during their siege of Boston had made matters worse. Now with the arrival of the Convention Prisoners, Mrs Winthrop complained that 250 cords will not serve them for a week and that prices had already risen to five pounds ten shillings per cord. The commanding general in New England, Major General William Heath, had already written to General Washington saying, "Wood is now $12 and $14 per cord on the wharves and the inhabitants cannot obtain a supply at that price."[106]

Firewood was not the only problem facing the prisoners. Winter clothing to cope with a New England winter proved impossible to obtain. In an effort to see that his men were looked after as much as possible, Burgoyne issued an order that, "every favour and preference was to be refused by the officers in general till justice could be done to the private men."[107]

Prices of everything were soaring. As early as January of 1777, the New England states had tried to control prices of commonly used commodities. Their efforts had failed. No one took any notice of John Adams who had opposed mandatory controls. He forecasted correctly that ". . . after a time the evils will break out with greater violence." His solution was to stop the issue of more paper money and to draw in some that was already out. He urged that taxes be increased and interest rates be raised from four to six percent. The Continental Congress was however, not prepared to face the political consequences of such a policy and inflation took hold.[108]

Heath, forty years old, was a farmer turned soldier. Writers have described how closely he resembled in appearance, the Marquess of Granby of "charged bald-headed" fame. Although the only time he commanded an army in the field resulted in failure, his efficiency as an administrator, subsequently led to his promotion to second-in-command of the American forces under General Washington. He had no illusions as to the task of being responsible for the Convention Prisoners. He stated it was a "wide and difficult field." He was a strong disciplinarian and would brook no nonsense from either the prisoners or his own men. At the same time, he seems to have been eminently fair and among other things, strived to do his best to alleviate the conditions under which the prisoners were being forced to exist.

It did not take long for the first official dispute to take place between the British and Americans concerning the treatment of the prisoners and such disputes were to continue over the next five years. By 14th November, Burgoyne was writing expressing his dissatisfaction over the lack of accommodation provided for the officers. While the seniors found suitable houses, Heath was unable to secure any for the junior officers. This was due to what one historian described as the Great Cambridge Conspiracy, designed to thwart Heath's efforts at finding housing. Burgoyne protested at the situation the officers found themselves in and in doing so he used the words, "the public faith is broke." Those words were to have far reaching political repercussions and Congress referred to them when they subsequently suspended the treaty.

Harvard College was the ringleader in stopping the officers obtaining housing. When protesting to the College concerning what was going on, Heath used language very similar to that of Burgoyne. With the continued obstacles placed in the way of his providing accommodation, Heath now found himself in an embarassing situation. Unable to publicly support the British, he wrote to Burgoyne stating the Convention had not been broken, and that housing would be found "as soon as possible." He failed in his efforts to do this and most of the junior officers had to spend the winter with their men in the ramshackle barracks. In retaliation, several of the officers refused to sign their paroles, and in turn, Heath cancelled their parole arrangements.[109]

Neither the fledgling Congressional government or its army could be directly blamed for the lack of accommodation. At best, the administrative control over any local area was fragile. In many instances the population went about their affairs in their own manner. The country was a long way from the point where any instruction would be obeyed promptly and without question. Most inhabitants continued to think of themselves as citizens of individual colonies or states, rather than as citizens of a unified country.

Heath had a much greater problem to solve than accommodation. He had to find the supplies to meet the required rations for not only the prisoners, but also for his own men. Gates had agreed in the Convention, that the British and Germans were to stay in Massachusetts until they left for Europe. He had omitted to consult with the Massachusetts government about this arrangement and they had little warning of the prisoners' arrival. They did their best to make arrangements and had appointed "persons to buy and deliver provisions." The make-shift arrangements meant that ration requirements often failed to materialise.

There was no dispute between Congress and Britain over the interpretation of article five of the Convention. Britain agreed that as the men were not prisoners of war, the British government was liable to pay for anything supplied to the Convention Prisoners. A dispute did arise, however, when the Americans refused to recognise their own paper currency and Congress demanded payment in specie. By February, Doctor Hayes at the British hospital in Albany, had to protest when asked to pay for supplies for the invalids, which caused great hardship. The American Commissary in the area was also writing, asking how he should act in view of the resolutions of Congress that supplies had to be paid for in gold or silver. Neither the doctors nor the patients possessed such funds.[110]

The British inevitably found difficulty in finding the monies required for the purchase of provisions. Heath thereupon agreed to provide the food, if the British would agree to replace them "in quality and quantity." He had no authority for making this arrangement but subsequently, Congress approved his taking this action.[111]

After several months, Congress also approved a further arrangement, proposed by Sir Henry Clinton, for food supplies to be transported through British-held Rhode Island. The quantities were quite insufficient to meet requirements and reliance on the purchase of local supplies continued. The Council of Massachusetts, following the instructions of Congress, demanded payments be made in gold. They said the gold was to be paid into their treasury, but it seems that much landed in the pockets of the merchants. Delays in making payment were also caused by disputes as to what were legitimate charges. The British Assistant Quartermaster General objected to the Americans including charges for the cost of maintaining the guards over the prisoners. Later, another argument broke out concerning some prisoners of war who, at the American's request, were lodged in the barracks, this being due to the absence of alternative accommodation. Major General Phillips refused to pay for their upkeep saying, "I have nothing to do with prisoners of war—I received a number of them into my care at the request of the Commissary of Prisoners and with your consent. I did this as a relief to your prisons and prison ships and as an act of humanity to the prisoners of war, but I never stipulated for the delivery or payment of provisions for them."

The Americans were not referring to authorised temporary lodgers at all. They were alluding to British prisoners of war who had "disappeared" by blending in with the Convention Prisoners. These prisoners of war had the incentive to do this—better rations and repatriation. Burgoyne was annoyed at what was happening as it could be considered a breach of the Convention. He suspected his junior officers were involved and he issued an order stating it was,

> an unwarrantable proceeding, and consequently supposed to be without the knowledge of the officers . . . and if any prisoners of war are with the troops, their names are to be reported to the General in order to their being delivered to the Commissary of Prisoners.

No record remains as to who these prisoners of war were. Probably they were soldiers of Burgoyne's army, captured before the making of the Convention, who had been classed by the Americans as prisoners of war. The support given to these soldiers by the junior officers, indicates the extent they were prepared to go outside the terms of their parole, in defiance of Burgoyne.[112]

The impact of the gold, plus the sheer volume of supplies required to feed several thousand prisoners and guards, caused the local economy to go awry. Heath had foreseen the shortage of food and appealed to the Governor of Connecticut for cattle, who let him have 70 head, but only on the condition that the hides would be returned there since the, "soldiery of this state, are almost totally barefooted." States from Pennsylvania southwards, were asked to send supplies of foodstuff to Boston, but this produced nothing. Despite Heath's efforts, the men often went hungry.

Inflation, which had first caused firewood prices to rise, now affected all forms of supplies. One officer complaining at the level of Cambridge prices and the profit tradesmen were making on their wares said, "If I buy anything at fourth hand, i.e. at the fourth remove, I can figure that I have had to pay almost sixteen times more for it than it cost at first hand in Boston". Heath tried to ensure the prisoners were treated fairly. He bewailed the fact that "the Yankee traders were unable to resist the bewitching allurements of gain and the expectation of catching hard money". Hearing what was going on, a British officer in Rhode Island commented, "That army has proved a mine of gold to the rebels, and the quantity of cash thrown into circulation by these means, has in great measure kept up the value of the paper currency, and enabled them to make remittances which has given them some credit with foreign nations."[113]

Another factor affecting the quantity and quality of the food received by the men, was fraud. Heath had appointed a Major Browne as quartermaster for the barracks. Browne was a former British private, who had deserted the 47th Foot some years previously. Burgoyne protested at his appointment. Heath sympathised, but said that there was nothing he could do, not having another officer available. The British soldiers complained Browne was dishonest. In addition, they said he often discriminated against the British in favour of the Germans.[114]

Notwithstanding the tedium and monotony that goes with being a prisoner, the officers, taking their lead from their commander, were outstanding in their care of their men. They constantly visited the wretched barracks and personally assisted in strengthening and weatherproofing them. They supplied the men with money for food and clothing under the pretence of buying their rags of old clothes and cast-off boots. Despite the harsh discipline imposed by the eighteenth-century British Army, there were close ties between the men and the regimental officers which is not reflected in official documents and records. As will be seen, the officers were prepared to risk their own privileged parole status to assist their men to escape.[115]

Regular drills were maintained for the men; the surrendered arms were represented by stout sticks; on holidays and accustomed anniversaries they turned out the "whole motley crew for a pathetic parody of a dress parade." This conduct, plus the lifelong discipline and ingrained morale, led Batchelder to add it was a source of mystification to the Americans, with their loose militia system and,

> it enabled the officers, in spite of every effort to break their spirit by insult, deprivation, extortion, and chicanery, to preserve their professional pride, and even now and then to play the gentleman in the midst of our conquerors.[116]

The lack of clothing also caused severe hardship to the men throughout their incarceration, but especially so during that first New England winter. British regiments were clothed by their Colonels, who by this time owed them two suits of uniform. There was plenty of warm clothing in Canada but that was now out of reach. Continuing a practice, first started when the regiments were in Canada, coat tails were cut off so as to provide material for repairing jackets and other items. Phillips wrote to Clinton "the soldiers are quite naked."[117]

During the winter, between 1st November 1777 and 31st March 1778, a further 17 men died. In the same period, 468 British soldiers also left their regiments, many to work in the area. Some of those that did leave, wrote to Burgoyne explaining they had no intention of deserting, but had gone into the country for food and shelter. Burgoyne accepted this explanation and in his orders dated 16th November 1777 said,

> The Lieutenant General is willing to believe that some of the Men who have absented themselves from their Corps, have not meant finally to desert, but have been induced to seek shelter from the present hardships, by offering themselves to labor in the Country for a limited time.

Finding temporary employment was nothing new in the eighteenth-century British army. As Houlding has described, it was customary practice to let their men eke out their pay by working away from their corps part-time. Disappearing for extended periods of time without official sanction was of course another matter. Lamb recorded that disciplinary action was taken against some men when they were caught by the Americans and returned to barracks, but even then it seems no severe penalties were inflicted by their officers. During the same period 57 men returned to their regiments with others following later. Many of those who did not return had made up their minds to try reaching the British lines in Canada, Rhode Island and New York.[118]

For the Convention Prisoners, getting out of barracks, or slipping away from marching columns, was for the most part a comparatively simple task. They were guarded by very inefficient militia or Continental regiments, who, in many cases, were as much dissatisfied with their lot as were the prisoners. Later in the war, an eyewitness described an incident where in adverse weather, 150 British prisoners were being marched into Lancaster, Pennsylvania. The guard, unwilling to continue under such conditions, had already lost 40 prisoners through escape. When four days later the guard were prevailed upon to continue the march, further escapes had reduced the number of prisoners to 50.[119]

A prisoner planning escape did face a difficulty not experienced by his counterpart in twentieth-century wars, when all British servicemen were instructed that if captured, it was their duty to attempt escape if that were possible. This was not so in the eighteenth century. Escape was frowned upon to protect the Colonels of the Regiments, who had paid good bounty money for each man when recruited. Whether or not the escaper reached British lines, the Colonel of his regiment had, invariably, lost the services of the man and expense would be incurred in recruiting a replacement. Some adjustments between regiments were often made but rarely to the satisfaction of the losing regiment. A case on record describes the treatment of one of Burgoyne's men, Private John Christian Fox (24th) captured at Schuylers House in Saratoga. Fox was classed by the Americans as a prisoner of war and was made to work on fortifications. He eventually escaped, reaching the British lines in August 1780, and then drafted into the King's American Regiment. His claim for pay for the period he was on the run was rejected. It was held that as a prisoner of war, he should not have escaped, but should have waited to be exchanged. That it was some years before any agreement could be reached between the antagonists for even limited exchanges of prisoners of war, was ignored.[120]

A regiment arriving back in England reduced to a skeleton through desertion, could only be rebuilt at great expense. Therefore, all men who left were described as deserters, regardless of their intentions. The word escape was never used. According to Sergeant Lamb, the orders issued to the Convention Prisoners on the subject, deterred many of the prisoners from an escape attempt, when an absence of one day or night could mean an accusation of desertion. After his return to England, Burgoyne himself drew fire on the subject. In Parliament, he excused the number of men leaving their regiments by saying they had acted with a view to get to Clinton or Howe and were "honourable deserters." In response, comments were made that his "imprudence" in saying this, "may be made use of to bad purpose." This referred to the possibility of encouraging soldiers elsewhere to escape after capture. When subsequently challenged on what he had said, Burgoyne considered it necessary to excuse himself by explaining,

> he would not be understood that he approved of their deserting, but on the contrary, if he had known of it, he would have hindered it.[121]

In May 1778 Major Frederick Mackenzie, later Adjutant General under Clinton, noted in his diary when in Rhode Island, that several officers of the Convention Army had arrived from Cambridge under their paroles and had informed him that,

> . . . there is great desertion from the British troops there; but as many of them are the best soldiers, it is generally supposed they go off with a view of getting into some of the posts occupied by the King's Army.[122]

Despite the opposition of senior officers to escape attempts, that view was not shared by the lieutenants and captains, who actively aided their men to leave. They gave the men passes and forged documents so as to satisfy the guards. There is evidence some officers were consulted before a man left. Lamb, before one of his escapes, informed his officer of his intention. Later in the war the officers, when learning their men were going to make a break for it, provided them with certificates stating the arrears of pay and clothing due to them. This was done to allay the fears of the men, doubtful of their reception if they were successful in arriving in New York. As Anburey commented,

> . . . we could refuse no more than we could their desertion, but to

be candid, rather than be witness of the hardships the men experienced, which were out of our power to redress, we rather connived at it.[123]

Burgoyne was very displeased with the aid his junior officers were giving their men to facilitate escape. In a General Order referring to desertion he added,

. . . but let officers reflect how much their own reputation is involved while this evil continues.[124]

Howe, the British Commander-in-Chief, had resigned his position early in 1778 and Clinton had been appointed in his place. Clinton was a realist and in desperate need of rank and file. An exchange of prisoners would have solved much of his problems, but no such arrangement was in sight. One of the early obstacles to reaching an accord on exchange was that the British needed additional rank and file—they had plenty of officers; the Americans wanted officers—under their short-term service system most of their rank and file in the hands of the British would be time expired by the time they returned and they would want to go home. This difference in their man-power requirements, added to political motives, delayed any agreements being made until much later in the war.

It did not take Clinton long to realise that escaping Convention Prisoners provided him with a ready stream of urgently needed trained soldiers. He moved from a passive acceptance of receiving them as they arrived, to actively encouraging them. He offered a bounty of one and a half guineas to those reaching New York. Later some received two guineas. After their arrival, the men were drafted into other regiments. Sergeants, corporals and drummers also received the bounty, with the choice of repatriation to Europe or transferring to a regiment of their choice. Any objections that might be made by the regimental Colonels to these arrangements, were overcome by Clinton ordering the receiving regiment pay one guinea per man to his original regiment.[125]

Hoping to take advantage of the desperate conditions under which the prisoners were forced to exist, and observing that they were going off on their own, led the Americans to establish recruiting parties just outside the British barracks. American officers did their best, by means of free drink, bounties and the prospect of sufficient food and clothing, to entice the British soldiers to desert their regiments and join the

American forces. Some really did desert. Burgoyne protested to Heath that these were parading in front of their more loyal comrades dressed in new American regimentals. Heath denied this. He asked why in any case were the British beyond the sentry line, since this was forbidden. No free liquor had been given, and he pointed out the Americans had worse barracks and no more fuel than the British prisoners. Moreover, recruitment was contrary to the express order of Congress.

It had occurred to many British soldiers that much of the danger of being picked up by the Americans, once they were on the run, could be avoided by joining American regiments. When the regiment moved near a British line, they could desert once again and join one of their own armies. It is not known who initially adopted this method of escape, but the first record of a British soldier making a "home run" to New York after joining the American forces, was not a Convention Prisoner, but a prisoner of war. Private James Burrows of the 55th Foot, was captured at the Battle of Princeton (3rd January 1777). After escaping, he enlisted in Colonel Innes's Connecticut Regiment, and by October 1777 had managed to reach New York. As Clinton took the trouble to have a personal record made of the method used, Burrows was probably the first to do it successfully.[126]

The Convention Prisoners reduced the same avenue of escape to a fine art. Local citizens called or drawn by lot for service in the militia, were allowed to hire substitutes to serve in their place. It did not take the British soldiers very long to make themselves available for this purpose, collecting a hire fee from the draftee; at the same time serving their own ends, by deserting their American regiment as soon as possible.

Robert Mansfield (47th) joined Crane's Artillery, and when that unit was posted to West Point, he crossed over into the British lines at Stoney Point. He was able to provide much information on the American artillery positioned at West Point. An un-named soldier of the 53rd arrived in New York after joining the 4th Maryland Regiment. Another from the 53rd, this time a German, Johan Keyser, served with Green's Corp of Artillery arriving in New York, was able to give valuable intelligence concerning the American dispositions.[127]

The use of this method of escape became widespread in a short period of time. When Burgoyne heard that many of his men were joining American regiments and not fully aware of their intentions, he

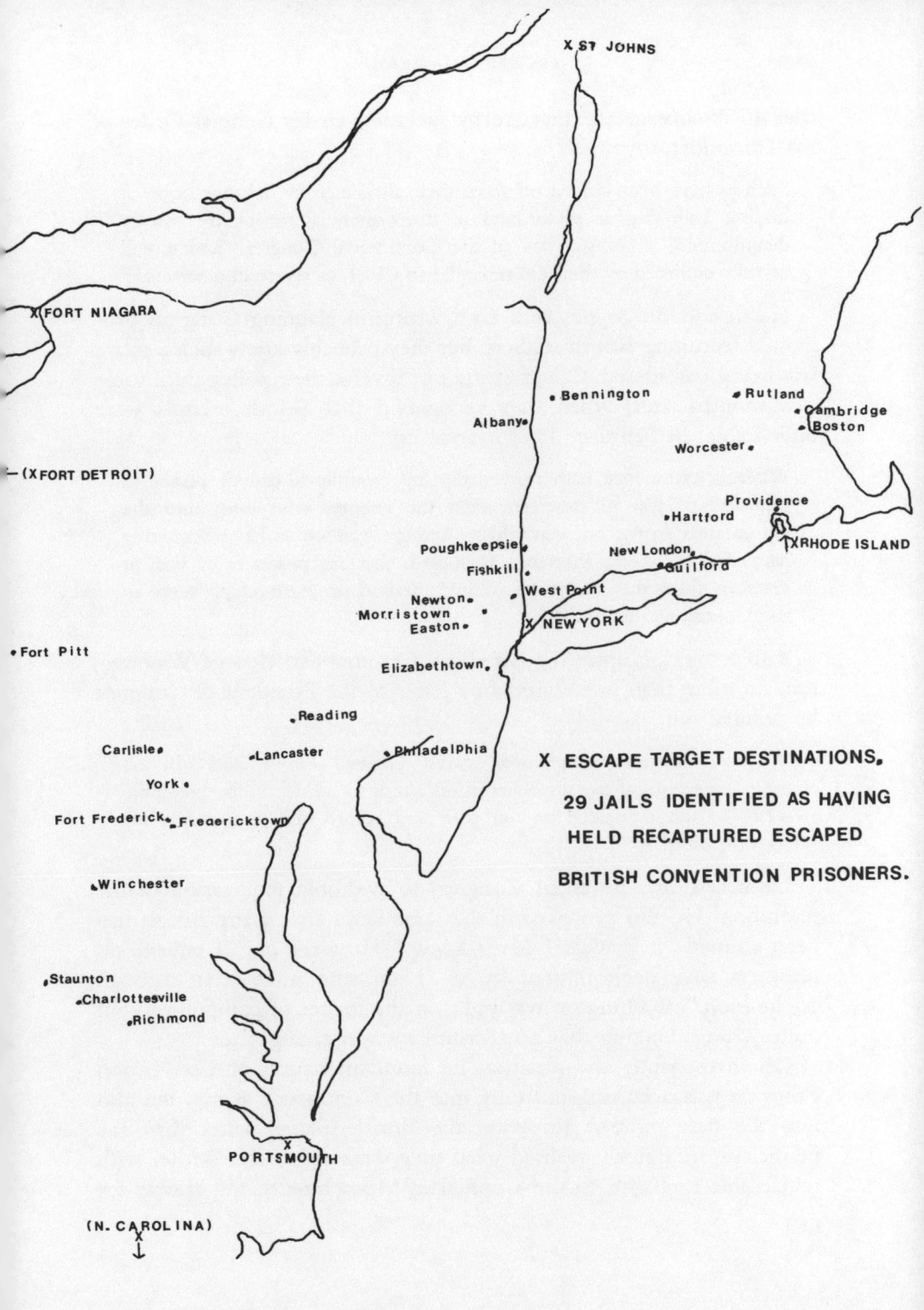

X ST JOHNS

X FORT NIAGARA

• Bennington   • Rutland
                              • Cambridge
Albany •   • Boston
              Worcester •

— (X FORT DETROIT)   Providence
                          • Hartford •
                                      X RHODE ISLAND
         Poughkeepsie•   New London •
              Fishkill•   •Guilford
                      West Point
         Newton•
• Fort Pitt Morristown•   X NEW YORK
         Easton•

         Elizabethtown•

            •Reading

Carlisle•   •Philadelphia   X ESCAPE TARGET DESTINATIONS.
         •Lancaster
York •   29 JAILS IDENTIFIED AS HAVING
Fort Frederick•Fredericktown
                                        HELD RECAPTURED ESCAPED
•Winchester
                                        BRITISH CONVENTION PRISONERS.

•Staunton
  •Charlottesville
    •Richmond

         X
      PORTSMOUTH

(N. CAROLINA)
      X

tried to discourage the practice by including in his General Order of
4th December 1777,

> Such as have been drawn off from their allegiance by delusive hope of
> finding high pay or preferment in the provincial troops are equally
> disappointed, it being a law of the Continental Congress, and it will
> be fully enforced by their Commander in Chief, to reject all deserters.[128]

Heath and Burgoyne were both wrong in claiming Congress pro-
hibited recruiting British soldiers, but they probably knew such a move
was being considered. Congress did not reverse their policy until some
two months later, when they recognised that British recruits were
undesirable. In February 1778 it resolved:

> Whereas experience hath proved that no confidence can be placed in
> prisoners of war or deserters from the enemy, who inlist into the
> Continental Army; but many losses and great mischiefs have frequently
> happened by them; therefore Resolved, that no prisoners of war or
> deserters from the enemy be inlisted, drafted or returned, to serve in
> the Continental Army.[129]

This resolution upset the American Commander, George Washington, on more than one count. In a letter to the President of Congress
he pointed out,

> We have always complained against General Howe and still do
> for . . . permitting the prisoners in his hands to inlist . . . the preamble
> seems to admit practice on our part (and) afford him opportunity for
> recrimination.

Unsuccessfully, he asked Congress to withhold publication of the
resolution. He also protested in the same letter that if any British had
been enlisted "it is what I never knew." He went on, "I believe no
prisoners have been inlisted by us. I am sure none have through
compulsion." Washington was right on the matter of compulsion, but
quite wrong thinking that no recruitment was taking place.[130]

On investigating the situation he found induction of Convention
Prisoners was occurring not only into the Continental Army, but also
into the state militias. Knowing the British soldier better than the
politicians, he quickly realised what they were up to. He wrote, with
remarkable foresight, to the Council of Massachusetts, responsible for

the recruitment of their militia, telling them that their town and district committees were enlisting deserters from Burgoyne's army and warning,

> . . . you may be amused for the present with the flattering idea of speedily completing your battalions, they will be found at or before, the opening of the campaign, reduced, by the defection of every British soldier, to their original weak condition, and the accumulated bounties of the Continent and the State will have been fruitlessly sacrificed. Indeed Mr. Burgoyne could hardly, if he were consulted, suggest a more effectual plan for plundering us of so much money, reinforcing Mr. Howe with so many men, and preventing us from recruiting a certain number of Regiments.

Apart from the impact on regimental strengths due to British soldiers deserting, he also expressed his fears that American militiamen would be affected. He went on,

> . . . to say nothing of the additional losses which may be dreaded, in desertions among the native soldiers, from the contagion of ill example, and the arts of seduction, which is more than probable will be put in practice.

Washington went on to ask that not only the practice of recruiting British soldiers be stopped, but to apply a retrospective remedy and discharge those who had been enlisted.[131]

George Washington's fears were soon realised. Two weeks later he again wrote, "The evils which I apprehended has already made its appearance" and continued,

> One of the Colonels informs me, that every British deserter sent to his regiment, except one, is already gone off. One of these people, a few nights ago, took off a light horse with his accoutrements from an advanced picket. I hope upon this proof of the infidelity of the above described class, that a total stop will be put to the hiring them. It is now prohibited by an express Resolve of Congress, passed a few weeks ago.[132]

Heath did his best to stop the recruiting. The American officers were experiencing much difficulty in filling their ranks, but they were not the only culprits. When French officers began to arrive in Boston to help the Americans, they were also being misled by the British. In a letter to Major General Phillips, Heath stated he had "broke up" a rendezvous established by them at Watertown and protested that,

> . . . the arts and deceptions made use of by your people, by dressing themselves in sailors & peasants habit and by the most solemn protestations of having no connections with the army are constantly imposing upon the recruiting officers, to their great embarassment.[133]

There was no quick reaction to Washington's appeal. At the end of April he was complaining again to Heath, that it was astonishing that officers will, in direct violation of his recruiting instructions and the most evident principles of policy, founded in experience, persevere in enlisting deserters from the British Army. He went on,

> Supposing it might be done in any case, yet there is every possible objection to the measure in the instance of deserters from General Burgoyne's army. These troops did not originally come into our hands thro choice, they were conquered, brought into our possession by compulsion. Those apprehensions of punishment in case of return, which may operate on the minds of "deserters", they feel nothing of. So far from the most distant chance of punishment they will be applauded by the commanders of the British army, for the fidelity and attachment to their Prince, and their inlisting with us, will be considered as a high stroke of policy and the only probable mode they could adopt to effect their escape. We are counting on men, who cannot be confided in, and who will embrace the earliest opportunity to leave us and strengthen the enemy, at the expense of arms, cloathes and bounty on our part.

In support of his arguments, he quoted a case where Convention Prisoners had been recruited into two detachments and very few now remained. Washington added, "they are gone."

With his ire mounting over the conduct of his officers, Washington went on,

> If we would wish to reinforce the enemy with the whole of Mr. Burgoynes army, we can not pursue a mode that will be more effectual or more certain, than to inlist it in our service; but it may be done with less injury by sending them the men, unarmed, without cloathes, and without paying them an exhorbitant bounty. If nothing else will restrain Officers from pursuing such a pernicious, ruinous practice, they must be made to pay for all expenses for this injury.[134]

Brigadier General Count Pulaski also received a "rocket" from Washington,

> I am exceedingly concerned to learn that you are acting contrarily to a positive Resolve of Congress and my express orders, in engaging British prisoners for your Legionary Corps . . . the British prisoners will cheerfully inlist, as a ready means of escaping, the Continental bounty will be lost and your corps as far as ever from being complete. I desire therefore that the prisoners may be returned to their confinement, and that you will for the future adhere to the restrictions under which I laid you.[135]

Washington's ADC, Alexander Hamilton, also aided his chief by writing to the Governor of New York, linking the attempts at recruiting the prisoners and the impact on their own militia of the failure to allow ordinary soldiers to be exchanged. He pointed out,

> . . . we have enlisted prisoners of war. This silences all our complaints against the enemy for a similar practice, and furnishes them with a damning answer to anything we can say on the subject. This is at least an instance of folly and inconsideration, and serves to prove the general charge.

He continued,

> . . . it can never be our interest to exchange; the constitution of our army, from the short term of enlistments and the dependence we are obliged to place in the militia, are strongly opposed to it . . . (but) I may venture to assert there never can be a time more proper than the present, or rather a month or two hence . . . and I would ask whether, in a republican state and a republican army, such a cruel policy as that of exposing those men who are foremost in defense of their country, to the miseries of hopeless captivity, can succeed? [136]

Washington's pressure began to show results. On 19th May 1778 he was able to write he was happy to see the steps taken, adding,

> No practice has been more impolitic, nor injurious, in proportion to its extent. But few of (them) have proved faithful, and I believe there is not a single instance when the (they) have not deserted, when they had an opportunity. The inlisting of prisoners or soldiers in the circumstances of those of Mr. B's Army, is far less justifiable than inlisting deserters.[137]

Later in the war, Washington convinced Von Steuben, the "Father" of the new American army, that he should not countenance the recruitment of the Convention Prisoners. When Von Steuben prepared the instructions for a Recruiting Bill and sent it to the Governor of Virginia, he was careful to note that under no circumstances were any Convention Prisoners be allowed to join.[138]

Throughout the war, Washington could never leave this subject for long. As late as April 1781, after learning that recruiting had started again in Massachusetts, he told Heath he had flattered himself the "imposition" had been guarded against, "but since it has happened again, we must prevent this evil from proceeding any farther, by confining those (deserters) until handed over to the Commissary of Prisoners."[139]

The energy which Washington expended on this subject appeared to have made lasting impressions on the American army with regard to the recruitment of former British soldiers. Some 70 years later, long after the War of Independence and the War of 1812, any recruit attempting to join the American army admitting he had served as a British soldier, was required to provide documentary evidence he had not deserted the British service.[140]

William Beatty (20th) was one of those who were recruited by Americans at Prospect Hill, when he joined the Congress's Own Regiment. He served some seven months before being able to desert at Deanbury, and crossing the sound, was able to meet up with a Loyalist regiment, the Queens Rangers, at Oyster Bay. Beattie was one of many of the Convention prisoners who, after escaping to New York, was drafted to another regiment, only to be captured for a second time when Cornwallis capitulated at Yorktown. Beatty again escaped, managing to join the very same American regiment, the Congress's Own. He repeated his desertion, and within little over four months from the date of his second capture was back into New York on 1st January 1782.[141]

Auguste Barrete (24th), a German, first escaped on his own, but was recaptured after four weeks. Confined in an American prison ship in Boston harbour for six months, he accepted enlistment in Colonel Jackson's regiment. After eighteen months he was able to desert and got into New York.[142]

Andrew Smith (9th) suffered three jail terms for repeated escapes. Some Loyalists advised him to enlist in an American regiment which was going into the line opposite the British on Rhode Island. He took their advice and within a month, he, with four others, managed to steal a guard boat and reached safety.[143]

Others, using Massachusetts regiments to travel to New York, included Corporal William Terry (20th) who deserted the 1st Massachusetts; John Sutherland (47th) and George Molton (20th) both chose the 15th.[144]

Using American regiments as a means of safe transit across enemy occupied territory, had the disadvantage of not being able to control their destination. The regiment might not go anywhere near the British. One who was disappointed in this manner, was Private William Mason (47th). He first tried enlisting with the Americans so that "it might give him an opportunity of making his escape to Rhode Island." They refused to enlist him, but gave him permission to work in the country as a prisoner of war. He worked for twelve months, then bolted with another British soldier. He was accepted by an American artillery unit, but two days later, instead of moving towards the British, they marched westward in order to campaign against Indians, who were harassing the frontier. It was another twelve months before he could desert the Americans and find a way into New York, not reaching there until 6th July 1780. He made up for the delay by appropriating 16 head of cattle, 2 horses and 5 other animals, which he was able to take with him into short-rationed New York.[145]

When the war finally came to an end in 1783, there were still some men serving in the American army who had failed to reach freedom promptly. As these soldiers finally found their way into New York, Carleton, by then the British Commander-in-Chief, castigated them "rascals" for not moving more quickly, but did not punish them.

The American Army was not the only American institution to provide a means by which prisoners could reach their own lines; there were the American navies. With the exception of New Jersey and Delaware, all the colonies possessed naval organisations. In most cases the vessels were very small, although Massachusetts, South Carolina and Virginia possessed some larger ships. Despite this proliferation of naval organisations, Congress decided to form a Continental Navy.

They found great difficulty in manning their ships with efficient crews. Not only had many sailors joined the army, others were attracted to the state navies which continued their operations. The main difficulty facing the Marine Committee established by Congress, was the loss of skilled sailors to the privateers. No fewer than 2,000 of such vessels put to sea during the war, preying on British merchant ships. The possibility of sharing prize money obtained in this way was an attraction which was hard for the common sailor to resist. The outcome was that the quantity and quality of crews available to the fledgling Continental Navy was insufficient to maintain the number of vessels putting to sea. To meet their requirements, the Captains of the Continental frigates were forced to find crews where they could. Some came from the American army, where the penalty for desertion was often one hundred lashes and transfer to the Navy. Others came from press gangs, criminals, British prisoners of war and escaped Convention Prisoners.[146]

The Continental Navy had been given authority for the construction of thirteen frigates. Their record was not good; one was sunk in battle; two were burned on land by the British; three were destroyed in port by the Americans to avoid capture; the remaining seven surrendered themselves at sea, without much of a fight. It was the latter that provided the opportunities for some of the Convention Prisoners to make successful escapes.[147]

As has been seen, George Washington did his best to stop escaped prisoners being accepted by American regiments. No similar expression from the American navy is on record, but there soon developed a recognition by the ship's captains that the British were up to no good. The best of the American naval officers, Captain John Paul Jones, found British ex-prisoners to be a "sinister influence on his crews."

Private John Major (24th) first tried the American army in an unsuccessful effort to reach safety; failing this, he tried their navy. Major had fallen sick at Williamstown on the march to Cambridge. On his recovery six weeks later he tried to reach his regiment at Prospect Hill, but was intercepted and gaoled in Bennington for nine months as an escaper. He then accepted being bailed out for work in the locality, but after three months, on hearing the Convention Troops were on the march to Virginia, he ran away. He surreptitiously approached the column and managed to speak to his company commander in the 24th,

Captain Ferguson. Ferguson told him not to try rejoining the column, but to make a bid for New York. This he tried, but was caught again at Poughkeepsie and this time spent seven months in prison. In order to regain his freedom, he with two other British prisoners, volunteered for an American regiment. All three deserted after two days.

Deciding a better way would be to make for Philadelphia and the sea, he worked his way across country. Some two years later he was accepted as a sailor aboard the frigate Trumbull. The crew consisted, in part, of British deserters, the remainder were disaffected Americans, who were described by the captain as "a sorry lot." It was evening when the ship fell in with the British frigate Iris (itself the former American frigate Hancock). Immediately many of the crew deserted their action stations and went below. The battle lasted an hour in heavy weather during which the Trumbull was dismasted. The official American record states the damage was due to the weather, but Major claimed that it was he who came up from below and cut away the top sail ties to preclude the ship escaping. The fight had resulted in sixteen American casualties and with only a handful remaining determined to fight, the Captain surrendered the ship.[148]

Another man left sick at Williamstown, Private Robert Sanders (9th) had a somewhat similar experience, except he landed on the frigate Confederacy as a victim of a press gang in Philadelphia. After two months, the ship was taken by the Royal Navy vessels, Roebuck and Assurance. He with 9 other British soldiers were taken to New York, where it seems he spent 15 days without going ashore. It may be that the British Navy had ideas about keeping him. However, he managed to leave the ship and presented himself to the nearest regiment, the 17th Foot. They immediately accepted him into their own regiment with which he spent the remainder of the war.[149]

Private James Steel (21st) also spent several periods in American prisons before serving on the Jason, which the Americans had captured from the British. His aim in serving was, "in the hopes of falling into the hands of a British cruiser." This duly happened and with thirty other British and Germans, he was taken into New York.[150]

One of the first groups to succeed in leaving by sea were 13 prisoners of various regiments. They were William Wheatley (9th); Patrick Innis (20th); John Frazier (21st); Thomas Jackson, Patrick Maloney, Thomas

Fee, George Lane (all 47th); John Adams, Edward Frell, John Stoddart and John Patten (all 62nd). Two others, Edward Hubbard (35th) and William Allen (45th) were also described as being Convention Prisoners. These last two must have come from Lieutenant Nutt's detachment of recruits as their parent regiments were not part of the Convention Army. They had all been serving on the American brig Angelica, which was taken by the Royal Navy frigate Andromeda on the 30th May 1778. On board the Andromeda was General Howe, who was returning to England to clear his name in the uproar which was going on following the Saratoga defeat.[151]

At least one group, also a party of 13, travelling by sea died. They were among the 30 or 40 passengers and crew drowned when a sloop, on its way from Virginia to New York, was wrecked off the New Jersey coast. Next day, it was found bottom up on a sand bar. When the bodies were searched for identification, it was found they had papers purporting to show that they had been paroled.[152]

Some of the men who joined the American army and navy were true deserters. Among those were, Private Jones (24th) employed by the Americans as an informer on escaped prisoners; Washington referred on one occasion to an unnamed British sergeant who also was assisting the Americans. Anburey reported that the whole of the band of the 62nd, excepting the "Master," deserted in a body and were playing for an American regiment in Boston. Although they were ranked as soldiers and were under Articles of War, the bandsmen were not trained soldiers. Usually they were German civilians in uniform. It was not until 1803 that bandsmen in the British army were ordered to be trained as soldiers; even then the order was often ignored. Anburey also reported another case where a soldier had deserted and sent an American into the barracks to get his ten year old son, a drum-boy, to join him. This, the boy refused to do.[153]

At that time, the usual number of lashes for desertion did not exceed one hundred in the American army. In the British army the punishment was usually in the range of five hundred to one thousand lashes. The difference in the imposition of pain and the wounding of the victim was not so great as might be first apparent. The Americans used raw-hide whips, while the British used the "cat." A soldier who served in both armies and saw the results of such punishments, calculated that fifty

American lashes inflicted the same physical suffering or damage to the constitution as three hundred British lashes.[154]

Using the American army to transit American-held territory was not without its risk of punishment from the British. If they did not gain their own lines promptly, or were captured by the British while still serving with the Americans, there was a considerable likelihood of being charged with desertion. Private William Seals (20th) was so accused, found guilty and sentenced to 500 lashes. Fortunately for him the court added to the sentence ". . . it plainly appears, that the desertion was committed with the laudable intention of joining the army at New York," following which, the Commander-in-Chief pardoned Seals.[155]

Another case on record, concerns Private Reid (21st), who had left the marching column of prisoners before they reached Cambridge. He had joined an un-named American unit in the company of a Loyalist. They did not reach St John's in Canada until early 1780. He was never charged with desertion but was clearly under suspicion. The interrogating officer, in his report to Quebec, referring first to the Loyalist, stated, "His reasons for entering into the service was with a view to come in. The soldier tells the same story, with less appearance of sincerity."

The Seals case shows the risks the British soldiers were taking. The situation they found themselves in, must have made many nervous about their reception when reaching British units. Clinton watching events closely from New York, suspected more "deserters" were joining the American forces than were eventually finding their way back to British lines. Using his imagination, he perceived that some of those using that method might be reluctant to take the final step of placing themselves back in the hands of the British army, after serving in an enemy regiment. In order to overcome their fears in that respect, he issued a proclamation on 23rd February 1779, offering a free pardon to any escaped soldier serving in the American army providing they surrendered themselves by 30th April 1779. This notice seems to have produced little increase in the numbers coming in. In order to make the offer "more generally known," on the 15th April he repeated the offer, extending the final date to 1st July. Now achieving better results, on the 14th June he issued a further proclamation,

Whereas the well known anxiety of the enemy to keep from the

knowledge of their troops every information, which might give them
a just idea of their situation, may have prevented some deserters from
this army from reaping the benefit of my late proclamations of the 23rd
February and 15th of April last. I have thought fit to extend the term
of the said proclamations, that the grace therein offered, of which so
many have already accredited themselves, may be more generally
known—and I do hereby promise a free pardon to every deserter, who
will voluntarily surrender himself to any of His Majesty's troops before
the first day August.[156]

His offer of pardon appears to have been continued regardless of the
date set. Two years later, Carleton after taking over as Commander-
in-Chief, continued the policy of pardoning the late-comers, but as
will be seen he was not happy about the time it had taken for many
to respond.

Those escaping and who tried crossing American-held territory,
declining to use either the American army or navy, could aim for one
of several places. Canada was the target for many, particularly in the
earlier years. The disadvantage in taking that direction was not only
finding sustenance while passing through a wilderness of forest. There
were also large areas where the occupation by either side was not
clearly defined. Patrol clashes and ambushes were frequent. An escaped
prisoner was just as likely to meet up with an American patrol as a
British one. Despite that difficulty many succeeded in getting through,
often receiving assistance from Loyalist units. Rogers' Rangers, who
had distinguished themselves during the French and Indian war, acted
in a defensive role in the War of Independence and were based on
St John's; for many years they were instrumental in helping many
escapees.[157]

While the British occupied Rhode Island, it was a very convenient
place to aim for, since the distance from Cambridge was not great;
several successful escapees took that route. Philadelphia too, was also
occupied for a time and that city also became a target. Later in the
war, British armies operated in both Virginia and the Carolinas, and
some Convention Prisoners were successful in reaching British regiments
in those directions.

Throughout the war, the most favoured destination for those heading
for British lines was New York. Captured by the British in 1776, the

city remained the pivot of British strategy until the final withdrawal from America in 1783. Although the Convention Prisoners had no way of knowing future intentions, there seemed to be no doubt that for most, it was the best place to reach. In view of the number of other places captured by the British, only to be subsequently abandoned, the prisoners seemed to have exercised good judgement. There would be little to gain struggling to reach a British-occupied town, only to find they were not there when the fugitives arrived.

Among those who escaped from Cambridge and journeyed on their own was Private John Sudders (47th), who left in November 1777. Recaptured and jailed several times, on one occasion he almost reached Philadelphia. On recapture, he was carried back into New Jersey, but obtained permission to work in the country. He claimed his work pass was given him by George Washington. He finally reached the British Lines in November 1780, and joined the 17th Dragoons.

Private John Dewhurst (20th) was jailed in Boston after an escape attempt. He obtained release, by agreeing to work. On hearing a rumour that prisoners of war from the 71st Foot were to be exchanged, he went to Hartford in Connecticut, but the rumour proved unfounded. He was re-arrested when informed upon by the Private Jones mentioned earlier. This time, he spent seventeen months in Hartford jail, but broke out with a Loyalist named Robinson and reached New York on 1st August 1779.[158]

Private John Deering (47th), who we met being flogged on the way to Saratoga, escaped in March 1778. On recapture, he first spent nine months in Easton jail and then was moved to Philadelphia jail where he spent two years and four months. With 18 other British soldiers, they broke out by digging, with no other instruments than their knives. They were successful in making a home run to New York. Another, following Deering's trail, was Private Richard Barker (24th). He spent periods in Easton and Philadelphia jails and after working for a time in the country, he reached New York in August 1780.[159]

Thomas McNamara (20th) chose Canada. He got as far as Skenesboro and after recapture was sent to Albany jail. He then tried going south. Re-arrested again, he was taken to West Point. This gave him the opportunity of crossing the river and reaching freedom. John Ennis

(21st) did well in reaching North Carolina, where he joined the British 84th regiment.[160]

Others known to have escaped successfully from Cambridge were Thomas Swindle (47th) who had been badly wounded at both Lexington and Bunker Hill; Thomas Barnsley (47th); Edward Hayes (20th); Philip Leaklighter (9th); Paul Thompson (21st) and William Thornton (62nd). The latter was recaptured and incarcerated in Rutland, but was able to bribe a sentry with 10 dollars to let him out.[161]

An unnamed corporal of the 9th Foot takes the prize for the quickest transit of enemy territory, at the same time avoiding the difficulties of an overland journey. Accompanied by an escaped Loyalist soldier, they were able to secure a boat, sailed it round to Rhode Island, arriving there on 19th November 1778. The whole journey from the barracks took but a couple of days.[162]

By mid 1778, individuals and groups began to arrive in Rhode Island and New York in a steady stream. Initially, there was no organisation to receive the men in an orderly fashion, and after what they had been through, some may have attached themselves to various British units to enjoy a little rest and recreation. Clinton had to issue instructions that all arriving NCOs must apply to the Town Major for orders. In July, a group of escapees consisting of 2 sergeants, 1 corporal and 27 men from eight of the convention regiments were collected together and drafted unceremoniously into the 52nd Foot. Two weeks later Clinton announced the appointment of an officer of the 20th Foot, Captain Farquhar, to command a new unit consisting of exchanged officers and escaped men of the Convention Army. These orders included the invalids waiting repatriation to Europe. He excluded any soldier under the description of Prisoner of War.[163]

Gradually a routine was established to process the escapees in an orderly fashion. On 3rd September, those arriving who had served in the Canadian Companies, (i.e. the flank companies of the 29th, 31st, 34th and 53rd Foot), were ordered to Canada by sea. They were probably pleased to get back to their own regiments, while Clinton, in view of the grave shortage of men he was experiencing, must have regretted losing them to the Canadian army. Two days later the men from the flank companies of other regiments at Cambridge coming into New York were drafted to the "weakest regiments of the second brigade."[164]

The men pronounced unfit, were to remain under the command of Captain Farquhar. A month later they left for Europe for examination by the Chelsea Hospital Board.[165]

Some of the men arriving, found the re-imposed discipline irksome. David Taylor (29th), Patrick Shanley (47th), William McGill (53rd), John Hughes (24th) and Thomas Piersall (47th) were all charged with mutiny. The first three were each sentenced to one thousand lashes and remaining two to five hundred lashes apiece. Despite their sentence, the court recommended them for mercy in consideration "of the long and uncommon hardships the prisoners have undergone from want of their pay and every other necessary and from the good character given of some of them." Clinton accepted the recommendation and pardoned them.[166]

The continuous reduction in the numbers of Convention Prisoners remaining, raised the problem of the status of the regiments concerned. By mid 1778, Phillips tried to grapple with the problem. He proposed to Clinton that as the strength of every regiment was so very considerably reduced, they could no longer be considered battalions. He recommended that it would be preferable to have most officers and the staff of each regiment exchanged; the British sent to Europe; the Germans to Canada. There they might reform afresh the battalions to which they belonged. In this way the King again would have the service of the several regiments which at present were totally broken and separated from the army. He went on to suggest that the remaining Convention Troops might then be considered as detachments of those regiments.[167]

Phillips's proposals were not accepted. As the British officers were exchanged, many transferred to new regiments. Except for some of the men of the Canadian Companies, all escapees were drafted into new regiments. NCOs either went back to Europe or transferred to regiments of their choice. No change was made to the status of the incarcerated regiments remaining in the hands of the Americans.

CHAPTER 5

The Convention
is Suspended

FROM the moment Congress received the delayed news concerning the Convention, there were expressions of dissatisfaction with the liberal terms granted. Suspicions were harboured that the British would never abide by the restrictions placed on the future use of the troops, and would endeavour to circumvent the terms of the agreement. George Washington also saw difficulties for himself if the Convention terms were carried out. As early as 5th November 1777 he wrote to Major General Heath saying it was not in the American interest to expedite the departure of the prisoners. If they sailed for Europe in December, the garrisons they replaced could sail for America, and arrive by May, in time for the summer campaign season.[168]

On the same date as Washington's letter to Heath, the New York Committee of Safety addressed a letter to Congress, raising additional concerns about the treaty. It expressed the view that the British had already broken the terms of the Convention by not giving up all the arms, standards, and equipment as required by the agreement. The Committee also added that it was imprudent to leave the prisoners so near the coast and the British base at Rhode Island. At the same time, individual members of Congress were raising their doubts about the whole transaction.[169]

Responding to the growing unease and dissatisfaction with the agreement now being freely expressed, Congress ordered Heath to record the name and rank of all Convention officers and men, and in the case of the latter, their place of origin, occupation, size, age and description. The object in compiling this list was to identify any Convention Prisoner who might, in breach of article two of the Convention, be returned to America to again participate in the war. Burgoyne ignored the request and refused to provide the information.[170]

Congress also appointed a committee to investigate the meagre stores which had been obtained on the surrender of the British. This committee confirmed that, in their opinion, something was amiss. While some muskets had been surrendered, these had proved unfit for service. There was very little powder and fixed ammunition, with only 638 cartouche boxes. Further, there were no trace of regimental standards, the military chest, medicines or tents. As part of their investigation, Congress wrote to General Gates asking for his version of what had happened. At the same time they carefully added that their enquiries were "by no means intended to throw any slur on your acceptance of the Convention; but to come at a true idea of Burgoyne's conduct."[171]

After several days spent mulling over the evidence which had been accumulated, Congress on 8th January 1778 resolved, with four members voting against, to suspend the embarkation of the army. The stated reasons were the failure to obtain the supplies and equipment intended under the treaty; the failure to receive the descriptive lists of the other ranks; Burgoyne's letter dated 14th November 1777, wherein he charged a breach of faith and therefore, his "personal honor is hereby destroyed." Congress then added that the suspension of the Convention and the retention of the troops in America would remain until,

> a distinct and explicit ratification of the convention of Saratoga shall be properly notified by the court of Great Britain to Congress.[172]

Since this resolution of Congress was the justification for the Convention Army being held for over five years, the merits of the American action in suspending the Convention need to be examined in some detail.

On the matter of supplies and equipment, Gates's response to the enquiries of Congress left very little doubt on the matter. He stated that there was no military chest. In this he was right because before the signing of the Convention, Burgoyne had detached Canadian Captains McAlpin and McKay with a large party of their men and some Indians, together with the chest, to go through the enemy lines and find their way back to Canada. While Lt. William Fraser and some 50 men were captured, the two Captains and the money arrived safely in Canada.[173]

Gates also pointed out that drummers did not carry muskets and therefore there were always fewer weapons than men. The bayonets had been stolen by the American militia and that a considerable quantity of cartridges and powder had been surrendered. Medicines had been left at the hospital at Freemans Farm. He went on expressing his confidence that there had been no destruction of military stores. He pointed out that it was unusual for a British army to surrender, so it was not surprising there were some irregularities, but not enough, "to justify our charge of their having violated the Convention."[174]

Gates admitted that he had overlooked mentioning "accoutrements" in the Convention, but that many had been left and others had been sold for drams on the road to Boston. There is additional evidence on the substance of this complaint. Major Kingston, the Deputy Adjutant General, supported by an officer of the 21st Foot, in testimony given at the subsequent parliamentary enquiry on the surrender, disclosed that as the British troops stacked their arms and were marching off, Gates noted they were still wearing their cartouche boxes. Kingston replied that there was nothing in the agreement relating to accoutrements and that the Americans had no right to anything not in the document. He claimed that Gates turned to him and said "you are perfectly right," and turned to some of his officers saying "If we meant to have had them, we ought to have inserted them in the convention." Major Kingston was of course, quite wrong in claiming the failure to mention the accoutrements in the agreement meant they were not to be included. European precedents clearly indicated that when arms were surrendered, the accoutrements went with them. But rightly or wrongly, Gates had agreed he had no title to them.[175]

Gates also reported that Burgoyne had given him an assurance that all military colours had been left behind in Canada. This was certainly not true in the case of the German regiments, as Baroness Riedesel the wife of General Riedesel explained in her memoirs, they were hidden in a mattress and smuggled into New York by a British officer, who then sent them on to Canada. There is also evidence, that of the British colours, at least those of the 9th Foot found their way to England and were presented to George III. Others may also have been returned because, according to a statement signed by two of the German officers, Burgoyne had ordered all colours to be hidden away. They might have been referring to the colours being taken when the Canadians left before the signing of the Convention. Having taken the war chest, it is conceivable they also took them at the same time.[176]

The Americans were on stronger ground when the British refused to supply the descriptive lists of their men. The British themselves had demanded and received similar lists after the surrender of the American force two years before at The Cedars in Canada. However, as Laurens wrote to Heath on 23rd December, the matter of the descriptive lists became a "mere bagatelle," when compared to Burgoyne's letter stating that, because of the American breach of faith to provide suitable accommodation for the officers, "the public faith is broke." This gave the Americans the opportunity of claiming his comment was unfounded and, "betrays a disposition of availing himself of such declaration in order to disengage himself and the army under him," of any obligation under the Convention.[177]

After the expenditure of considerable effort to find reasons for breaking off the Convention, including much researching of international law, Congress had come up with two minor breaches on the part of the British, i.e. on the matters of the descriptive lists and the colours. Despite the paucity of their case, Congress pressed on with it. The political advantages to be gained by demanding ratification of the Convention of Saratoga by the British Government were substantial. Agreement by Britain would mean that Congress would be recognised as the legitimate government of a sovereign power. If Britain refused to give such ratification, as indeed she did so refuse, then America had found what to them, was a legitimate reason to keep the troops in America.

As Trevelyan wrote,

> . . . they soon had made up their minds to do the wrong thing. There were two ways of doing it; and they chose the worse. They might have boldly proclaimed that no servant of the State had power to bind the State by an engagement to the public interest; and then they might have repudiated the Convention, and made a scapegoat of Horatio Gates. So they would have acted if they had had the courage of their unscrupulousness; but Gates was their spoiled child, and their chosen instrument for persecuting and displacing better soldiers than himself. Intent upon throwing over the Treaty without sacrificing the reputation of the general who made it, they deliberately confused the issue by raising a series of petty and vexatious quibbles.[178]

The decision of Congress also caused confusion among many Americans. William Fitzhugh of Maryland protested to Washington,

> If the Convention was broken, as I have no doubt it was, why comply with any part or article of it? Does it not imply a contradiction unfavourable to the wisdom or justice of Congress?

He went on to suggest that if the prisoners were treated as prisoners of war, the officers could be separated from the men, the latter could then be mingled with the population.[179]

In taking their decision, Congress had been driven by a more immediate anxiety. The British might not even send the troops back to Europe, but endeavour in some manner to get them into New York, so as to have them readily available for the 1778 campaign season. One of the committees had already drawn the attention of Congress to the request (made at the instigation of General Howe), to change the port of embarkation from Boston to Rhode Island, on the grounds of the difficulty for sailing ships to tack into Boston harbour at that time of the year. Howe had already despatched to Rhode Island 26 transports but it was pointed out that they were insufficiently victualled for an Atlantic crossing.

During the course of the following 150 years, Americans endeavoured to find an answer to the allegations of historians such as Trevelyan, who criticised the actions of Congress. In 1932, a letter from Howe to Burgoyne was discovered, which indicated that while the Germans were to go to Europe, the British artillery men and infantry were to be transported to New York. Howe's rationale for this change was that the Americans had not returned to him an equal number of British prisoners of war in exchange for 2,200 American prisoners he had repatriated to them during the winter of 1776/77. Since its discovery, this letter gave a more substantial case to suspend the Convention. At the time of the suspension however, Congress had no sound or honest case for their action and the "stain" on their history remains.[180]

American historian John Bigelow Jr. in 1908, probably best summed up the the American viewpoint, when he wrote that Burgoyne should have foreseen that the Convention would never be carried out and "should have known and considered that Gates could not guarantee anything but the conditions under which his army should march out, and give itself up." Precedents just before Saratoga indicate otherwise. Surrenders negotiated between opposing generals which took place during the twenty-one years before, and involving the passage of troops through enemy-held territory included; the French surrender to the British, Minorca 1756; the Polish surrender to Prussia, Konigsteen 1756; the British surrender to the French, Fort William Henry 1757; the French surrender to the British, Montreal 1760; the French surrender to the British, Pondicherry 1761. Of all these, only the Fort William Henry instance was dishonoured, when the Indian allies of the French massacred the British survivors.[181]

Congress still had not completed the devious course it had taken. Having made the release of the army contingent on the British Government recognising Congress as a sovereign power, they now grew concerned that perhaps the British Government might just do that. In his covering letter, when sending the 8th January resolution to Heath, the President of Congress directed him to give one copy to Burgoyne, but there was to be no official communication to the British Government. They were to be kept ignorant of the resolution for as long as possible. The letter, with the copies of the resolution did not, in any case, reach Heath until 3rd February. Burgoyne immediately requested permission to send a copy to New York. A delay in complying with this request was gained by Heath, he making the excuse that there could be no such communication until Congress had received his certification that the letter and resolution had been duly delivered to Burgoyne. In the end, in classical American style, it was the American press which let the cat out of the bag. Much to Heath's mortification, on 16th February, the Boston Gazette made a front page issue of the resolution.[182]

The fears of Congress were unfounded, because the prevailing view within the British Government at that time was that they would never allow the recognition of Congress as a sovereign body. The nearest the matter came to resolution was six months later, when British commissioners, meeting with their American counterparts, endeavouring to negotiate an exchange of prisoners, offered a ratification signed by themselves. This was rejected by Congress. There for the time being the matter rested.[183]

The suspension of the Convention placed the officers and men in a curious situation. From this time on, Americans generally, no longer spoke of "Burgoyne's Army," but often referred to them as "Convention Prisoners." Their special classification was maintained, for the time being, so as to enjoy the financial benefit of the British paying the cost of their maintenance. However, to all intents and purposes the Americans henceforth, treated them as prisoners of war.

In a letter Phillips later wrote to Clinton, he drew his attention to the American use of the term "prisoner", when referring to the Convention Troops. He wrote,

> I think it my duty to represent to your Excellency, that the American Congress, as well as many others of the Americans have industriously use the word 'prisoner' . . . Burgoyne always asserted the contrary—that we were not prisoners—I have ever both in sentiment and conduct done the same. Whether the Troops of the Convention being called "prisoner" by the American officers and the American Congress proceeds from accident, from pride, from assurance or from policy, I am as Senior Officer of the Troops of the Convention, under a necessity of protesting against the term . . . We have considered ourselves as passengers under the sanction and virtue of a treaty, not as prisoners.[184]

The inconsistency of the Americans also caused difficulties. As Batchelder has said,

> they spoke of the troops as prisoners, but carefully kept the various units together, and allowed them to be paraded, inspected, and disciplined by their own officers, in a manner totally at variance with the usages of an ordinary prison camp . . . They bragged about their prisoners, while treating the entire force as a species of 'paying guests'. Military history has seldom recorded a more anomalous state of things.[185]

Expecting trouble, which was already brewing, Heath was authorised to increase the guard to 1,500 men.

CHAPTER 6

The Prisoners Rebel

THE Convention Prisoners were not only punished by their own officers for infractions of regimental orders and discipline. They were also subjected to punishment from the Americans for a wide range of crimes including; the direct insult or disobedience to sentries or guards; breaking out of camp; attempting escape or forging gate passes. Americans would quickly arrest the offender, who would immediately be incarcerated in the American guard house at the barracks or at Fort Hill if caught in Boston. If offences were repeated or where more serious cases were involved, the soldiers would be removed to the prison hulks in Boston harbour, for an indeterminate term.

Even before news of the suspension of the Convention had spread, the temper of the British soldiers had begun to wear thin. As Hudleston has said

> Anglo Saxons do not make good prisoners of war. They do not take captivity easily, and they do their best to make it as unpleasant as they possibly can for those who have taken them captive.

Their undisguised contempt towards the Americans steadily increased. As Knepper explained, they had to put up with the "comically unsoldierlike militia who loved to lord it over the haughty Lobster Backs." A German officer commented "there is tremendous animosity between American and the English soldiers, and there have been many vexatious occurrences which render our stay here even more unbearable." The British soldier, in addition to not making a good and docile prisoner, is notorious for his "back chat" and sarcasm. Such conduct during the American War usually generated immediate retaliation, because in most cases, the Americans could understand what was being said or implied. By mid-December of 1777 this conduct, and the American retaliation, led to a series of incidents which escalated into a dangerous situation.[186]

From the start, both sides appear to have been in the habit of hurling verbal abuse at each other. Even the townspeople did not escape the rancour. One soldier addressed by a shopkeeper as one of "Burgoyne's Lobster Backs," retailiated with a physical attack. The American officers also complained of what is now known in the British forces as "dumb insolence" and they found difficulty in finding the means to stop it. As matters deteriorated, a situation developed where the Americans started to ignore legitimate complaints, treating all requests with derision.[187]

Heath felt constrained to protest to Burgoyne about the deteriorating discipline,

> . . . prisoners being rescued from the guards—centinels abused and insulted on their posts—passes counterfeited, and others filled up in the most frontive manner; and of late, several highway robberies committed in the environs of the garrison—one of the last evening, on which a gentleman was robbed of between 7 and 800 dollars, and a watch. The robberies I do not charge to your people, as it is unknown who were the perpetrators; but there are several reasons to suspect it.

The passes referred to, were those required to make visits into the town of Cambridge on various duties. Very few of the American militia could read and it was a comparatively simple task for such passes to be written by officers, NCOs or men who could write. In addition, an American officer named Keith, was also selling passes to the prisoners. The men going into the town, was in direct conflict with Heath's standing orders. When forty of the prisoners were caught without official passes, they were sent to the prison hulks in Boston harbour. In view of these accusations, Burgoyne, always fearful that legitimate reasons would be found to end the Convention, found it necessary to issue an order in which he stated that much of the growing discord was due to,

> Indiscretion of our own troops: of this the attacks upon the provincial sentries, and the forging of passes, are particularly glaring.

In the same order, he went on to say that the officers should detect and punish offences of this sort, and by such examples, they would strengthen their claims for the redress of legitimate complaints. It seems that on at least one occasion the officers paid only lip service to his orders. A British soldier was sentenced to 50 lashes for assaulting a guard. The American was invited to watch the punishment, and when he unexpectedly attended, he found it had been cancelled. To improve the level of discipline, Burgoyne ordered that in addition to the existing daily roll-calling parades, there would be an additional two general parades to be held at 12 noon on Sundays and Thursdays.[188]

There was very little trouble from the German troops, which General Riedesel attributed to the better discipline maintained by the Germans when compared to the British. This was only partly accurate. Before the advent of the war, there is evidence of friction between soldiers of the former Colonial and British regiments. Under the conditions now being experienced, this rancour developed into a deep hatred for each other. This is readily understandable in the midst of a guerilla war. What is not so easily understood is that despite their common heritage, antipathy between the ill-educated rank and file of both countries, for a variety of reasons, continued to exist into recent times. Despite their being allies, the number of cases of friction and trouble experienced in World War II is evidence of this. It is only since that war, with better education and the increase in travel between the two countries, has their dislike of one another been reduced or eliminated.

The situation on Prospect Hill became increasingly tense. Cases were reported of American sentries being attacked by British prisoners, beaten up, and their firelocks stolen. In a subsequent search of the barracks, the guns were never found and one American statement supposed they had been broken up. A more likely reason was that they had been sold to local civilians. There were also several cases where British prisoners being escorted to and from the guardhouse by American soldiers for a variety of offences, were forcibly released by other prisoners and spirited away into the barrack blocks.

Heath had appointed Colonel David Henley as the commandant for the British barracks. His friends acknowledged his quick temper and that he was a poor choice to have been placed in charge of several thousand recalcitrant prisoners who were not prepared to accept discipline from any officers except their own. He clearly found difficulty in coping with a situation of dealing with the British, who apparently followed a policy of keeping occupied as many of the enemy as possible, and who were determined to cause as much trouble as they could.

On the 19th December 1777, Henley, accompanied by troops went to the guardroom to release some dozen British soldiers who had been incarcerated for a variety of disciplinary offences. After reading their names and reviewing their conduct, he came to Corporal Reeves and told him he had insulted a Provincial officer. Reeves acknowledged having done so, stating he had not known him to be an officer. Henley losing his temper said "By God, Sir, had you served me so, I would have run you through the body, and I believe you to be a great rascal." Reeves retorted "I am no rascal, but a good soldier, and my officers know it." Henley demanded silence, but Reeves repeated the same words adding that he hoped soon to carry arms under the command of General Howe and fight for his King and country. Colonel Henley then replied, "Damn your King and country; when you had arms, you was willing enough to lay them down." Henley again ordered silence, but Reeves once more repeated his words about hoping to fight for his King and country.[189]

Henley then ordered one of his guard to run Reeves through with his fixed bayonet, but the soldier obviously reluctant to commit such a cold-blooded act, did not obey. Henley then dismounted from his horse and seizing a firelock and bayonet from one of the guard, he stabbed Corporal Reeves in the left breast, saying if he said another word he would have it through his body. Reeves retorted he did not care; he would stand by his King and country till he died. Henley then made a second dart at him with the firelock and bayonet, which Corporal John Buchanan (9th) and Private Alexander Thompson (29th) managed to get their hands on and throwing it up, it passed over Reeves shoulder. Buchanan told Henley that Reeves was his prisoner and not to take his life. At this, Henley returned the firelock and ordered both Reeves and Buchanan back into the guard-room and dismissed the rest of the prisoners. Even then Reeves was not finished. Inside the guard-room, but by the window where all outside could hear, he made disparaging remarks about Congress and "King Hancock" (the then President of Congress).

Reeves was not seriously wounded by the thrust, it not penetrating deep enough to be of any consequence, but later evidence indicated that if it had penetrated an inch further his life would have been in danger and two inches further would have meant certain death.

Disorder became more wide-spread in January, when several British soldiers were bayoneted, but only lightly wounded. On one occasion some prisoners were standing around the guard house at the gate, when about 100 men of the regular Continental army passed by. The American version of what happened was that one of the British soldiers swore at them. Private Thomas Page (24th) gave the unlikely explanation that he stood on the toe of Private Thomas Trudget, also of the 24th, standing next to him, who then swore. Whatever occurred, the sergeant of the American unit turned and bayoneted Trudget lightly in the breast. The sergeant then clubbed his firelock and hit Trudget on the side of his head. The incident immediately led to turmoil and a mêlée ensued. One American soldier running up to assist the sergeant, lunged with his bayonet at Private Wilson (9th), who parried the bayonet with his hand, but immediately, another Continental soldier bayoneted him through his arm into his left side. By chance, Corporal Buchanan, still in custody since the December incident, was returning to the guard house under escort of two Americans. In the confusion he took the opportunity, with the assistance of others, to escape into one of the barrack blocks. For his part Trudget proved to be no friend of the Americans. He escaped in September of 1779 and arrived in New York on Christmas Eve 1780.

While the fracas was going on, Colonel Henley happened to be inspecting some works behind the guard-house and he immediately gathered some American troops ordering them to load their weapons. Coming among the British soldiers with his sword drawn, he ordered them to disperse. They did not move fast enough, and Colonel Henley pushed his sword into the side of Corporal Hadley with sufficient force to bend it. He then endeavoured to chase Private John Winks (9th), but was delayed while trying to straighten his sword over his knee. An American Sergeant came to his aid and knocked Winks down into a ditch.

By chance, no one was grievously hurt, but tempers were growing raw on both sides. Incidents were reported where sentries threatened to bayonet British officers when endeavouring to visit the camp offices on business. There was also a reported shooting at British women who did not obey sentries' orders fast enough, which also endangered the lives of passers-by. On one occasion, American troops surrounded a barrack block and found a dozen British soldiers inside ready to defend themselves with cudgels. Another complaint was made of Colonel Henley going into a fit of rage, when a soldier tried to address him in a respectful manner.

Matters came to a head on 9th January 1778, when Burgoyne wrote to Heath,

A report has been made to me of a disturbance which happened at the barracks Wednesday afternoon, for which I am much concerned; and though the provocations from your soldiers, which originally produced it were of the most atrocious nature, I was desirous the offender on our part should be properly punished. The suspected persons were confined accordingly; but Colonel Henley thought proper to make prisoners eighteen innocent men, and to reject the guilty one. The innocent men are sent on board guard-ships, as alleged by your order.

It is not only a duty to my situation to demand the immediate discharge of these men, together with a satisfactory apology, but I also mean it as an attention to you, Sir, that I give you an immediate opportunity to disavow so unjustifiable a proceeding, as committing men to the worst of prisons, upon vague report, caprice, and passion.

Insults and provocations, at which the most placid dispositions would revolt, are daily exercised by your troops against the officers and soldiers of this army.—regular, decent complaints are received by your officer, sometimes with haughtiness, sometimes with derision, but always without redress. These evils flow, Sir, from the general tenor of language and of conduct held by Colonel Henley, which encourages his inferiors, and seems calculated to excite them to the most bloody purposes.

For want of sufficient information, and not bringing myself to believe it possible the facts, as related by common report, could be true, I have hitherto declined taking public notice of this man; but, upon positive ground, I now, and hereby, formally accuse Colonel Henley of behaviour heinously criminal as an officer, and unbecoming a man; of the most indecent, violent, vindictive severity against unarmed men, and of intentional murder.

I demand prompt and satisfactory justice; and I will not doubt your readiness to give it. Whenever you will inform me a proper tribunal is appointed, I will take care that undeniable evidence shall be produced to support the above charges.

Heath did not take long to react to this letter. He suspended Colonel

Henley from his post and appointed a Court of Enquiry to investigate the charges. This did not satisfy Burgoyne. Heath again responded by elevating the enquiry into a full scale Court Martial. The trial began its sittings on 20th January 1778 and consisted of 13 Continental officers. Burgoyne was appointed Prosecutor and the Court was to be assisted by the American Lt. Colonel Tudor as Judge-Advocate.

At the hearings, there was some indication that witnesses from both sides had been coached. In referring to one of the disturbances, all British witnesses numbered those present as being between 50 and 70, while all American witnesses numbered the crowd between 200 and 300. Henley only asked witnesses a few isolated questions and in his own defense read a short prepared statement. He did not subject himself to cross examination by taking the witness stand.

With a court consisting only of American officers the outcome of finding Henley not-guilty was a foregone conclusion, but the proceedings were notewothy for historical reasons. It is probably the only instance in military history that a captive officer was allowed to act as prosecutor against an officer of his captors. It is a remarkable testimony to the efforts of the American military, and Heath in particular, to act in an impartial manner as possible.

Burgoyne was not a lawyer, but he did a remarkable job in presenting his evidence. At one point, he quoted Blackstone, the English legal authority (who of course was, and still is, referred to by Americans), on the legal definition of threatening behaviour. He was so successful, the Judge-Advocate, who would normally act as prosecutor, had to admit to the Court that he had turned himself into the defense attorney, so as to be fair to both sides.

Most importantly, the trial provides irrefutable evidence that the British soldiers were no friends of their American captors and that most remained loyal to the Crown. This evidence makes a mockery of any accusations, that widespread "true" desertion of the colours was taking place.

Colonel Henley was restored as commandant of the prisoners, but it is clear that his superiors did not think much of his conduct. Within a week, he was quietly transferred back to regimental duties. An American report states that Henley then challenged Burgoyne to a duel. This was accepted by Burgoyne but he refused to have it on American soil, so Bermuda was chosen. Even if the report was true, the duel never did take place.

Henley's troubles with the Convention Prisoners were not over. After his experiences with them, Henley should have known the British soldier better. He thought he had found sixty of them who had deserted and who he had assumed were prepared to serve with his regiment. George Washington angrily related what the British did,

> . . . a detachment from Colo. Henley, which marched from Boston 60 strong arrived here two or three days ago with 13 men only, and had it not been for a detachment of New Hampshire troops, it is highly probable, one of them would not have been seen. Thirty of the 60 are now in Easton Jail, having formed a plan at that place to go off in a body. The rest except 13 had escaped before.[190]

The record of one of Henley's recruits has survived. James Cuff (62nd), a barber by trade, spent three months in Easton jail before being able to escape with another British soldier. He was again apprehended and this time was put into jail at Philadelphia. He spent six weeks there, before being sent to Providence. He was court martialled and received a sentence of 100 lashes for deserting the American regiment. Less than a fortnight later he again escaped and was successful in reaching New York in company with another soldier.[191]

Although still short of officers Congress placed Henley on the supernumary list in March 1779. After the war ended, he commanded the State of Tennessee's troops.[192]

Shortly after these confrontations, Burgoyne, on 3rd March, while still on parole and subject to recall, received permission to go to England. Congress, however, added a price-tag. Before he could go, all monies due to the Americans for supplies had not only to be settled, but paid in specie. He was incensed saying, "if Congress could be serious in their resolution, requiring in specie the same sum which they had expended in paper money." He was told by Heath that that honourable body was serious in all their resolutions. Burgoyne protested it was unjust and appealed to Heath to say whether he thought it just himself. Heath extricated himself from embarassment, by saying he was an executive officer and it was not for him to judge or determine whether the orders of his superiors were just or not. He did add, however, that if the British did not want to send money, they could replace the provisions which had been supplied by the Americans. Congress approved this arrangement and both methods of settlement were used during the first twelve months of the prisoners' captivity. For security, when gold and silver was paid, it was transported on wagons to Cambridge, labelled as supplies. When by May, the British did supply some food, it came through Rhode Island.

Burgoyne sailed on 15th April. His earlier applications to return to Europe had been refused by Congress and their change in policy pleased Washington, who writing to Heath commented,

> Glad to hear General Burgoyne is gone, and wish his departure had been much earlier. At capture he certainly must have entertained very favorable impression of our force and perhaps in good policy he should have been allowed to depart, before they were in the smallest degree done away, and before he could have obtained any accurate idea of our affairs. He must yet in vindication of his conduct, speak largely of our powers.

Although Burgoyne's leaving was ostensibly on grounds of ill-health, he wanted to be in London to answer his critics. When he arrived there he received a cold reception from the King, who refused to see him. Later, at the King's instigation, he received orders to return to America to be with his troops. When he did not go, he received a warning,

> your not returning to America, and joining the troops, prisoners under the Convention of Saratoga, is considered as a neglect of duty, and disobedience of order, transmitted to you by the Secretary of War.

He refused to return to America, but was never charged with any offence.

In place of Burgoyne, Phillips became the commander of the Convention Prisoners. He was a volatile and short-tempered officer. Of undoubted ability, he was a Royal Artillery officer who had distinguished himself at Minden. Phillips's career in the artillery was accidental. He had commanded a company of miners who were converted to artillery and, as a result, he had jumped over longer-serving officers to the rank of Captain-Lieutenant. This gave him a good start towards reaching his rank of Major General. At Burgoyne's insistence, he became second in command of Burgoyne's army, at a time when artillery-men were not usually permitted to command infantry. As will be discussed later, there is some evidence that he was prepared to ignore official British policy and at the same time go outside eighteenth-century standards of conduct of paroled officer prisoners. Although like Burgoyne and four others of the Convention officers, he was a Member of Parliament, he did not possess the diplomatic skills of Burgoyne and it did not take long for Anglo-American relations to deteriorate further.[193]

The change in the American camp commandant had first improved matters to some extent, but it was by no means an end to serious trouble. On 17th June, Richard Brown, a second lieutenant in the 21st Foot, accompanied by two young women from Boston, drove a chaise at a fast pace down Prospect Hill. At the foot of the hill he was challenged by an American sentry. Brown, perhaps having some trouble with his horse, made a gesture which the guard took for a threat or an insult and who raising his musket, shot the officer who died that night.

Ever-ready to show their anger towards the Americans, some British soldiers immediately retaliated by seizing the sentry and dragging him by his heels up the hill, which tore open his face. To add to the confusion, the adjutant of the 21st, on hearing of the incident, set off furiously on horseback, but his horse stumbled, pitching him off, breaking his collar-bone.[194]

Phillips immediately wrote to Major General Heath in the following terms:

> Murder and death has at length taken place. An officer, riding out from the barracks on Prospect Hill, has been shot by an American centinel. I leave the horrors incident to that bloody disposition, which has joined itself to rebellion in these colonies, to the feelings of all Europe. I do not ask for justice, for I believe every principle of it is fled from this Province.
>
> I demand liberty to send an officer to Gen. Sir Henry Clinton, by way of the head-quarters of Gen. Washington, with my report of this murder.[195]

Heath would have none of this language. Replying the next day, after describing steps he had taken to arrest the sentinel and for a coroner to conduct an enquiry, he added:

. . . that duty which I owe to the honour and dignity of the United States will not allow me to pass unnoticed such expressions as are contained in your letter; and I cannot put any other interpretation upon them, than that they are a violent infraction of your parole, most sacredly given.

Heath then described a new parole for Phillips, limited to the area between his house and the quarters of the troops. If he refused to sign the parole, he would be restricted to his quarters. At the same time, he would not authorise an officer to go to New York, but would allow Phillips to send a copy of the coroner's report with any "just and decent representations . . . after I have examined such letters."[196]

The argument which ensued, revolved around whether the Convention officer prisoners were responsible for the discipline of their own men. Heath, however, would not give way and insisted on the right for the United States to discipline the prisoners as they thought fit. This had never before been so forcibly put to the British officers and from this time on the status of the prisoners steadily declined.

Phillips refused to sign his new parole and he was restricted to his house and gardens with three sentries posted around the perimeter. This situation continued until Heath was relieved by Gates as area commander in November. Gates and Phillips had served together in the British Army and they very quickly found ways to renew their friendship, with the full parole area being quickly restored to Phillips.

The sentry involved in the Brown shooting was court-martialled and acquitted. He was judged to be following orders regarding the action to be taken when a prisoner did not stop on being challenged by a sentry. He turned out to be a fourteen year old boy, which is a commentary on the make-up of the American troops, about which General Schuyler had complained the previous year.

Later, another riot broke out in Boston, this time between American troops and their new French allies, in which a French officer and several sailors were killed. Some Convention Prisoners, who it seems, were still successful in absenting themselves from the barracks, were accused of instigating the disturbance.[197]

With the British always ready to cause trouble, the local residents refusing to co-operate in matters concerning the prisoners, and fellow officers prepared to criticise his management, Heath's tenure as area commander could not have been easy. He kept his humour; when writing his memoirs some twenty years after the events, he related,

> A wag, coming from the barracks, was asked if anything was found; he answered, "Yes—in one of the rooms a large brass mortar." This spread, and was alarming to be sure. The fact was that in one of the rooms there was a large bell-metal pestle and mortar, for family use. Jealousy, like other passions, although a virtue in itself, may exceed its bounds; and when it does, "trifles, light as air to jealous minds are as strong as proofs of holy writ." [198]

CHAPTER 7

The March to Virginia

Having suspended the departure of the Convention Army, Congress now feared that Clinton would organise a rescue attempt from New York. One correspondent wrote that the enemy would regard the decisions of Congress as an open rupture of the Convention. He thought a strong British force from Rhode Island could drive through the countryside and converge on the camp. The possibility of this occurring was no idle concern. Clinton had in January of 1778, prepared a memorandum with this in mind, detailed to the point of allocating units which would take part in such an effort. American Major General Sullivan in New Hampshire, either from intelligence he had obtained, or by intuition, speculated that with 10,000 men which were available to the British, and by forced marches, which they had demonstrated they were capable of, they could not only rescue the prisoners but also crush all opposition in the area. For various reasons connected with the need for troops, nothing came of the British planning and the fears proved groundless.[199]

Apart from security, Heath had the problem of feeding twenty thousand extra mouths in New England. These included not only the prisoners, but also their guards and the American army facing the British in Rhode Island. This, added to their apprehension of what the enemy might do, led Congress to resolve moving the Convention Prisoners inland, away from the coast and out of reach of a raid. Authority was given to disperse the prisoners throughout Massachusetts. Following this decision it was agreed that only the British should be moved. No similar preparations were made for moving the German troops, since the Americans considered them "so tame and submissive." The place chosen for the British was Rutland, a remote town 60 miles from Boston where there already existed some barracks, housing prisoners-of-war captured before the Convention was made. The first ordered to leave were the battalions of the grenadier and light flank

companies, together with the survivors of the Royal Artillery detachment. Most, but not all of them departed from Cambridge on 15th
April 1778. Small pox had spread throughout the town causing Harvard
College to cancel its commencement exercises. 300 of the prisoners
went down with the disease; men delegated to be moved that survived
that ordeal had to follow on later. The choice of these particular units
to move first was no accident. The Americans recognised these men
were the most highly trained and therefore, the most valuable to the
British.[200]

The 9th Foot followed in June. When a fleet was sighted off Boston
in September, the 21st and 47th were sent to join them. The fleet
thought to be British, proved to be French. The last of the British
Convention Prisoners, consisting of the 24th and 62nd Foot, marched
early in October. The German troops remained in Cambridge, but the
infamous barracks which had housed the British troops on Prospect
Hill since the end of the previous year were now finally empty.[201]

The Rutland prison proved to be a much more secure place than
the barracks at Cambridge. The huts were surrounded by a picket fence
which rose to a height of nearly twenty feet. An American militia guard
described the place:

> The prisoners were all confined in a large piece of ground with high
> strong pickets round it so that they could not escape, and this space
> was occupied by barracks. Duty was to stand guard by turns around
> this picketed enclosure.[202]

The barracks were insufficient to accommodate all the men and
throughout the summer the prisoners laboured to erect additional
quarters. The warmer weather made this task easier to bear than they
experienced at Cambridge. Although a vessel had arrived under a flag
of truce with "some necessaries," by this time the men were described
as "almost naked", due to the failure to obtain uniforms or materials
with which to clothe the men.[203]

The high stockade surrounding the barracks brought home to the
soldiers their unenviable status as prisoners. The remoteness and bore-
dom took their toll. Escape was more difficult, but although the numbers
of men leaving slowed, it did not stop. An army strength return shows
that between April and October when regiments were spread between

Cambridge and Rutland, 416 men left while 69 returned, making a net reduction of 347 during the seven month period.[204]

Patrick Kelly (31st) escaped from Rutland by breaking two of the pickets making up the fence surrounding the prisoners. Accepted by Colonel Draytons Regiment of militia, he stayed with them for over six weeks until he could desert. After feeding himself by taking employment, he reached New York in June of 1780.

Another man who did not stay long in Rutland was George Holmes (53rd) who escaped as soon as they arrived from Cambridge. He worked at his trade of shoemaker to support himself and when he succeeded in getting through to New York he brought with him two other British soldiers and a Loyalist.[205]

An unsuccessful effort from Rutland was made by John Ward (31st). He was recaptured by the Americans and put in jail in Providence, Rhode Island. He stayed in jail until the British evacuated the island in October of 1779, when he was let out to work at his trade of breeches maker. He made a new attempt and arrived within the King's lines at New York in November 1780.[206]

One of the young recruits from Lieutenant Nutts detachment, Private Christopher Weir, escaped from Rutland in November 1778, but was recaptured at Newhaven where he was put in jail. He was allowed out to go farming, but left after two weeks. On his way to New London, he fell in with a man conducting ten other escaped British soldiers and sailors to safety. The intention was to go by boat, but the effort failed, and Weir finished up in the jail at New London where he stayed seven weeks. He was bailed out by a farmer for whom he worked six months, but was then arrested for trying to enlist American soldiers for the British army. This time he was put into Hartford jail for eleven months. In company with seven Loyalists, he escaped from prison and worked farming at Salem in New York State for eight or nine months. He then went back to New England, intending to surrender himself to his regiment in Rutland, but found them gone. After a year in New England, he travelled to Providence. There he was arrested by an American Colonel, who said he had seen him in the American service. After a period in jail and further farming work, he was arrested once again trying to get into New York with three loyalists. He was not only put in jail for nine months in Poughkeepsie, but also charged with murder and robbery. With 11 others he broke out of the jail; and after a further period of work, arrived in New York in May of 1782. There he finally joined the 33rd Foot, the regiment he had been recruited for so many years previously.[207]

Philip Quick (29th), like many others, tried for Canada, where the rest of his regiment was stationed. After a first arrest, he spent nine months in Bennington jail. Promising to behave as a prisoner of war he was allowed to work. Then with a Loyalist, he made a second attempt to reach Canada. After six weeks on the road, he was caught once again and this was followed by another jail sentence. He seems to have decided that Canada was impossible and after a period of working to keep himself, he was successful in reaching New York.[208]

William Warren (47th) escaped from Rutland in the spring of 1778 and went to work in Salem. After being jailed, he escaped five days later and spent two months on the road reaching Paulus Hook and then on into New York in August 1780. There he was drafted into a Loyalist regiment, the King's American Provincial Regiment.[209]

One of the best group escapes of the war, was made from Rutland by five of the prisoners. Led by Private Michael Tiffin and accompanied by Privates James Robinson and William Heslop (all 47th), they together with James Fenton and Peter Gordon (both 21st), escaped 17th September 1778 reaching Newport in Rhode Island by 9th October. They were frequently examined on the road, but never arrested since they were able to pass themselves off as Americans. Travelling by night, they lay up in woods during the day. Like some others, in typical British soldier fashion, years later they claimed from the British army ration money to cover the period they were not fed properly during the retreat from Bemis Heights. Although the army did not in general, treat the escaping prisoners well in terms of monies due, this group did succeed in getting paid! [210]

Private Loughlin Murphy (9th) spent nine months in Fishkill Jail, after which, he was sick for eighteen months, but finally made it to New York on Christmas Day 1780.[211]

In Cambridge, because of its proximity to the villages around Boston with their concentrated population, there was always something going on. Not so at Rutland. It consisted of just a few houses and there was a considerable distance to the next village. The men began to call the place "Siberia." There was further discouragement when two recaptured men, together with the wife of one of them, were hanged by the Americans for the murder of a man at Worcester. The guards also had their problems, but their lot was relieved by their tour of duty being limited to three months' service.[212]

While these moves were taking place, Clinton realised that no matter what was said or done, the Americans were determined not to carry out their commitment under the Convention. In response to the intransigence of Congress, he had since early June, with approval from Germaine, delayed supplying some provisions. This brought great hardship on the Convention Prisoners because it made the Americans responsible for finding the supplies and they were often in difficulties in meeting the required quantities. Having abandoned a military solution to the problem, Sir Henry now resolved to take the course recommended by Phillips to cease permanently the supply of rations, or more importantly, gold for the purchase of supplies. This development had repercussions, probably unexpected by Sir Henry. The Massachusetts merchants, who despite the hardship on their local population caused by food shortages and supplies, had been very happy to earn substantial profits in hard currency coming from the British. With the supply of gold now drying up, their opposition to the prisoners being moved elsewhere evaporated.[213]

As early as September, Congress had resolved that if passports for supply ships to enter Boston were not granted by the British by 5th October 1778, it was deemed justified to move the prisoners out of Massachusetts to another part of America, where food was more plentiful. Moving the prisoners from Massachusetts would be in direct contravention of Article 4 of the Convention. When Pennsylvania refused to accept them, the western part of Virginia seemed to be the place. The south had seen little of the war. More importantly, it was remote, far from the sea, and unlikely to provide a tempting target for the British to stage a rescue attempt. The area had already been used for a few prisoners of war and for exiled Quakers and others who had refused to take up arms against the British. While passing through Winchester, some Quakers had met John Harvie, a Congressman from Charlottesville and after talking with them it was probably then he conceived the idea of recommending his property as a safe place to incarcerate the prisoners.[214]

John Harvie, was Trustee to the estate of Thomas Jefferson's father. He had been one of the four members of Congress to vote against suspending the Convention, saying the British might attempt to rescue these troops. Despite that, he appears to have been astute enough to recognise the financial opportunities which would be created by with-holding the departure of the prisoners. He offered Congress the use of some of his land near Charlottesville in Virginia, on which to locate barracks for the prisoners' accommodation. Congress accepted the offer, and later they paid him $23,000 to cover the cost of construction of sufficient barrack blocks to accommodate both the British and German prisoners. Harvie never completed the buildings. When the prisoners arrived, they found for a third time, they had to complete the con-struction of their own prison camp. It was claimed that failure to comply with the contract was due to the construction being left to the inefficient brother of John Harvie. This may be true, but John Harvie enjoyed, apart from the money, another substantial benefit from housing the prisoners. By the time the prisoners left Virginia, their insatiable demand for firewood and building materials had cleared his land of timber for several miles around, making it ready for farming. There was also a still further advantage. Since December 1777, he had been trying to obtain the use of prisoners of war to help Thomas Jefferson complete the buildings at Monticello, his home just outside Charlottesville. He was now able to write saying if the prisoners were sent to Charlottesville, "some tradesmen of the professions you want may be found amongst them and procured."[215]

With a complete disregard for the problems involved, Congress instructed Washington to move the prisoners with all convenient speed. He could not spare Continental troops for the escort, since they were fully occupied investing the British armies in New York and Rhode Island. His frustration with this order is evident from his letter to Heath dated October 21,

> I know of no way of conveying the troops to the place of their destination but by calling upon the several states thro' which they are to pass for a proper guard of militia and carriages sufficient to transport their baggage. You will therefore apply to the State of Massachusetts

for the number necessary, and when you have fixed the time of march and the Route, inform Governor Trumball that he may be ready to receive them upon the borders of Connecticut.

At the same time, Washington applied to the Governors of New York and New Jersey for their escorts.[216]

Although it was now a year since the battle, special arrangements needed to be made for a number of prisoners still suffering from wounds received at Saratoga. Many of these, especially those with leg and thigh wounds, were incapable of making the march. Six British officers, 138 men, 38 women and 36 children were unable to join the columns. Phillips, still at Cambridge, was able to report to Clinton that Gates had done all in his power to assist in examining these men to be candidates for exchange and moving them to New York. If exchange could not be effected, then they would be moved by sea to Virginia, in the cartel ship which had just arrived for that purpose. Both sides recognised they held men with wounds or with permanent ill-health, making them incapable of further military service. A limited agreement for exchange was quietly made between the generals. In this way, many of those who had to be left behind, found themselves in British hands in New York. There, one of them, Robert Hewart (21st) seems to have recovered very rapidly. He was not repatriated to Europe but spent the rest of the war serving with the Loyal American Provincial Regiment.[217]

The exchange gave at least one escaper freedom. Sergeant John Jackson (20th), after spending some time in Providence jail for escaping, either at Rutland or on their journey towards New York, managed to intermingle with the invalids of the Convention Army, and reached New York with them.[218]

One of those who was sick, but not sufficiently so as to be exchanged, was Private Charles Stephens (24th). He was left at Rutland in the care of a group of prisoners of war from the 53rd. He remained there until 1780. When he heard that German Dragoons, prisoners of war, were to be exchanged, he tried to have himself included. This failed, as a German sergeant refused to help him. Subsequently, with four other British soldiers he escaped. In the company of some black slaves owned by farmers at Middleton, they took a boat and with provisions, got as far as Seabrook, when they were caught by a guardship. After nine months in Hartford Jail, he enlisted "stark naked," as an artificer in an American unit. Later, he protested that all they gave him was an old coat! He marched south with this regiment and then deserted. He succeeded in reaching the British in Yorktown on 29th September 1781, just in time to be captured for a second time with Cornwallis's army three weeks later.[219]

Another left sick at Rutland, was Private James Gray (9th). He managed to reach St. John's in Canada, where he requested to join Rogers' Rangers. That famed regiment was instrumental in intercepting many escaped Convention Prisoners in the thickly wooded country on the Canadian border, and Gray's preference for that regiment was probably due to their finding and helping him.[220]

On receiving the news of the intended move to Virginia, there was great concern among the allied senior officers; the prisoners had neither proper clothing or money to sustain themselves on a winter march. They asked they be allowed to notify Sir Henry in New York. They drew attention to the problem of marching in winter and in particular the need for clothing and blankets for the men, as well as their concern about accommodation on their route of march. Washington wrote a letter of reassurance on these matters to Phillips, requesting at the same time, that he ensure the discipline of their soldiers to prevent disputes, either with their conductors, or "the countries thro' which they may travel."

On hearing of the intention of the Americans to remove the prisoners from Massachusetts, Clinton drafted a proclamation ordering the taking and transportation of civilian hostages to England. Part of the purpose in taking such a drastic step was to place pressure on the Americans to comply with the Saratoga Convention. Good sense seems to have prevailed and the proclamation was never published or put into effect. The only retaliation adopted by Clinton was to recall to confinement all the American officer prisoners who were on parole in New York.[221]

Washington's reassurances on the prisoners' welfare proved wrong and the apprehensions of the Convention Officers materialised. The columns had barely started when snow began to fall "by day and night." Once more in the mountains, the men lay out in the open with only a blanket apiece and "snow upon us ½ yd deep." Two men of the 9th Foot were drowned when crossing the Connecticut River, due to the volume of the water and "the wind being high drove them over the falls." During this portion of the march another 50 British left the columns, but Phillips was able to report that "the rest had behaved with very good order, and pursued the march in health and spirits."[222]

The ever-present danger of British troops making a sally out of New York to intercept the columns made Washington take a great personal interest in the route to be followed. While movement through Massachusetts and Connecticut was fairly safe from interception, the recognised point of greatest danger was when the column had to cross the Hudson. He stipulated this was to be at Fishkill, which was the nearest point the column would come to New York City. For that part of the march, he planned to use one of his scarce Continental regiments as an additional escort. Heath, on Washington's instructions, kept the route secret from the prisoners. Washington then felt that all possible precautions had been taken and was able to write to him,

> I thank you for your caution in concealing the route from the officers
> of the Convention, altho', in the present situation of the Enemy's affairs,
> I do not think any danger is to be apprehended.

Although the Convention Officers were unaware of the route they were to take, the British in New York had information on at least one part of the journey. A British intelligence officer at an outpost of the New York army, picked up information which later proved correct. The American camp at Valley Forge in Pennsylvania was being rehabilitated for the prisoners while en route. The Americans had vacated the camp in June 1778 and had left, what the informant described, as a scene of desolation.[223]

Washington did find an efficient Continental officer to superintend the movement. He was Colonel Theodorick Bland Jr. and efficiency was not his only quality. A descendant of the Indian, Pocohontas, and a former doctor who had studied medicine at Edinburgh, he had very early in his life advocated less government from the mother-country and was now an enthusiastic supporter of the War for Independence. Despite his firm views in that respect, and his being perhaps a little pompous, he had the ability to gain the co-operation and respect of the senior British officers. The American General Henry Lee, described him as "noble, sensible, honorable, and amiable, but never intended for the department of military intelligence." Notwithstanding ceaseless differences and his insistence on discipline and correct behaviour from the prisoners, he was able to develop long lasting friendship with many of them. Even when he and Phillips were in the midst of a dispute over British escapes, it seems that Phillips had lost a bet of 500 pounds with him.[224]

Bland's efficiency in both planning and executing the march rapidly proved itself. Soon after the columns had moved out of Rutland and Cambridge, and despite the bad weather conditions, Washington was able to report to the Board of War that the troops have made good progress towards the North (Hudson) River and hoped they would continue to do so in the future.

Washington's fear of intervention from New York led him to order Major General De Kalb's division to constitute an additional Continental escort, during the most risky part of the march. He instructed De Kalb to select five or six hundred men to be divided into 6 detachments, each commanded by an officer not above the rank of a Lieutenant Colonel, "that there may no interference with Colo. Bland on account of rank." Washington wanted no confusion in command in the event of an attack by the British from New York.[225]

Although Washington did not think such an attack was likely, he was taking no chances. He was also concerned with the volume of escapes that might take place. In his instructions to De Kalb, he stated

> It is probable that many of the Convention Troops may, under the pretense of desertion, attempt to get into New York. I therefore desire you will order a strict watch to be kept, and if any of them are found stragling any suspicious distance from their corps, that they may be taken up and returned to them.

After giving some thought on what he had written, he decided that it would not be advantageous to return the escaped prisoners to their units for punishment by their officers, as this would discourage those deserters who truly wished to disappear. He therefore added a postscript,

> Upon reconsidering the matter, it will be better to post two Regiments at the Continental Village where Genl (George) Clinton was posted, and if any of the Convention Troops attempt to pass that way let them be stopped and informed that they must go back into the country.

Lieutenant General John Burgoyne.

William L. Clements Library.

Major General Philip Schuyler.

William L. Clements Library.

Major General Horatio Gates.

William L. Clements Library.

You will have heard, & for I doubt not long before this can have reached you that Sir W. Howe is gone from hence. The Rebels imagine that he is gone to the Eastward, by this time however he has filled Chesapeak bay with surprize and terror.

Washington marched the greatest part of the Rebels to Philadelphia in order to oppose Sir W.m Army. I hear he is now returned upon finding none of our troops landed but am not sure of this, great part of his troops are returned for certain I am ~~[struck out]~~ ter[...] must be owing to them. I am left to command here, half my force may I am sure defend every thing here with as much safety I shall therefore send Sir W. 4 or 5. Bat.ns I have too small a force to invade the New England provinces, they are too weak to make any effectual efforts against me and you do not want any diversion in your favour I can therefore very well spare him 1500 men I shall try something certainly towards the close of the year notwithstanding at any rate It may be of use to inform you that report says all yields to you. I own to you I think the business will quickly be over now. G.l W.s move just at this time has been lasfiled Washington have been the worst he could take in every respect I sincerely give you much joy on your success and am with great sincerity your &c &c &c

A secret message from Clinton to Burgoyne. A seemingly innocuous letter turns into a military opinion. Clinton Papers.   William L. Clements Library.

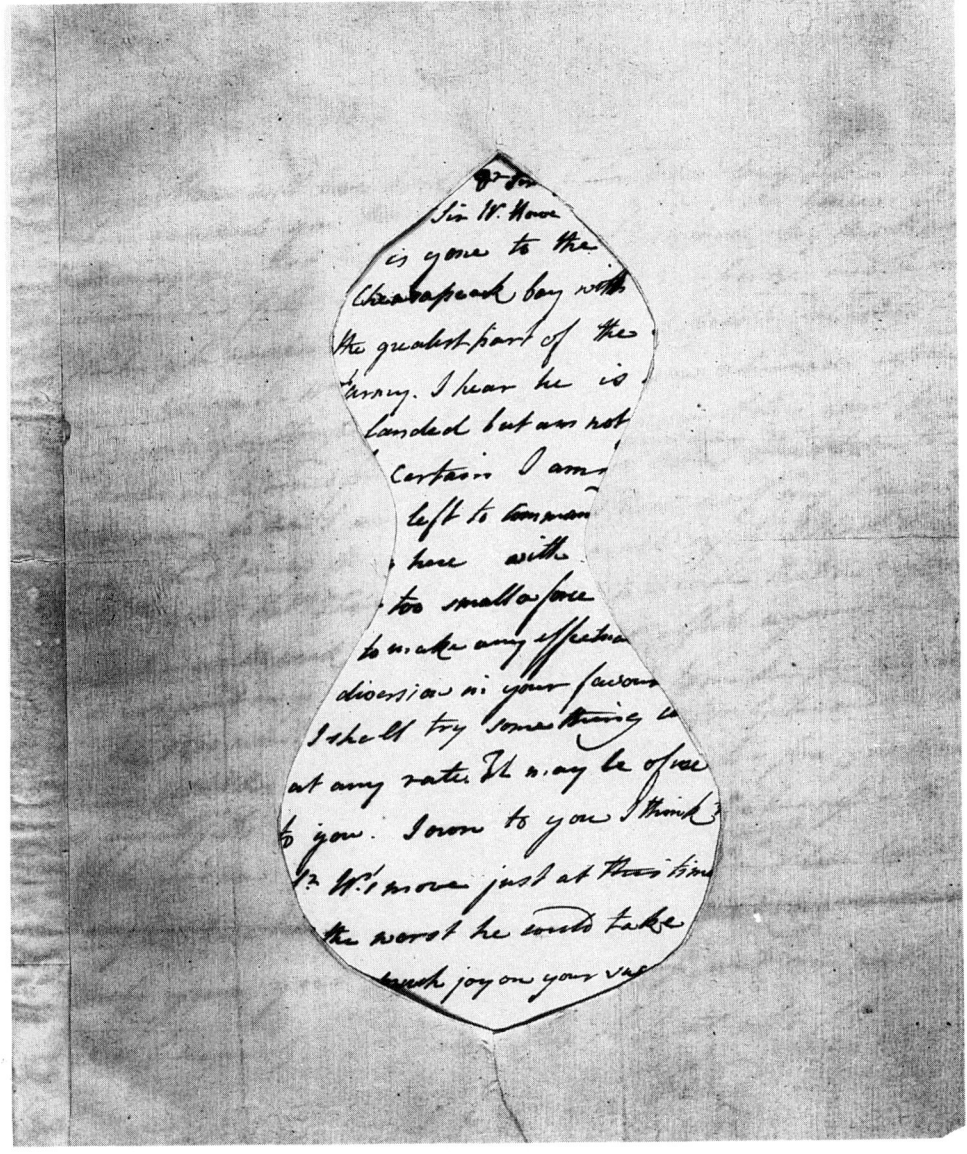

Message reads: Sir Wm. Howe is gone to the Chesapeak bay with the greatest part of the Army. I hear he is landed but was not certain. I am left to command here with too small a force to make any effectial disertion in your favour. I shall try something at any rate. It may be of use to you. I own to you I think Sr. W's move just at this time the worst he could take.

General William Howe.   William L. Clements Library.

Lord George Germain.

Major General George Washington.   William L. Clements Library.

Major General William Phillips, R.A.
Described by George Washington as "a dangerous man".

National Army Museum.

Major General William Heath.

William L. Clements Library.

Major General Clinton.
Always a friend of the Convention Prisoners.

Lieutenant James Moody rescuing Private Robert Maxwell from Newton, Sussex County, New Jersey Jail. From a 1785 painting.

National Army Museum.

Returning them to their corps will have a bad effect to those who really mean to desert in earnest.[226]

Washington was still not satisfied he had taken all the steps he needed to reduce escape to a minimum. He wrote to Brigadier General Poor, changing his previous orders and instructed him to move to Fishkill with as much expedition as you can, "without injuring your men."

To Brigadier General Jedidiah Huntington, he also wrote referring to the prisoners escaping to New York,

> It is more than probable that many of these under the pretense of desertion, will endeavour to find their way into New York; I would therefore wish you to stop all that may happen in your way and detain them until you think their release may be safe, or send them back into the country, provided there will not be a probablility of accomplishing their aim, should they mean to get into the city, with a threat that if they are detected again under the slightest appearance of making their escape that they may rely on the severest treatment. It would not be amiss to warn the magistrates convenient to you in this matter, who may frequently have an opportunity of intercepting such when it would be out of your power to do it.[227]

It was as well that Washington had taken precautions against a possible rescue attempt by the British. Orders had been issued for troops on Long Island to make a foray coinciding with the columns crossing the Hudson. This was a powerful force as it included all the Grenadier and Light Companies on Long Island. Leaving New York on 4th December they moved up the Hudson as far as Kings' Ferry, hoping to intercept the prison columns, but they failed to find them. They were two days late in reaching the river; the prisoners had already crossed and were out of reach.[228]

This time, the Germans were also moved and the allied army was divided into six divisions. The three British led the way from Rutland, followed by three divisions of Germans from Cambridge. As they proceeded, the weather again improved and the columns made good progress. It did not take the prisoners long to take advantage of the scarcity of escorts. The period of the march fell mostly in November and December of 1778 and for these two months, an army return indicates that no less than 294 British left, with only one man rejoining.[229]

Many of those who made successful attempts to reach British lines could not have done so without the active support of Americans. John Adams, second President of the United States, many years after the war, gave his view of the attitude of the inhabitants of America during the revolution. He estimated that of the three million people settled in the thirteen colonies at the time, one third supported the revolution, one third supported the British, and one third "didn't give a damn." Another comment came from John Harvie, who wrote in 1777, that two thirds of Delaware are "notoriously known in their hearts to be with our enemy."[230]

Those supporting the revolution had been much better organised and more prepared to take up arms; they had quickly gained control of the political structure in each of the colonies. Having political control they were able to administer the laws to their own advantage. Those accused of being actively opposed to the revolution were charged with treason, sedition or aiding the enemy and subjected to penalties ranging from tarring and feathering, the confiscation of property, exile and death. One Maryland group was sentenced to be hanged, drawn and quartered, later reduced to simple hanging.

Many of the inhabitants who may have been quietly sympathetic to the British cause were just not prepared to risk their lives to assist an escapee. Those fearless, but unfortunate inhabitants caught helping escaped prisoners, were often hanged. Many from New England, were sent to the Simsbury mine in Connecticut and had to exist under conditions quite as bad as the notorious British prison ship Jersey. The derelict copper mine, was first used for incarcerating Loyalists in December of 1775, when George Washington sent the first group from elsewhere in New England. Americans quickly dubbed the place Newgate, referring to the London prison. After passing through a guardhouse and down into a basement, prisoners were forced to descend a forty foot vertical ladder. Those that would not climb down were forcibly winched down. At the bottom a tunnel sloped down to a series of caverns. Here, seventy feet below ground, in chambers hewn out of solid rock, no natural light, dripping water and limited ventilation, the prisoners existed for years on end. As could be expected, under those conditions many died. Tired of British soldiers escaping, and knowing of the conditions existing on the British prison ship Jersey, Congress passed a resolution that the Simsbury mine also be used for "the reception of British prisoners of war and for the purpose of retaliation." Fortunately for the British soldiers, the war came to an end before any could be sent there.[231]

Known Loyalists avoiding retribution by fleeing to the British lines, lost all their belongings and property, receiving very little or nothing in the way of compensation from the British authorities. Eventually, and usually penniless, they had to seek exile in Canada, the West Indies or Britain.

Under these circumstances the lot of the British prisoner was very similar to the escaper on the run in the occupied countries of Europe during World War II. If they took the risk of going from house to house for food or assistance, they never knew whether they would receive it, be turned away due to fear, or handed over to the local Committee of Safety or army unit.

During the American War the escaper would be put in jail for an indeterminate period; as in World War II the civilian could expect much worse. Sergeant Roger Lamb (9th) has left the most graphic description of the problem of clandestinely seeking assistance from civilians. Lamb, after successfully escaping when a Convention Prisoner, declined repatriation to Europe and joined the 23rd Foot. He was then captured for a second time at Yorktown and once more successfully escaped again, receiving a bounty on both occasions when he reached New York. On his first venture with two companions, he eluded the guards before they crossed the Hudson River. The woman in the first house they tried, hid them for the rest of the day and pointed the way to a Loyalist who would guide them to New York. When the Loyalist's wife learned what they wanted of her husband she point-blank refused to let him do it. The offer of a $20 gift made no difference. Expressing the fear, which the prisoners found in many of the inhabitants, she said,

> Do you mean to break my heart, by foolishly running into the jaws of death, depriving me of a husband, and my children of a father? You know that there are several camps and garrisons between this and New York, that you would not be able to go ten miles before you would be taken up, and then you would be hung up like a dog.

After two others had given help they finally found a couple who welcomed and fed them but would not have them in the house. The husband first refused to act as a guide, saying, "that it would be an hundred chances to one, if we were not taken." He then relented saying, he would go if a young man living nearby agreed to act as a second guide, and adding, "but I will not go by myself, as I well know the dangers which we shall be exposed to without a second guide."

After ten hours on their way, they were deserted by the young man who had demanded a payment of $40 which they did not have. Creeping past American camps and troops, they again fell in with a couple who looked after them and hid them in a hay stack for thirty hours. The three were now forty miles from Kingsbridge, the nearest outpost of the British army, and they decided to try to complete the journey in one night. This they did, arriving before dawn at a house one mile from the British line. The inhabitants were terrified at an order to light a candle saying, if a light were seen the British would immediately open fire on the house. Realising it was too dangerous to make for the fort in darkness, they waited in the house before traversing the last mile to the fort. At last in response to a challenge by a British sentry they were able to reply, "We are British soldiers, who have made good our escape." It had taken them a week to cover the 100 miles from the point of their escape.[232]

During his second escape from Yorktown, Lamb was recaptured twice for short periods of time. He was very badly handled, beaten and starved by the Americans after they had been told by a British deserter of his previous escapes. On what was his fourth and final effort in eluding his captors, he received financial assistance from one of his officers. After experiencing several adventures, and suffering severe hardship, he led a party of 3 sergeants and four privates of the 23rd, all of whom, after dividing into two parties, eventually reached New York. One of the escapees with him was one of the men who had accompanied him on his first successful escape effort during the march to Virginia.[233]

Private Ambrose Fox (24th) was another man who left the column on the way to Virginia. His company officer, Captain Jamison, gave him a $60 bill to carry him forward, and it seems that this money enabled him to make a successful journey into New York.[234]

Charles Pocock (24th) also made a very quick escape on his own.

He took only ten days to get into New York. Another of the 24th, James Bond, escaped at Goshen and arrived promptly in New York.[235]

Colonel Bland experienced a serious escort problem when the first division arrived at the Connecticut/New York border. The Connecticut militia refused to go on and Bland had to rely on 500 Continental troops which Washington was forced to order up from Fredericksburgh, New York. It was at this time that popular General Anthony Wayne, their commander, expressing the disdain that regular troops often show for reservists, wrote to Bland saying, "I find the Connecticut militia are but a militia; I send you soldiers." [236]

The Governor of Pennsylvania found the required number of militia, but only with difficulty. He had to call men who had already served. Even then he had to countermand this order for York County which was to cause problems for Bland. By the time the lead division had reached Lancaster, Pennsylvania, the weather had once again deteriorated. A temporary halt had to be made to await the arrival of militia from other parts of Pennsylvania who would, with a small detachment of Continental cavalry, form the escort to the Virginia border. No sooner had the halt been ordered, when fighting broke out between the British soldiers and the townspeople. Bland, choosing the lesser of two evils, decided to risk the bad weather and continued the march to York, although with the knowledge that no militia would be waiting for him at that place. His main reason for taking this risk was the realisation that if the first division failed to move, the other divisions following, would be forced to stop where no provisions were available.[237]

In Maryland, Bland had an easier time of it as they had 500 militia with supply wagons ready to take over as escort. The weather continued to deteriorate. While the first and second divisions of British troops were able to proceed, albeit slowly through the thick snow, the third division on reaching Frederick Town experienced a massive snow storm, which lasting all day, brought the march to an end for several days.[238]

The day the columns entered Virginia, men were sinking to their knees in snow, cutting shins and ankles on hidden obstacles. After a march of over 16 miles the men had to sleep in the open on the snow.

Virginia had also made adequate provision for the escort and by mid-January 1779, all six columns had arrived at Charlottesville. Here the prisoners were handed over to Colonel William Harvie, who was to act as the Commissary of Prisoners. Bland, who came from Virginia, immediately wrote to Washington asking permission to spend the winter on leave. With a barn burned in New York State, the fracas in Lancaster, and with a large number of prisoners escaping from the columns, his command had not been an easy one. Although many of the escaped prisoners had been recaptured in New Jersey and other places, an impression is gained that Bland was pleased to be relieved of the responsibility for the prisoners. It was not to be for long.[239]

CHAPTER 8

Charlottesville

C HARLOTTESVILLE, described as being, "in a dreary region of woods and wretchedness", proved to be a very small town. It consisted of the Court House, one tavern and a dozen houses. The barracks were situated in an area permeated with ticks and snakes. Ten miles from the town by road, but by using a cross country path, the distance to the barracks could be shortened to five miles. That path today is a road and still bears the name Barracks Road.[240]

Anburey left a graphic description of the scene of misery and confusion which awaited the men on their arrival,

> As to the men, the situation was truly horrible, after the hard shifts they had experienced in their march from the Potowmack, they were, instead of comfortable barracks, conducted into a wood, where a few log huts were just begun to be built, the most part not covered over, and all of them full of snow; these the men were obliged to clear out and cover over to secure themselves from the inclemency of the weather as quick as they could, and in the course of two or three days rendered them habitable, but by no means a comfortable retirement; what added greatly to the distresses of the men, was the want of provisions, as none had as yet arrived for the troops, and for six days they subsisted on the meal of Indian corn made into cakes.

Most of the officers shared the men's problems. Phillips reported to Germaine that,

> (The officers) finding no shelter nor any habitations whatever contiguious to the miserable sheds in which the soldiers were placed, they cheerfully undertook to build huts at their own cost, in order to take care of the men, and encourage them, by their example, to sustain the many but unavoidable difficulties they were exposed to.

Anburey did not criticise Congress for the mismanagement. He squarely blamed John Harvie, who he said had misguided and duped

Congress. Colonel Bland quickly handed over the prisoners to William Harvie and left for home. After failing to carry out the barracks construction contract, Harvie proved just as inefficient in his role as the officer in charge of the prisoners.[241]

The prisoners had to set-to providing themselves with elementary protection from the severe winter weather. For several weeks to come, they had to endure the roofless, doorless, windowless snow-filled barracks. In addition, the lack of food and provisions immediately became apparent. For the first ten days nothing was supplied. The men had to exist on the little remaining food left over from the march and what they could beg or steal from the few area inhabitants. Anburey commented, "Never was a country so destitute of every comfort, provisions were not to be purchased." Immediately, the Virginia deputy quartermaster suggested to Congress that the men be moved from Charlottesville and closer to navigable rivers so that food supplies could be more easily provided. Since this would mean separating the officers from the men, Thomas Jefferson was opposed to such a move. In his opinion, it would be a breach of the Convention which he would not countenance. Saying the prisoners had arrived at a particularly unfortunate time regarding weather, he pointed out the cost of moving them again,

> the expense of building barracks, said to have been £25,000, and of removing the troops backwards and forwards, amounting to, I know not how much, are not to be permitted, merely because they are Continental expenses; for we are part of the Continent; we must pay a shilling of every dollar wasted.

Jefferson also noted the benefit to the local economy,

> The sums of money which, by these troops, or on their account, are brought into, and expended in the State, are a great and local advantage.[242]

It was assumed this time, that their stay would be prolonged, so several hundred huts were constructed. A broad space was left between those occupied by the German troops and those of the British. This became a main street dividing the two areas. The huts were completed in regular lines with "streets" between. Each regiment had its own area, eventually there was sufficient accommodation to limit the number of prisoners in each hut to six. When the living accommodation was completed, a guard-house, hospital and theatre, complete with scenery and curtain, were added. The 21st Foot built themselves a church. Space for a cemetery was cleared and a fence constructed around to protect it from incursions by animals. Wells were sunk, and orders were given for all men to develop vegetable gardens, the latter proving to be a wise decision in view of the grave shortages of food which developed after their arrival. Two enterprising Americans erected taverns outside the barracks. Dabney noted that a runaway female slave named Patt was suspected of being kept at the barracks.[243]

In an effort to reduce calls on their militia, the Virginia legislature asked Congress to raise a special regiment of 600 men. This regiment, The Convention Guards Regiment, would guard the prisoners; officers would be selected by Virginia; service would be for one year or until the prisoners left the state. Many of the recruits were very young. In at least one case, a guard was only thirteen years of age. Their lack of training was demonstrated when a sentry accidently shot one of his own officers.[244]

Although food was desperately short, it seems the unusually cold weather for Virginia halted the number of deaths. Jefferson commented on this, at the same time making an interesting reference to eighteenth-century frontier demographics. After the men had been at Charlottesville for three months, he wrote, of a population of 4,000 (i.e. British and German prisoners) there should be one death per day, but that there were only four during the three months. Of these, two were infants. Phillips also reported to Clinton that in spite of the short rations, the men "are extremely healthy—the barracks are become by some labour tolerably commodius." [245]

The clothing and ration problems were relieved to a limited extent by the arrival in May 1779 of a vessel from New York, containing clothing and stores for the prisoners. The British Commander-in-Chief had now realised his previous tactics of refusing to supply provisions had failed to gain the release of the prisoners. His shipment was a belated effort to relieve their misery. A delay in the vessel's arrival was due to Washington, knowing of Phillips's propensity for taking any advantage, laying down stringent conditions as to its route and conduct. By the time it arrived, trouble by the British troops caused by the lack of food and accommodation, had again stirred. The

American Board of War were of the opinion that the situation required an officer "having sufficient weight and knowledge of business to regulate the uneasy and discordant spirits among the prisoners." George Washington, desperately short of officers, had no alternative but to ask Colonel Bland to cancel his leave and return to Charlottesville to take command again. Bland acceded to the request.[246]

Bland quickly summed up the problem. Recruiting for the Convention Guards Regiment had been a failure. Jefferson, now Governor of Virginia complained that he had been unable to raise more than half a battalion of infantry for guards. Instead of 600 men, Bland found only 200 raw recruits, all undisciplined and poorly clothed. He made a request to the Virginia Council, warning them of the difficult situation with the prisoners, and asking for a troop of light horse to "procure deserters and be ready for emergencies." The Council would have nothing of it and recommended that he send for 15 men from his own 1st Continental Dragoon Regiment. This he was forced to do, and there arrived in Charlottesville two troops of his very ragged, but well-drilled and disciplined Dragoons. A week later, Bland's words came home to the Virginia Council, giving them second thoughts on what should be done,

> reflecting on ye exceeding great dangers that might result fm an insurrection of ye Convention Troops, & on ye weak condition of ye Militia, for want of arms, to oppose any attempt they might make to join ye enemy.

They then resolved to arm the militia of the six counties around the barracks; they warned the Lieutenants of the counties,

> to discipline their militias in a particular manner & have them equipped & ready at a moments warning in case ye sh'd be called upon to counteract any dangerous designs these troops may have.[247]

When Major General Phillips arrived at the barracks some weeks after the men, he was incensed at the treatment they had received. Anburey commented that had Phillips seen them on the day of their arrival, his warmth of temper would have laid him under the same house restriction as he had endured at Cambridge. For his part Bland did promise to render the situation of the men as comfortable as possible, and with all expedition, but he was never able to resolve the problem of shortage of food.[248]

All the British generals concerned with the Convention went to great lengths to ensure that no conduct on their part could be the cause of giving the Americans any excuse for cancelling the treaty on legitimate grounds. Their correspondence and records were worded in such a way to support this policy. We have seen how Burgoyne criticised his officers in his orders for assisting men to escape. Carleton, commanding in Canada went to extremes in complying with the treaty which had already been suspended by the Americans. As the first British who had escaped to the north, straggled into Canada, he ordered them to Europe immediately, as required by the Convention. As far as the Canadians were concerned, to ensure they took no further part in the war, he ordered that "no one . . . should do duty of any sort." He even extended this to civilian workers returned to Canada under the treaty, not allowing them to caulk any boats or repair any military accommodation. His policies were only reversed on 2nd June 1778, when he came to the conclusion that the suspended treaty was unlikely to be reinstated by the Americans, and he declared the treaty "nul and void in this Province."[249]

Phillips's role as Commanding Officer of the Convention Prisoners needs to be examined in some detail to judge the extent to which he complied with the Convention. He always took an open and aggressive position with the Americans when matters arose affecting the discipline or treatment of the prisoners. That much is clear. What is not so clear, is the extent he played a double game with the Americans on matters of escape. Ostensibly, he strongly disapproved of it in his official correspondence with Clinton in New York. But the Americans had always insisted on censoring all letters going out and coming in, and much of what he wrote must have been for their consumption. In one letter, he blamed the Americans for the desertion, saying the severities and hardships gave the men no alternative but to leave, so as to avert starvation. In one letter to the Americans he described deserters as,

> miscreants, who will embrace any cause, and change from party to party, from fear of punishment or hope of reward.

Despite such expressions, he makes other statements which are difficult to believe. Furthermore, we keep getting glimpses of him doing things not expected of an eighteenth-century officer who had given his parole. The evidence shows that if he was not actively organising escape, at the very least he closed his eyes to what was going on around him.[250]

While at Cambridge, Phillips had engaged in what amounted to an offer of bribery to General Gates and the American politicians. He asked Gates to use his influence to have all the prisoners exchanged. He offered 2,000 guineas for Gates's interest in "bringing forward a negotiation." If those negotiations resulted in a general exchange taking place, a further payment of 6,000 guineas would be paid. As might be expected, the correspondence does not explain all that was going on. Phillips also asked that his proposal be kept private and Gates assured him he would ask Congress to treat it as such. In any event, nothing came of it.[251]

Phillips was also prepared to dabble in intelligence work. He had not accompanied the troops on their march, but had travelled to Charlottesville on his own, with but one American officer as his escort. In his usual belligerent manner, he ignored instructions he had received from the Americans regarding the route to take, and this made Washington furious when he learned what he had been up to,

> I view General Philips in the light of a dangerous man. In his march to Charlottesville he was guilty of a very great breach of military propriety, nay of a procedure highly criminal; for, instead of pursuing (the) rout pointed out to him, namely the one by which the Troops of Convention marched . . . he struck down to George Town in Maryland, from thence went by water to Alexandria taking as I am told the soundings of the river as he went, and from thence to Fredericksburg.

When Washington enquired why the American officer accompanying him had allowed Phillips to do this, he found that the American was a prisoner of the British and apparently on parole. Washington wrote,

> . . . the officer who conducted him was more culpable than he, but upon enquiry it is found that this officer is a person over whom I have no control as he is a prisoner of theirs.

Washington added there is, "the necessity of keeping a watchful eye upon these (British) officers." How Phillips had arranged for his escort to be an American officer on parole, rather than an active one, is unknown. The officer, in order to protect his parole, probably had to do what Phillips told him. What is clear is that Phillips, in breach of his parole, was obtaining intelligence which would be useful for an invading British army. It was almost as if he had known he would at some time in the future be commanding such a force.[252]

When Phillips arrived at Charlottesville, he immediately ordered a standing guard and patrol consisting of a sergeant, corporal and twelve men. As escape of prisoners escalated, Bland implied that the patrol had not done their duty in stopping escapes. Phillips, with tongue in cheek, refuted this by replying,

> I can never understand that the picquets could be intended to prevent desertion, but to correct any abuses and misbehavior which might appear growing among the soldiery towards the inhabitants of the country around.

This statement does not show any concern at the number of escapes taking place or any desire to stop them. Indeed, it could imply that soldiers deserting were none of his business.[253]

Phillips's record at both the Battle of Minden and at Saratoga, shows that he was an efficient officer and a leader of men. One is therefore, left with the question that if he was really interested in preventing men leaving the barracks, surely he could have taken steps to stop it. Even given the size of the barracks at Charlottesville, additional patrols could have made escape extremely difficult. It would also have kept more of the men busy. His denial that the police patrol was to stop escape is not the only indication of his attitude. Bland had intercepted evidence that many escapees were reaching New York and he maintained their conduct was in breach of the Convention. Phillips, expressing a highly unlikely attitude for a senior British officer, replied,

> I cannot possibly know anything concerning them [the deserters] after they have left the Troops of Convention; . . . nor is it a matter which concerns me, or any regiment of the Troops of Convention, whether they serve in General Washington's army or with Sir Henry Clinton; nor do I conceive it in any manner possible to construe desertion [unless

it can be proved to be by my orders] to militate against the treaty of Convention of Saratoga.

It was asking a lot of the Americans to believe that he did not care which side they joined! [254]

Others recognised the type of man he was. Before Major John André proposed to Clinton his plan to meet with Benedict Arnold, to arrange that officer's defection to the British, the suggestion was made that Phillips would, as an older and more experienced soldier, be more suited to the dangerous and complicated mission. It was suggested that Phillips then in Charlottesville, could be brought to New York on parole, and when passing through Philadelphia he could then confer with Arnold. In the event, it was André who met Arnold at West Point, which led to André's capture and execution. Even to consider the use of Phillips in such activity was in direct violation of eighteenth-century rules of war and parole conditions.[255]

One would suppose any efficient commander finding his army fast disappearing by desertion beyond his control, would accept the first opportunity to disassociate himself from such a situation.

We find Phillips doing nothing of the sort. When, in October 1780, he had been exchanged and appointed to command the army invading Virginia, the King not only approved his past conduct, but in addition he was allowed to continue as Commanding officer of the Convention Army. This despite the remains of that army being behind enemy lines. Not only had many of the successful escapees been drafted into the regiments constituting his new army on the coast of Virginia, but we find he was in active, secret communication with the remaining Convention Troops in Charlottesville. Joseph Jones, reporting to James Madison on British espionage from Richmond, Virginia wrote,

> Three other fellows were apprehended yesterday abt ten miles below this place the one a sergeant of British Grenadiers, the others soldiers and all deserters from the barracks the last summer and got into New York they were part of the British Army at Portsmouth (Virginia) and it is supposed were on their way to the barracks whether sent with written or verbal instructions has not yet come out.

Madison quickly reported this to Thomas Jefferson, who in turn, issued a warning that,

Some deserters were yesterday taken, said to be of the British Convention Troops who had found means to get to the enemy at Portsmouth and were 70 or 80 miles on their way back to the barracks when they were taken. They were passing under the guise of deserters from Portsmouth.

Phillips obviously wanted to co-ordinate the two armies under his command. Sending messengers to Charlottesville accorded with a letter he had received from Clinton, instructing him to inform the Convention Prisoners they were to obey his orders.[256]

While he remained in Charlottesville, Phillips had continued his aggressive attitude toward the Americans when the welfare of the prisoners was at stake. Just as he had clashed with Major General Heath, so differences arose with Colonel Bland. One concerned "worn out" men. The wounded and permanently disabled at Cambridge and Rutland had been exchanged, but there were now another 50 or 60 men who were "invalids and worn out". The Americans were prepared to have these men exchanged, but only after they had been certified as unfit by an American surgeon. Phillips ever jealous of procedures affecting the prisoners, proposed that the "Commanding Officers and surgeons of the respective regiments provide the certification, with no others other than invalids included and countersigned by the Surgeon General". There is no evidence that the Americans gave way on the point.[257]

A more serious breach took place over the responsibility for disciplining the British troops. Bland had ordered a Corporal King be handed over for trial before a Garrison Court Martial. Subsequently, Bland decided he was only wanted for examination on the facts laid against him. But Phillips had already gone into action, writing to Bland that for any offence within a miltary code,

> . . . I do protest against any officer or soldier of the troops under the Convention of Saratoga being tried before any Military Tribunal composed of American officers. I have been invincible in this determination ever since I have been at the head of the troops in their present situation. I well know that force & punishment are both in your power and the present situation of the troops under the faith of a convention which has never been in the slightest degree infringed on our parts put all resistance from us out of the question; and we must submit and we shall do it with patience and if necessary with fortitude

under any exertions and inflictions of force and punishment which you shall use.[258]

Bland's response to this letter contained a proposal that the two should meet and discuss such cases, which was welcomed by Phillips. It was at this point that Phillips defined two of the three types of desertion which were being experienced. This arose from the case of an escaper taken by the Americans and incarcerated in the American guard house at the Barracks. Phillips wrote,

> . . . there is now in the American guard house one of the Troops of Convention taken up attempting to desert and that you conceive he has by that forfeited the privilege he was entitled to under the Convention and comes under the predicament of a prisoner of war . . . You will allow me to explain . . . that any deserter from the troops of Convention must mean to desert from the cause of Great Britain into that of America and such men as you observe not entitled to any privileges under the Convention of Saratoga, and I am sir, to inform you that I will never suffer deserters to rejoin any corps of the Troops.

He then went on to define a second class of desertion, which he called "positive" desertion. In such cases he opined that punishment of the man should be left to him. He explained,

> I however, Sir, mean by the positive desertion, of men who may have straggled into the country, and by the enticements of women and liquor have absented themselves from their companies and regiments come under several particulars of our Articles of War and have always been treated accordingly by being punished & forgiven as the nature of their offence merited. As to the man in question I shall with great pleasure hold a conversation with you on the subject and find myself Sir, extremely obliged to you for so readily adopting that agreeable mode of doing business.[259]

He is silent on that other form of "desertion" i.e. escape. The written evidence of his attitude towards escape is quite contradictory. On 27th May 1779, he was writing to Clinton expressing the view that the men "behave well," yet in the first five months of 1779 his own figures show that 44 of the NCOs and men under his command have, "absented or deserted." Later the figures would soar. In June and July a total of 178 men disappeared. No figures are available for August, when the rate may have been even higher. It further seems that despite his letters to the Americans, he was continuing to do very little to stop it. On the other hand, he was careful not to openly approve anything which might give the Americans an excuse to claim he was breaching the Convention. In one letter he first pleads that having taken every care and caution to prevent desertion, "but I have been unable from various reasons to so do."

He then goes on, despite the evidence available to Bland that men were reaching the British in New York, "I must conceive, that in their desertion, they abandon the cause of Great Britain for that of America." There is no evidence that Bland, or any other American officer, took any notice whatsoever of these fictions.[260]

In the same letter, Phillips did claim truthfully, that any soldier who escaped came off the muster rolls of the Convention Regiments. He had issued an order on this, a copy of which went to New York. The Boards of Enquiry established by Clinton and Carleton to examine the men's claims for back pay while prisoners, used his order as an authority for sorting out these claims, and for the allocation of payments between their old and new regiments.

Phillips also thought the best defence to charges that the Convention was being breached by the British, was to accuse the Americans of encouraging the men to desert. He suggested it was they who were breaching the Convention.

> under what description may be put the conduct of several American officers in New England, who publicly had recruiting parties at the foot of the barracks at Cambridge, and took a variety of methods, persuasion, bribes and otherwise, to entice the troops of convention to desert; that in consequence many did desert, and two American regiments were nearly formed of such men, which joined General Washington's army,— serving against their country and the king. I will not call this militating against the treaty of Convention of Saratoga, but leave you, sir, to judge of it as you may think proper.

He omitted to remind Bland that most of the men recruited in this way had in turn deserted the American regiments and many were now in New York.

Bland would not give up, obviously knowing what was going on. Included in his letters to Phillips he raised concern over the

role the officers played in the escapes taking place, which he interpreted as,

> implied injurious suspicions of the Officers of Convention, and under
> that description, dishonorable to their parole.

Phillips, as usual, protested at the strong hint of retaliation and asked
to be allowed to send his views to General Washington who,

> I cannot conceive . . . can propose to use undeserved severities with
> the troops of convention, or to stigmatize the characters of officers
> which have been invariably irreproachable. At any rate, I shall do my
> duty by the troops, at whatever consequences may arise to me.[261]

So the war of words and the escapes went on, right until the day
Phillips was paroled and allowed to go to New York.

As the months passed, the accommodation improved, but the matter
of food supplies for the troops remained inadequate. On April 10th
1779, Anburey reported that,

> the men received meat only twice or thrice a week, and for some
> weeks none, what they get is scarcely wholesome, this is at present
> what the poor fellows term a fast, they not having any meat served
> them since the twenty-fifth of last month.

Later that year Anburey again described the worsening situation,

> Although we have been now near a twelvemonth in this province, the
> soldiers fare little better than on their first arrival; for the greatest part
> of the summer they have been thirty and forty days, at different periods,
> without any other provision delivered to them than the meal of Indian
> corn. Great quantities of salt provisions have arrived at the barracks,
> but owing to some defect in airing, and the heat of the climate, are in
> a state of putrefaction; some person advised the American Commissary
> to bury the meat in the earth for a few days, and it would regain its
> purity, which, when dug up, and although swarming with vermin, he
> insisted was exceedingly good, only a little tainted with the weather,
> which the utmost care could not prevent, and served it out to the
> soldiers as so many days ration of meat.

Fox confirmed Anburey's comments about the buried meat and says
Phillips appointed a jury of surgeons to condemn it. Also referring to
the food shortage, Fox described how local Indians helped them with

pounding the Indian corn between two stones. He stated in one period of seventeen days they went without meat. Another period of ten days without bread and lived on one quart of corn per day.[262]

Anburey commented that little redress could be expected from the Americans. He felt that the only possibility of improvement would occur if Clinton took up the matter with Washington personally. Despite the respect that the British officers had for Washington, Anburey did not even then anticipate much being done. He said that the only hope they could rely on is for a general exchange, adding,

> should that take place I may venture to affirm, that he [Clinton] will not have braver troops in his army; for the soldiers, from the cruelty and ill usage they have continually experienced, since they became prisoners, will fight to desperation.

In the following year Phillips expressed similar sentiments. Writing to Major General Frederick Haldimand, who had taken over the command in Canada from Carleton, he wrote, referring to failed exchange talks,

> Whatever part of the Troops of Convention that might have been exchanged, were by the King's orders to have been sent to Canada, by which Your Excellency would have gained a very fine detachment of the Royal Artillery and a number of men of other corps, perfectly inured to the climate of America, and whose patience and discipline have had very sever and long trials.

Germaine had already written a letter to Phillips indicating the King's approval of the men's conduct. Phillips read this letter to the men and he reported that,

> The King's general approbation of their conduct could not fail of making a deep impression on them and it has proved a most healing balsam to their weakened minds in the present situation.[263]

Phillips' figures showed another 14 men died in the four months of April through July 1779. With the coming of summer and driven by hunger and the failure of their officers to find a solution to the problem of supplies, the men now left the barracks in large numbers, leading to the escalation of escapes already mentioned. Some of these men have left a record of what happened to them.[264]

We have already met one James Robinson. Another of the same name, this time from the 9th Foot, succeeded in reaching the army under General Leslie, operating on the Virginia coast. After serving with the King's American Regiment, he was subsequently drafted into the 23rd Foot, and captured for a second time at Yorktown.[265]

John Cameron (29th) reported that his officers encouraged him to escape which he did on the 7th July 1779. Five weeks later, Sergeant John Macdonald of the same regiment, followed him and the two were able to get into New York. Cameron went into the Black Watch, while Macdonald served at the general hospital.[266]

Another of the July escapees, James Riley (31st) was quickly recaptured and served time in Winchester, Philadelphia and Frederick jails. Due to a confusion in records, he was able to pass himself off as a sailor and joined a group of naval personnel who were being exchanged under a flag of truce. After his arrival in New York he was also drafted into the 42nd. Another soldier successfully passing himself off as a sailor, was Corporal John Stubbs (62nd). He did not leave Charlottesville until 6th October 1780. After being recaptured by some American light cavalry and sent to Philadelphia jail, he adopted a fictitious name which allowed him to reach New York by 2nd March 1781. After his arrival he was appointed Drum Major of his new regiment.[267]

Another escaper who successfully disguised his true identity was William Woodsides (47th). After leaving Charlottesville he was incarcerated in jail, subsequently finding himself with a group of prisoners of war from the 17th Foot who had been captured at Princeton. They were later exchanged and a sergeant of that regiment included him on their muster roll and in this way he was successful in reaching New York.[268]

Two others of the 20th, Privates John Rhoads and John Hannagan escaped together on 14th June 1779. Both were recaptured the following day, and after spending two months in the American guard room at Charlottesville, they were taken first to Fort Frederick and then to Lancaster barracks. Rhoads was caught one night cutting one of the picquets round the barracks and was put in a dungeon in irons for a period of three months. After being returned to the general barracks he again got over the stockade. Later, a guide conducted him into New York which he reached on 3rd August 1781. Meanwhile, Hannagan was marched to Philadelphia jail where he spent seven months and became so ill he was included in an exchange of invalids made on 29th September 1782. Also included in the same exchange was Isaac Johnson (29th) who had been recaptured the day after his escape.[269]

John Clayton (20th) escaped by tunnelling. After leaving Charlottesville on 5th July, he was recaptured five days later and put into Winchester jail. He soon escaped again but this time landed in Frederick Town jail. He was marched in irons to Fort Frederick where he soon broke out again. He was caught once more in Philadelphia and spent eleven months in a dungeon there. He and six other British soldiers tunnelled beneath the foundations and went to the house of Abel Jones, a Loyalist, who lived near Frankfort. Here with the help of others, they were provided with a boat to cross the Delaware and after further adventures, the whole party succeeded in getting into New York.[270]

Escaping jail was sometimes dangerous. When Joseph Alcock (24th) reached New York, he reported to the intelligence officer who debriefed him, that he had broken out of Guilford jail with two others. One of the group was killed and Alcock himself wounded, both presumably by musket fire.[271]

Despite the distance, which was now much greater than when they were in Massachusetts, many still preferred making for Canada. Reaching New York meant having to cross Pennsylvania and New Jersey, both of which were heavily infested with American troops. By trekking several hundred miles north-westwards to the British-occupied forts at Niagara and Detroit, most of the way was through a wilderness of forest. However, there was always the risk of encountering hostile Indians, in addition to the American patrols working out of Fort Pitt (now Pittsburgh).

Based at Detroit was the most active and successful of the Loyalist regiments. This was Butlers' Rangers. They operated over a huge area of country stretching as far south as the Kentucky Valley and eastwards to the borders of New York, New Jersey and Pennsylvania. In a manner similar to that experienced by World War II Commandos, John Butler demanded fitness from his men capable of marching long distances, regardless of weather. They operated all year round at a time when it was the custom of regular troops, both British and American, to move into winter quarters by November of each year.

Because of the extent of his activities, Butler suffered heavier casualties than other Loyalist regiments, but he was always able to keep his Rangers up to full strength. He had a reputation of finding suitable men wherever he could, which much annoyed other commanders. At one time Sir John Johnson protested at Butler poaching men from his King's Royal Regiment of New York. Escaped Convention Prisoners, grown tough and hardy from their long treks and at the same time avoiding recapture, were just the sort of men he was looking for and he took full advantage of their arrival. Not only were British Convention Prisoners recruited, but Germans as well. So much so, that Major General Riedesel, after he was exchanged and commanded the German troops in Canada, asked permission of the British Commander to send an officer to Detroit to get back his German Convention Prisoners serving with Butler.

There is also some evidence that Clinton deliberately detached men from his army to make their way through American-occupied territory to join Butler. An intelligence officer left record saying that 30 soldiers who had joined Butler in a body "were sent by Sir Henry in the character of deserters." The report also said "a great many more are daily joining them." These probably included Convention Prisoners who had made their way north.[272]

Alexander Skirvin (21st) was one of the British Convention Prisoners who aimed for Detroit. After escaping in July 1779 he was first recaptured in Winchester. He broke out in May 1780 and concluded that New York was impossible to reach. Striking north-westwards for Detroit, at the Ohio River he fell in with Major Langstone, leading a patrol of some 60 Canadians and Indians. He agreed to serve with them. A month later, while on another patrol with a small party, he was captured by an American group of 17 men. Taken first to Fort Pitt, he was returned to Winchester. This time, armed with forged passes, he broke out as a member of Sergeant Major Gordon's large party, reaching New York with them on the 6th November 1780. His troubles were not yet over. He was drafted to a regiment and transferred to Charleston without receiving his back pay. Three years later he was still trying to obtain it.[273]

Others who escaped from Charlottesville included, Edward Byrn and Joseph Robertson (both RA), Thomas Barnes (9th), John Morris and Arthur O'Bryan (both 20th), Thomas Hollis (24th), Joseph Dixon (53rd), Samuel Fowkes (4th Foot), Richard Morris (34th), and Thomas Edwards whose regiment is unknown. William Fogarty and Sergeant Richard Nicholson (both 47th) also escaped. Nicholson, as an NCO, was not drafted to another regiment, but obtained a warrant to raise American recruits for a Loyalist corps. This he continued to do until the cessation of the war, when he had to ask for financial assistance due to destitution.[274]

The number of prisoners at large alarmed the Virginians, who now realised they had a substantial problem on their hands. On 17th July, Jefferson received a letter from Colonel Bland informing him of numerous desertions during the last fortnight. Exaggerating the number at 400, Bland said that he had reason to believe it was with the connivance of some of their officers. The men had armed themselves with forged passports, some with certificates showing they had taken the oath of fidelity to the State. Some of the latter had been forged, others really given by "weak magistrates."[275]

Governor Jefferson quickly took steps to intercept the fugitives. Those recaptured were going in a northerly direction, most obviously heading for New York. Many were caught at Winchester near the northern border of Virginia, but Jefferson knew that many would slip through the net. He wrote to Washington saying, perhaps it might be in his power to "have such of them intercepted, as shall be passing through Pennsylvania and the Jerseys." Washington's men caught many of them very quickly. At one point, there were so many recaptured in New Jersey that George Washington was forced to ask Governor of New Jersey to hold the escapees as they, "cannot be conveniently disposed of, I must entreat that measures may be taken for securing them." In trying to find space to hold them, three weeks later, he was shuffling them among the various prisons. Some had reached as far as Elizabeth Town very close to New York, and he now had to move them across to Morristown where he had to strengthen the guard to secure the recaptured men.[276]

All prisoners recaptured were incarcerated in jails across the several states. Some were taken as far north as Rutland, Massachusetts and

Hartford in Connecticut. No jail was more notorious than the one in Philadelphia. It was under the supervision of Thomas Bradford, a newspaper publisher and owner of a bookstore nearby. An educated man and close friend of James Madison, his regime was one of neglect. The British, during the period of their occupation of the city, had first set the standard at the prison, when hundreds of their American prisoners died from a variety of fevers induced by overcrowding, poor food, and general mistreatment. When the Americans re-occupied Philadelphia they carried on the tradition. They constructed an additional building, which was named the New Jail. Loyalist prisoners were housed in the old building and recaptured British prisoners in the new. The fact that it was a new building made no difference to the treatment received. Food was frequently unobtainable and the prisoners often had to rely on Quakers to bring scanty meals in for them. Many died. Their names are lost to posterity, with only slight traces here and there who some of them were.

Incarcerated in a specially built enclosed jail, made no difference to their escape efforts, which were spurred on by the inhuman conditions. There is a record of one group of 18 digging their way out. Others escaped from the so-called hospital within the prison. Some of these double escapees managed to reach New York and reported on the conditions prevailing in the prison. Representations were made to an American commissary of prisoners visiting New York and he wrote to Thomas Bradford the head jailer in Philadelphia saying,

> It is with no small degree of concern and reluctance that I mention the cruelty practiced on the prisoners last winter in Philadelphia; On the 18th day of January when the cold was at the extreme, they say, that they were removed from their apartment . . . to others with windows removed. I have hitherto suppressed publication because it might be the means of adopting measures here, which would be disagreeable to me.[277]

The American War Office was also receiving complaints from the British and the Board of War wrote to Bradford,

> The Board are informed that divers of the British prisoners are suffering greatly as well in the goal as the hospital, from the want of necessary cloathing and blankets. You are desired immediately to make an accurate

inspection into their situation and wants, and report the result of your examination to the Board.

Bradford was not the person to act or reply promptly. We find the American Commissary of Prisoners some months later writing with some sarcasm,

I have longed to hear from you some lines and cannot but admire at your silences pray write me shortly and if convenient furnish me with a list of your prisoners.[278]

Philadelphia jail was only one of many prisons known to have held escaped Convention Prisoners. Many others have been identified as holding escapees at one time or another. (See appendix 4.) Records of the incarcerations are very piecemeal or non-existent. Even in the case of Philadelphia, where Thomas Bradford left voluminous records, names are often omitted. However, some references to them can be found in both American correspondence and British records.

In the spring of 1779, Britain had made naval raids on several places in the Virginia Tidewater area and Washington expressed the view that in an emergency, our policy towards the prisoners, " . . . will be to remove the troops, perhaps to divide them."

The ever-cautious Bland, planned to supplement the weak Convention Guards Regiment with additional militia and at the same time call-in those Convention officers on parole in the countryside, to live nearer the barracks. Washington approved these precautions. When later Phillips heard what was intended he was not at all pleased. In a letter to Governor Jefferson he pointed out that the British Convention Prisoners had already had an extra move when they went from Cambridge to Rutland and if a further move should be made, "a removal now would be in regular turn given to the Germans." He did not want the British leaving Virginia, if, as it appeared, active warfare could occur in the area. As it happened, the alarm over the British raids quickly subsided when the British withdrew their ships, and for the time being, all the prisoners remained in Charlottesville.[279]

Notwithstanding the rapidly dwindling number of prisoners, Washington was still concerned with the possibility of a rescue taking place from the Virginia coast. After adding a further 450 militia to the guard while the threat existed, he wrote asking the Marine Committee of

Congress whether they could provide vessels on navigable rivers for a measure of protection. They replied this was impossible since they were facing a superiority of British ships.[280]

Changes now began to take place. Phillips and Major General Riedesel, the German Commander, were finally given their paroles to go to New York to await exchange and before the end of August 1779 they had left Charlottesville. Recalling what Phillips had been up to on the way to Charlottesville, Washington dictated his route, telling his escorting officer he did not want him to see the American encampment on the Chatham Road. Brigadier General Hamilton, the next senior British officer, then assumed command at the barracks.[281]

Before leaving the barracks, Phillips gave orders for the preparation of a General Return of the Convention Prisoners, which reconciled the number who became prisoners on the date of the Convention, 17th October 1777, with those at Charlottesville on 1st August 1779. The document is in considerable detail showing the numbers of each rank, and by regiment. It also shows by month, the number of men who had left and those who had returned to their units, the numbers who had died, and the numbers exchanged. It also notes various promotions, including, surprisingly, a promotion from the other ranks to commissioned officer. There now remained 1,484 British NCOs and men at Charlottesville. Thereafter, during the period of their incarceration, only very occasional strength returns appear to have survived with little information providing the cause of differences between them.[282]

Unlike Phillips's disputes with Heath, those with Bland seem not to have interferred with their good relationship. Bland had made a good first impression on Phillips when the two first met. At the time when Bland relieved William Harvie as commandant at Charlottesville, Phillips commented that Bland was "a good officer and seems to be a man of sense and judgement." More than eighteen months later, and after his exchange and return to active service, Phillips in command of a British army advancing in Virginia, gave orders that "no part of the property of Colonel Theodoric Bland receive any injury from His Majesty's troops," adding, "Major General Phillips is very happy to show this favor on account of Colonel Bland's many civilities to the troops of Convention at Charlottesville." Bland was very much taken with this consideration and mentions it more than once in his correspondence.[283]

Thomas Jefferson, since becoming Governor of Virginia, had the problem of balancing the state budget. He very quickly changed his attitude on the cost of maintaining the prisoners. He argued they should be supported by Congress and not by the state. Virginia was a tobacco producer, not a large food producer. The failure of the wheat crop in 1779 made it more difficult to feed the prisoners. The best he could get out of Congress, was the suggestion that Indian corn should be used instead of wheat. At the same time, the Congressional Treasury recommended steps be taken to get the British to bring their payments up to date, which would ease supply.[284]

While Phillips had been a prisoner in Charlottesville, he was frequently entertained by Jefferson at his home Monticello, 4 miles from Charlottesville. After Phillips's parole and subsequent exchange, this relationship deteriorated. A dispute seems to have started when Benedict Arnold, now a Brigadier in the British army invading Virginia, issued a proclamation that any citizen who had been paroled and who breached the law, would be proceeded against "with the utmost vigour and reprisals made upon them and their families." This caused rumours and exaggeration to spread as to what the British intended. The Virginia Council, making an assumption, wrote that should such a threat be carried into execution it would be deemed as putting prisoners to death in cold blood. The Virginians would retaliate by the execution of prisoners in their possession. This letter was addressed to "The Commanding Officer of the British Force at Portsmouth." At this point, having taken command at Portsmouth, Phillips entered the picture. He in turn wrote to the American officer Lafayette, warning of retribution should Loyalists be executed, saying he would, "make the shores of James River an example of terror to the rest of Virginia." Subsequently, in a letter asking for passage of a vessel with provisions for the prisoners, he explained that a British Officer would do no such thing to unarmed civilians. He addressed his letter to "Thomas Jefferson, Esq. American Governor of Virginia." This annoyed Jefferson to the point that he refused passage of the ship. He commented,

the Convention Troops in this State should perish for want of necessaries before any should be carried to them through this State till Genl Phillips either swallowed this pill of retaliation or made an apology for his rudeness.

In the same letter Jefferson gave his opinion of his adversary describing Phillips to be "the proudest man of the proudest nation on earth." Jefferson addressed his reply to "William Phillips, Esq., Commanding the British Forces in the Commonwealth of Virginia," perhaps knowing that Phillips was unlikely to open a letter addressed in such terms. It seems the prisoners had to forego their provisions.[285]

While he had been incarcerated, Phillips's personal affairs had deteriorated. On 1st September he was writing from New York,

> I shall certainly be exchanged and shall after a time return home a Bankrupt in everything but reputation, that last thank heaven, I have the great satisfaction to think it is preserved to me, at least I have received the King's approbabtion of all my publick conduct.

One can only speculate whether the official view included the approval of so many men escaping.

After Phillips had left and with winter approaching, the number of escapes diminished, but the prisoners still continued to slip away in ones and twos. With Phillips going and his own departure pending, Bland had already tried to make the guards more efficient. He introduced a weekly compulsory field day for them, ordering,

> Every officer will be present at his post, dressed and accutred in an officer like manner, that the soldiers appear in uniform hair combed, powdered and tied up, shoes blacked, clean linnen arms and accutrements cleaned and in the best order . . . and that they make in every respect a soldier like appearance.

Bland, in November 1779 was given leave to go home and he handed over the Charlottesville command to Lieutenant Colonel Taylor of the Convention Guards Regiment, giving him detailed instructions as to the manner in which he was to treat the British. They were not allowed to be at large; return to their quarters every night; prevent soldiers passing without permission by day, or in any manner by night.

On his part Bland, through devotion to his military duties, had also neglected his personal affairs and he too was in serious financial trouble. It was only through the personal intervention of Jefferson that the forced sale of his farm was cancelled. Shortly thereafter, Bland turned up as a delegate to Congress from Virginia and as will be seen, he continued to be much involved with the Convention Prisoners.

Washington remained nervous about the security of the prisoners. He warned Jefferson of a probable British undertaking involving the Convention Troops. At the same time he had already decided to restrict Taylor to the position of garrison commander and he appointed Colonel James Wood as overall commander in Charlottesville, telling him,

> I do not wish you to show [the British Prisoners] any unnecessary rigor, [but] I wish you to be extremely cautious not to grant any unnecessary indulgences.

Wood, describing his new job as a "disagreeable command," delayed his taking over until the last possible moment.[286]

For more than a year, intermittent talks had continued between the two sides on the exchange of prisoners, but to no avail. The problem of Americans wanting officers and the British wanting men remained. To overcome the obstacles, efforts made to create a scale valuing so many men for each grade of officer also failed. The matter of recognition of Congress as a sovereign body also intervened and interferred with the making of an agreement.

Not long after Phillips arrived in New York, still on parole, he arranged for Clinton to appoint him as one of the three British Commissioners to sit on a Convention Prisoner exchange commission. In view of his opinion of Phillips, this could not have been welcomed by Washington, but by 29th February 1780, the latter agreed with the appointment. After two delays, the joint commission began to meet on 10th March. To facilitate their meetings, an area with a three mile radius centered on Amboy in New Jersey, was declared "Neutral Ground." With four hours of discussion taking place daily, the sessions extended through 14th March. The meetings failed, disappointing the officers of both sides. Congress would not consider a general exchange of the Convention Prisoners, unless the British commissioners could produce a document from the Government in England, giving them authority to negotiate such an arrangement. The British Government however, had remained adamant in not recognising Congress. An offer of an authority signed by Clinton was rejected by the Americans. The captured soldiers of both sides had to remain prisoners.[287]

Although the official conference came to an end, Phillips and one of the American commissioners, Alexander Hamilton, Washington's

ADC, tried to reach a secret arrangement for the exchange of most of the Convention Prisoners. Both pledged their honour that no part of their conversations should become a matter of official record or publication. Needless to say, both left detailed records of the discussions. These, then culminated in "A Proposition" prepared by Phillips, which allowed for a carefully orchestrated, balanced, but limited programme of exchange. In preparing this he had to sacrifice by leaving out of the proposals, the men of the 9th and 47th Regiments. The total to be exchanged from each side under the arrangement would not be equal if they were included. In passing, it is interesting to note that the numbers in each of the British regiments to be exchanged, tie very closely with those reflected in the comprehensive return he had had prepared at Charlottesville during the previous August. In addition to the men, the Americans asked for a payment of £25,000, being an amount on account for the supply of provisions for the prisoners.

In the midst of these long drawn out negotiations the Americans received a jolt. Cornwallis's army in Georgia, after repelling the American attack on Savannah had quickly occupied Augusta, thereafter moving into South Carolina. On 12th May 1780, through a tactical blunder, the American army of over 5,000 men led by Major General Benjamin Lincoln, fell into British hands at Charleston. The absence of any large organised force between Cornwallis and Virginia caused agitation among the politicians. Major General Nathaniel Greene, the American commander in the south, had passed on to Jefferson that one of the objectives of the British army was to rescue the Convention Prisoners. Lafayette also passed similar information on to Colonel Wood. On 9th June, the Virginia Council wrote to Wood informing him that the enemy were advancing through North Carolina and suggested that they may mean to attempt a rescue. Wood was instructed to have everything ready to move the prisoners over the Blue Ridge Mountains into the Shenandoah Valley, where they could be marched northwards. At the same time, he was authorised to embody the militia "as he shall think necessary."[288]

Despite this set-back, Congress still would not change its attitude on exchange and by June the secret attempt between the generals to have the Convention Prisoners exchanged had failed. Phillips then asked the Americans for permission to visit the captured Lincoln, who like Phillips, was paroled but not exchanged. Washington refused to allow such a meeting to take place.[289]

That ended the most determined effort so far to have the Convention Prisoners exchanged. Although a few of the officers were beginning to be exchanged, the men had to remain where they were.

Some of the Convention officers had been staying in accommodation several miles from the barracks. Now, Colonel Wood acting on instructions from Jefferson, had given the officers orders to report to the Barracks within five days, but he protested this move saying,

> . . . at the same time I must beg leave to suggest it as my opinion, that in case it shou'd be necessary to remove the troops it wou'd have greatley facilitated their march, for the officers to have remained at their quarters; they will certainly when confined to the limits of the barracks, conceive themselves discharged from their paroles—will encourage desertion among the soldiery—and in case of being obliged to remove will throw every obstruction in the way. It will be altogether impossible to secure the troops, and prevent desertion with the guards I have.

He added that due to the level of provisions it would be impossible to call up many militiamen as escorts, but 200 from Albermarle and Augusta counties would be ready to march.[290]

The politicians continued to be alarmed about the situation. On 16th June 1780, Jefferson wrote, "The Convention Troops in our country renders necessary to be watchful of every movement of the enemy." At the same time he wrote to Wood that it was important to hide any symptons of fear from the prisoners, "It suggests to them that the attempt is thought practicable."

Their concern was not idle speculation. Jefferson referred to an attempted Tory uprising which planned to,

> over run the country with the assistance of the British troops, who they were made to believe would meet them, and to relieve the Convention Prisoners. These they were to arm and then subdue the whole State.[291]

Wood had already protested at the continuing lack of food supplies, with stocks reduced to a very low level. He received in reply, nothing except sympathy. At the beginning of June, the officers of the Convention Guards Regiment had addressed a memorial to Jefferson also complaining of food shortages, and on 12th June Jefferson had written to Wood

> I have heard with real concern the suffering of the guard and prisoners at your station, for want of provisions, and the more as it has been out of my power to afford relief.

A few days later Jefferson also referred to the distress at the Barracks and the need to find slaughter cattle. At the same time, he extended the powers of the Commissioners of Provisions, so as to extract more supplies from the countryside.[292]

The State of Virginia now issued an ultimatum to Congress. It would provide a further £50,000 for the purchase of food for the prisoners, but that would be the last since their Treasury would be exhausted. Jefferson sent to Washington letters he had received from Phillips and the German officers about the shortages. He said, "I have no reason to doubt the truth of the state they send, so far as it may be understood of animal food, for of meal they have had always enough." He assured Washington that the ongoing shortages were not caused by any want of attention by the Executive of Virginia. Jefferson blamed the Continental Army commissary for the lack of supplies saying it was the purchasing policies which were causing the supply difficulties, not actual shortages. He went on to say the commissary was buying in the lower and distant parts of the country where it was difficult to provide wagons.[293]

Despite Washington prohibiting a meeting between Phillips and Lincoln, the latter had become a champion for an exchange to take place. After all, because of his mistake at Charleston his own men were prisoners and unless something was done they had no prospect of being set free. Lincoln did meet with Phillips at Elizabeth Town while the latter was on his way back to New York. To assure Washington that he had not disobeyed orders, Lincoln wrote claiming that he had not raised the matter of exchange with Phillips. He said that Phillips had suggested that while the British remained uninterested in a group exchange for officers only, as a concession, the exchange of the privates might be left until the first of December, which would be after the current campaigning season. In supporting this suggestion Lincoln pointed out,

> The daily decreasing of the number of the Convention troops, by deserting to the enemy, for which we have no compensation, and the

great expense to which we are exposed for the support of them, and of our officers and men, prisoners of war with the enemy, must have their weight in urging to the propriety of an exchange.[294]

The American politicians remained intransigent. They considered the prize of being recognised as a sovereign power outweighed the suffering of several thousand of their own men in British hands. But neither Phillips or Lincoln were yet finished. Each in his own way continued the pressure. Each were exchanged with the other on 25th October 1780 which strengthened their respective hands. Lincoln was supported by most of the American generals, who expressed opinions that they could not ask their men to fight if the prospect of capture meant indefinite incarceration without any prospect of exchange. The secret talks continued. Finally yielding to pressure from their own side, Congress had to change its position but did it in a way which still exerted the political pressure at a cost to the Convention Prisoners. On 20th December 1780, Phillips was able to report to Germaine that a general exchange of prisoners of war had been agreed, but that Congress had refused to include the Convention Prisoners. In taking a half-way measure, Congress removed a considerable part of the agitation for the release of their own men, but at the same time maintained their demand for recognition. Their refusal to include the Convention Prisoners in the arrangement meant, however, that many of the 5,000 of their men captured by the British at Charleston had to remain in British hands. As Germaine commented to Phillips during the course of the negotiations,

> It is not easy to imagine upon what ground the Congress attempted to justify their refusal to exchange the privates of the Convention Troops in the same manner with other prisoners of war. For if they will not allow them the benefit of Convention their claim to it might not, at least, to be made a plea for treating them with more severity than others. But, indeed there is no judging of the conduct of those men by any rules of reason [or candor].

In a subsequent letter Phillips wrote,

> The rejections of the proposals for that purpose by General Washington was as unexpected as his conduct upon the occasion appears irreconcilable to every principle of sense and justice . . . (the) liberality of Clinton . . .

contrasts with the total disregard and unfeelingness shown by Mr. Washington for his own prisoners; at the time that reason, humanity, and justice dictate . . . by exchange from the long captivity they have endured . . . but it seems when policy interferes, or whatever motive it may be that induces them, not to comply with our requisition, that he and the American Congress are equally regardless of the satisfaction of those who are without our lines as they are of the fate and sufferings of those within.

For his part, Germaine replied to Phillips,

. . . (I am) happy to learn you have effected a general exchange of the Kings troops who were prisoners of war tho you were not able to prevail that the Convention Troops should be exchanged against the rebel forces taken in Carolina. I most heartily sympathise with thos unfortunate brave men in their sufferings, from so long a captivity and removal from places so very distant from each other, and think every attention should be shown to render their hard condition as little irksome as possible consistent with the army rules.[295]

That was the end of efforts to obtain a general exchange of the other ranks of the Convention Prisoners. From enjoying an advantageous position over other prisoners of war as far as the prospects of exchange was concerned, they had now been reduced to the status of hostages for political ends. The British, recognising that the prospects of reaching an agreement were remote, allowed the Convention Officers to be exchanged at a faster rate than hitherto. It was soon reported that no less than 90 officers and personal staff had been exchanged.[296]

Even while the negotiations were in progress, the concern of the Americans over the security of the prisoners had continued to escalate during the second half of 1780. The British experienced another victory in August, when Gates was defeated at Camden. Widespread disaffection then occurred in Washington, Montgomery, Henry and Bedford counties of Virginia. Many of the inhabitants were going over to the British, and Bedford county was only 60 or 70 miles from Charlottesville. This led to a decision by Congress in September, responding to a plea from Jefferson, that if the situation warranted, the prisoners could be marched north to Maryland. This alarm was followed by a British fleet of 60 ships appearing in the Chesapeake in October. Shortly thereafter, there followed the British landing on the coast of Virginia near Portsmouth and Newport News. Although the British force had no such instructions, the Americans interpreted the move as an attempt to release the prisoners. Having written a "ready to move letter" in June, Jefferson now wrote he could wait no longer, and he gave instructions to Wood to commence marching the British west across the mountains and then north. This again proved to be another instance of politicians giving the military orders that were impossible to carry out. Colonel Wood did not have the supplies, transport or escorts to comply. Moving the troops out of state also caused problems with the Convention Guards Regiment. They had been enlisted for one year, or until such time as the prisoners had left the state. If the prisoners departed Virginia, the guards would go home. In the end, it was agreed that since the Germans were quiet, and for the most part bailed out to local farmers, they could, for the time being, remain where they were. This solution enabled Jefferson to remove the truculent British prisoners and at the same time keep the guards enlisted.[297]

Jefferson continued to harass Wood. He knew Wood was thinking of quitting, but he maintained pressure on him. On 1st November he wrote of the prisoners influence on the disaffected inhabitants,

> . . . (they) furnished a perpetual fuel to that smothered fire. The discontented build on their assistance whether they have or have not a right to expect it. We are not without hopes that their removal will contribute greatly to the cure of that spirit.

The following week he again impressed on Wood the need to watch the prisoners,

> I have no doubt of the candour of General Hamilton's endeavours to prevent desertions by his orders, but nothing less than stone walls can effectually do this among the British, while a British army is cantoned in our country.

On 16th November he continued to express concern, saying he would,

> be exceedingly glad to hear the British division is gone, as their presence gives uneasiness.[298]

Finally, it was decided that Colonel Taylor would remain in Charlottesville with 260 unhappy men of the Convention Guards Regiment to keep the Germans secure. A scratch militia escort, mustered by Wood, would go with the British on their march north. For the third time, the Convention Prisoners were starting out on a winter march. On the 20th November, the remaining prisoners, with their escort, passed through a gap in the Blue Ridge Mountains, and turned north. This time they were not to go far.[299]

CHAPTER 9

Intelligence and
Clandestine Warfare

BEFORE turning to the final phase of the story of the Convention Prisoners, we should take a look at what was happening in the countryside through which escapees had to pass.

The war had not gone well for the regular British army. While they had proved they could recover almost at will any territory chosen, the forces at their disposal were not sufficient to hold what they gained. In addition they had failed to inflict a decisive defeat on the American army. As Houlding has so aptly put it,

> . . . government attempted to subdue a rebellion by conquering a map; the venture was risky in the first place and, when the Bourbons intervened and sent their fleets into the Atlantic and Caribean, it was doomed to failure.

By the end of 1780, while they had been successful in holding intact the Canadian border and remained in possession of New York, large scale operations had virtually ceased in the north. Only in Virginia and North and South Carolina, were operations of any size taking place. The British command had neither the forces or the solutions to their problems in the northern states.[300]

Curiously, the apparent stalemate in the north was aiding the British far more than had been achieved by regular military action. A large part of the American civilian population was growing war-weary. In Albany, the New York leaders met to discuss a separate peace; Vermont, "the 14th State," still refused to take sides and remained neutral; riots took place in New Hampshire over the state debts incurred. In this atmosphere, intelligence and counter-intelligence operations became increasingly active. With the polarisation of views held by the inhabitants, intelligence work often extended into small scale guerilla operations against each side. Inevitably, escaped Convention Prisoners on the run became involved.[301]

Based on their experience in World War I, the British, early in World War II, established MI 9, an intelligence department designed not only to aid the escape of prisoners of war, but to channel the information they brought with them into productive use. 160 years earlier, in the War of American Independence, the British had developed an organisation with identical objectives.

The large numbers of escaped Convention Prisoners and prisoners of war arriving in British hands after having crossed large areas of enemy-held territory, were quickly recognised as a valuable source of military and economic intelligence. As they arrived they were closely questioned by officers about what they had seen and experienced. The value of information received in this way was mixed. Edward Montgomery (62nd) gave outstanding details on the location and move-ments of American regiments as recently as two days before he arrived in New York. Sergeant Major George Gordon, who commanded a large party which reached New York, was able to give some noteworthy information of what he had seen and experienced. Not every escaper could help. On the same date as Sergeant Major George Gordon arrived, Private Martin (9th) also came in. He may have been one of Gordon's party, but the apparently frustrated intelligence officer noted that he was unable to offer much in the way of information. When the flow of incoming men increased they were often quickly absorbed into regiments desperate for men, causing some to slip through the intelli-gence net without being interrogated. In order to make sure nothing was missed, Clinton ordered the Commanding Officers of all battalions to examine the ex-prisoners drafted to them, and record the names and addresses of the persons who had assisted or conducted them through the country.[302]

Two British officers managed the intelligence work. Major Frederick Mackenzie at first in Rhode Island and when that place was evacuated, he continued his work in New York. The second was Major John André, at first ADC to Clinton and then his Adjutant General. In both roles he was instrumental in extending the work started by Mackenzie, going beyond the passive taking of intelligence information from the prisoners. Both officers worked in establishing a network of spies throughout the northern colonies, charged not only with gathering of intelligence, but evidence shows some agents were appointed specifically to assist Loyalists and escaped prisoners. This activity included the establishment of safe houses throughout the north.

André himself had been a prisoner of war, when captured with the 7th Foot during the American invasion of Canada. After being exchanged, and before he was appointed Adjutant General, he had organised a rising of Loyalists in Pennsylvania. His knowledge of the German language undoubtedly proved very useful in that state where so many Germans had settled. It was probably André that George Washington was referring to when the latter complained about an officer of the 7th who had infiltrated his ranks.[303]

The British command in America divided intelligence responsibility into four departments; the Northern Area which extended as far south as Albany in New York was directed from Quebec; the Eastern Area was directed from Nova Scotia; the Southern Area had responsibility for Florida, while New York directed the Central Area. André's direct responsibity was for the latter department. His intelligence work involved the selection and appointment of agents, the establishment of safe houses and security of communications. As part of the latter activity he developed a series of simple but secure codes.[304]

André worked closely through two Loyalist officers. Colonel Beverly Robinson controlled the Hudson Valley area, while Brigadier Cortland Skinner directed a spy ring across New Jersey to the Delaware River and further south. Under these two men, much clandestine activity took place. One of their later successes was to infiltrate William Peters into the headquarters of General Greene in the role of his personal steward. He was discovered when caught recruiting volunteers for the British army. Both officers had a host of agents, many of whom were women. Ann Bates, a Philadelphia school teacher married to a British armourer in the Royal Artillery, has been described by one American historian as probably the most successful female spy in history. Her exploits included, when disguised as a pedlar, penetrating Washington's headquarters and obtaining a complete count of the artillery and ball held by his army. Ann Bates's fate was also intertwined with the escape of prisoners. Her historian records that,

It seems clear she was still using the secret chain of "safe" Tory houses the British had established across the Middle Atlantic states. This was so effective that British prisoners, escaping in Virginia could secretly return across-country—not with one guide, but with two—going undetected straight through the American forces.[305]

The establishment of the intelligence network soon produced results. As early as April 1778, a party of escaped prisoners, consisting of two Royal Artillery men and 15 others of the Convention Army, had been conducted safely into Rhode Island. Sergeant Lamb on his first escape with his two companions, travelling without organised assistance, claimed to be the first escaped Convention Prisoners to arrive in New York (at the end of November 1778). They were closely followed by a party of no less than 50 Convention Prisoners, conducted by one of the British agents, who, for each man rescued, received a guinea paid by the Commander-in-Chief.[306]

On that first escape, Lamb had very little information as to who might help him on his way. It continued to be much a matter of chance. Things had changed by the time he undertook the final leg of his second escape from Yorktown. He mentions the men had been provided with a list of people, with addresses, who would be prepared to help. He does not say where the list came from. Although by that time André was dead, it undoubtedly was the result of the undercover organisation which he had established to assist escaped prisoners.[307]

As might be expected, the surviving records of British agents in the American War of Independence are sparse. What has survived lifts a corner of the curtain hiding how the fortunes of many of the prisoners were closely linked with some of the agents.

In December of 1778, Chace, a spy employed by the British arrived in Rhode Island with a sergeant and private of the 47th Foot. They had been incarcerated in Taunton jail after being recaptured in a previous escape attempt. They were able to give news of the number of escapes that had taken place while the prisoners were being marched to Charlottesville.[308]

James Pearce, who was active as a "Pilot," brought in on one occasion, John Webster (RA), Samuel Troth (21st) with several others. After escaping from prison in Philadelphia and arriving in New York, they described in detail the limited rations given to the prisoners in Philadelphia.[309]

On 13th August 1781, 25 British who had been prisoners in Lancaster, arrived in New York. 19 of them had escaped in a body and were conducted the whole way by a single agent. Mr. Thomas Welsh who lived in Marlborough County, Pennsylvania was described as,

> a very steady loyalist, and very active in assisting the British prisoners to make their escape. He has built a place in the woods for their reception, where he subsists them until there is an opportunity of sending them off with a trusty guide.[310]

Another British agent, John Maguire, operating out of Lancaster, helped the prisoners by first concealing them in his house, then supplying them with guides to reach safety. His undoing came when he was informed upon after providing guides to an escaping British officer, jailed for fighting with an American colonel.[311]

The extent of the activity undertaken by agents helping escaped prisoners can be judged from the record of James Deegan and his wife. He kept notes about the prisoners to whom he had given shelter and other help. His record totalled 238 names. His work came to an end when an American guard boat intercepted him on a crossing into New York. They had to run ashore and in doing so, lost his records. However, he was able to call on several NCOs stationed in New York as witnesses to the extent of his help. His work came to official attention when, on getting into New York himself, he was called up by the British to serve in their New York militia. He asked for exemption on account of the clandestine work he had undertaken.[312]

The work of a conductor or pilot was extremely dangerous and American counter-intelligence responded quickly to the clandestine operations being carried out by the British. The Americans were able to crack at least one escape chain. Captain Andrew Lee, an American counter-intelligence officer, put on a British uniform and managed to mix with a group of British prisoners released by an old woman who had been selling fruit at their prison. Over a period of twelve nights, they moved from house to house, being sheltered in barns, cellars and caves. Before crossing the Delaware to reach the British lines, Lee was able to attract American soldiers to the scene and the whole group was captured. Subsequently Lee retraced the route taken and 15 Loyalists who had assisted the prisoners were arrested.[313]

Among those who assisted escaped prisoners and were caught at it, included a number of Pennsylvania citizens. These were John Coogler and his wife Susanna, Abraham Harvey, Phinneas Paxton, George Spangler. The last-named was executed. Paxton got off fairly lightly. He kept a public house and apart from the deposit of bonds totalling £40,000, his only other punishment was a ban on keeping a public house in the future. On the other side of the fence was Francis McHenry. He received £690 expenses for securing two British escapees on their way to New York.[314]

Glimpses remain of intelligence work carried out by the prisoners themselves. One of the active British spies was William Rose. A Loyalist soldier serving in Burgoyne's Army, he was able, under the Convention, to return to his home in Saratoga. He continued to work for André until 1780, when his activities made it too dangerous for him to stay; he then went to Canada and continued to work out of the forward post at St. John's.[315]

Private Edward Miller (20th) escaped from Charlottesville and made for Richmond hoping to join Colonel Banastre Tarleton, then making his mounted raid into Virginia. Miller was recaptured and sent to Staunton jail. After being bailed out by a wheelwright, he worked at that trade for some thirteen months. On hearing the Convention Prisoners were marching north, he deserted his employer and fell in with a British agent at Brandywine in Pennsylvania. The agent asked Miller to assist him in arranging the escape of some Convention Prisoners then at Lancaster. They were successful in getting 31 prisoners out. The agent then fell sick, and Miller, not knowing the road, arranged for the party to be divided into groups of twos and threes, to be hidden by local inhabitants who were mostly Quakers. Subsequently, the inhabitants gave each man five days' rations. After rowing across the Delaware River using rails taken from fences as oars, they reached the British in Amboy, New Jersey.[316]

Men of the Convention Army in the far north, also took part in operations behind enemy lines. On 3rd September 1780, the commanding officer at Fort St. John's, reported that

Taylor a soldier of the 47th. I have got two men to go with him as guides. One of them he new when in Vermont State that he is a good man I can depend upon him the other has been several times in the

Colonies and brought in men. I have got fourteen dollars change for Taylor with great dificulty.

Taylor was on an intelligence mission and needed American currency. Again on 4th October, the officer referring to escaped prisoners wrote, he had sent a man of the 47th on to Quebec, but,

the man of the 21st being acquainted with the country, . . . is gone with the Indians . . . I have permitted him to go with them at the request of the Chiefs, who are answerable for his return.

In another report, an escaped Grenadier of the 53rd had obtained and gave information about a notorious American spy, Captain Gosslin, being "in the country", which led to a massive man-hunt taking place. On another occasion three men, one a recruit from Lietenant Nutt's detachment, came in from the "Indian country" and was able to give information on the movements of Butler's Rangers and the British-commissioned Mohawk chief, Captain Joseph Brant,who both were very active in attacking American units. The three escapees had been serving with them.[317]

A sergeant of the 47th on arriving in New York gave information that while trying to cross the lines, three British prisoners serving with an American regiment, gave him secret information about the location of an attack shortly to take place.[318]

A letter survives from William Attlee, an American commissary of prisoners stationed at Lancaster. He wrote to Thomas Bradford, the head jail-keeper at Philadelphia,

Among the prisoners who lately broke the gaol of this town, one John Edwards of the Convention Troops—by an intercepted letter to his wife [but this is not to be mentioned as I expect further intelligence thro that channel] I find this fellow to be met with near Philadelphia as he orders her to direct his letter to the care of Mrs. Calhoon at the Free-Masons Arms over Schuylkill Bridge near Philadelphia' and desires his wife not to leave Lancaster till his further directions. I wish this fellow could be taken, as I suspect some persons were busy in that affair, who ought not to have meddled with such things—if you get him do examine him closely—he is a taylor by trade—a pretty neat made fellow—has dark hair and I think rather a dark complexion and wears sometimes a green and sometimes a brown coat—he worked at his trade hear a considerable time with one Tweed, and I confined him on suspicion of his being employed as an intelligencer—as he made one or two journeys from Lancaster, in the last of which he was absent about two weeks, and on his return I had him apprehended and confined after examining him to no purpose—We retook three of the chaps who escaped from the gaol with him, but there twelve yet missing, some of whom he may know about Philadelphia.

Attlee then added,

I opened your letter to enclose one I have just got hold of from Edwards' wife to him—do seal it and send it by some clever fellow, who by pretending to be friendly to their party may get something material out of him. It has transpired from Edwards' wife, that the others who went from this gaol are still about Philadelphia [she says among the Quakers] and that they purpose getting tools into the gaol, and to assist the prisoners there, if they can, in making their escape.
If she moves from here, I shall have notice of it and intend to secure her then; but not till she offers to go away, that I may have a chance of more letters.[319]

The counter-intelligence work by Attlee and Bradford appears to have been successful, because we next hear from Edwards in the jail at Philadelphia. In a letter addressed to one Aaron Levy in Lancaster, Edwards wrote that both he and his wife were now in good health but he had been very poorly, adding,

I return you ten thousand thanks for troubling yourself so much upon my account trying to get me my liberty.

He went on,

If your business should lead to Philadelphia I would be obliged to you if you took the trouble to call. There is some talk here of an exchange. If not I should be very proud if I were living along with you again.[320]

John Edwards (20th) had been caught with seven others at Paulus Hook on 19th August 1779 and taken to Lancaster jail, where, as related above, he again escaped. His letter to Levy was never delivered as it is still filed in Bradford's jail records. Edwards's eventual fate is unknown.

The treatment of Loyalists caught helping prisoners on the run was not pleasant. As early as 1777 a dozen spies had been hanged. In

February 1778, the Continental Congress had passed a resolution con-
demning those that actively assisted the British,

> Resolved, that whatever inhabitants of these states . . . shall, by giving
> intelligence, acting as a guide . . . he shall suffer death by the judgment
> of a court martial . . . if the offence be committed within seventy miles
> of the headquarters of the grand or other armies of these states, where
> a general officer commands.

This definition covered most of the settled areas of the 13 colonies.
The resolution gave the power to the army to try such people in the
form of courts martial. It seems however, that individual states were
also very active in prosecuting offenders. General Stark writing from
Albany in June 1778 said,

> They [the people] do very well in the hanging way. They hanged nine
> on the 16th of May, and on the 5th June nine; and have 120 in jail,
> of which I believe, more than one half will go the same way. Murder
> and robbery are committed every day in this neighbourhood. So you
> may judge of my situation, with the enemy on my front, and the devil
> in my rear.[321]

Two early casualties in the intelligence war were British officer
Henry Mansin and Wendal Myer. They were executed at Lancaster
on a variety of charges in March of 1778. Another case on record is
that of an old man being hanged for "piloting", who left a widow and
nine children.[322]

Despite the harsh penalties for spying and assisting prisoners, many
Loyalists were prepared to go even further by taking the war into the
enemy's camp. The most noteworthy of these, was Lieutenant James
Moody, who became closely involved with the Convention Prisoners.
Moody, known as "Bonnell" Moody, was a farmer living quietly about
6 miles outside of Newton in Sussex County, New Jersey. He recalled
he had no intention of taking up arms when the revolution broke out.
He admitted that since 1774, he had been maddened with the "Asso-
ciations, committees and libertypoles and all the preliminary apparatus
necessary to a revolt", when the general cry was, "join or die". He
relished neither of those alternatives—remaining on his farm as a silent,
but not unconcerned spectator, and took every possible precaution not
to give offence. Despite this he was once assaulted when attackers

flourished tomahawks over his head. Finally, in March of 1777, he saw a number of armed men marching towards his house and guessed what they had in mind. He escaped with a neighbour, but not before shots were fired at him.[323]

Newton lies to the west of some hilly and broken country, full of caves and rocky eminences about 50 miles west of New York. Moody knowing the area, adopted it as his hide-out. There is a cave, still known today as Moody's Cave, reputed to have been used by him. By the following month, he had managed to recruit some 73 neighbours and make their way to New York, losing only four on the way. There, he joined one of Courtland Skinner's battalions with the rank of Ensign.

Before he learned the safety of small groups, he returned to New Jersey and raised 500 volunteers for the Loyalist cause. When they heard of the British withdrawal from Philadelphia, most lost heart. Only 100 accompanied him towards New York. At Perth Amboy they were forced to disperse. Moody with eight others succeeded in reaching New York. Of the remainder, 60 were incarcerated in Morristown, two of them being immediately hanged. Thereafter he restricted himself to small groups. Making sally after sally into American-held territory, he became a specialist in robbing the American military headquarters' mails. He succeeded in this four times, one of which contained reports of a meeting which Washington had with Count Rochambreau, the French commander. On other occasions he was able to abduct groups of politicians and army officers and take them as prisoners into New York. On still another occasion he was able to rescue 42 Loyalists, some who had just broken jail. A man named Martin, who had been made responsible for confiscating Loyalist property, was also taken by him when accompanied by four others. Although they had to release him when attacked by 60 militia, thereafter it seems the man conducted himself in a much more mild and humane manner. The British rewarded Moody handsomely for his work behind the lines, but he passed all of it on to his helpers. The only recognition he kept for himself was his promotion to lieutenant.[324]

As soon as he struck, the cry would go up among the American militia, "Moody is in the country," and it was inevitable that he would experience failures. On his thirteenth mission, he was betrayed. Although he escaped, his younger brother John Moody was captured and hanged. On still another occasion, Moody himself was captured and taken to West Point, then commanded by Benedict Arnold. There he was badly treated, put in irons, and incarcerated in a dungeon dug out of rock, filled with rain, mud and filth, covered only with planks of wood. All this, despite the fact that Arnold was himself negotiating to desert to the British later in the year. Moody was then transferred to Washington's camp where he was to be courtmartialled, but in the meantime he was treated much more humanely. With his irons removed, he took the opportunity of counting their artillery before escaping.

Moody, with other Loyalists in Sussex County, became involved in helping escaped Convention Prisoners concealed in the broken country around Newton, waiting their opportunity to get into New York. Many escapees were accommodated and given food by Loyalists in that area. The records of two women helping prisoners have survived. In one, a British Officer in New York wrote,

> I beg leave to intercede in behalf of the bearer Mrs. Margaret Skaden an old faithful friend and 'Pilot' to numbers who have made their escape from the persecutions of the Rebels. But being at last detected in harbouring and conducting some of the Convention Troops into this City she has been obliged to fly here for shelter and leave little substance behind. I hope she comes within the . . . of such as are allowed rations for she really deserves much from Government. She has often fed the (British) and concealed them. It will be doing an act of benevolence if in your power to allow her rations.

A second record concerns Nancy Nevil, which stated she had been of great service in conducting and guiding a number of General Burgoyne's men into New York, "for which she has suffered."[325]

One of the Convention Prisoners at large in the area, was Private Roger Clansey (47th) who escaped from Charlottesville in June 1779. Working as a weaver as he trekked northwards, he was helped and hidden by Loyalists in Sussex County. Moody, having failed in an effort to capture the Governor of New Jersey, recruited Clansey with several other Convention Prisoners in an enterprise to blow up the military magazines at Succasunna. In Clansey's words, Moody was "on private service", eighteenth-century words for secret service. Clansey volunteered to join him and was given arms.[326]

Another of the Convention Prisoners in the same area was Richard Cosgave (53rd), who had also escaped from Charlottesville. After recapture in Maryland he again escaped, but was arrested in Sussex County. He was bailed out for farming. It was then that Moody recruited him into his group.[327]

The Succasunna venture had to be aborted when it was found the Americans had posted a substantial guard over the stores. Clansey then left for New York, but Cosgave stayed with Moody. At this point they moved back into Sussex County, where they heard of a Convention Prisoner languishing in the jail in Newton under a sentence of death. That prisoner was Private Robert Maxwell.

Maxwell and Private John M'Coy had been waiting in Sussex County for their opportunity to get into New York, when a house in Greenwich was burgled, and the two were caught and charged with the crime. Although in the area at the time, there was little evidence they were guilty. The local American press reporting the case, believed they were innocent and that someone from British-occupied Staten Island was the guilty party. While waiting their trial, the Church of England minister in Newton frequently visited them and spoke up for them. The prosecutor, however, told Maxwell "though he might not perhaps deserve to die for the crime for which he had been committed, there could be no doubt of his deserving to die, as an enemy to America." The two prisoners decided that silence would be construed as obstinacy, whereas an admission of guilt would not operate against any clemency they might expect. Despite the intervention by the minister, the jury very quickly found the two guilty and they were sentenced to death. The judge lamented the fact that it was not in his power to appoint counsel for the prisoners, as the only practitioner of law present in court was the representative of the attorney general.

John M'Coy was hanged the following Friday, but Robert Maxwell was given a stay of execution until 9th June. Both, at the place of M'Coy's execution, "made the most solemn protestations of their innocence of the accusation for which they were to suffer. The unhappy man died in charity, he said, with all men, and hoped that after his death the world might have due testimony of his integrity."[328]

Maxwell was again given a stay until 7th September but on the night of 21st May, Moody, Cosgave with five others, knocked on the jail door waking the jailer upstairs. They had come to rescue Maxwell. Moody told the jailer they had a prisoner to deliver. "What, one of Moody's fellows?" Yes was the reply. "What is his name?" One of the party, impersonating the character of the prisoner, gave his own name. The jailer still refused to open the door saying he had strict orders not to do so "in consequence of Moody being out." Moody then admitted it was indeed himself and threatened the jailer saying he had a large party of men with him. His men then gave loud Indian warhoops which panicked both the villagers and jailer, allowing Moody to gain entrance to the jail. Maxwell had slept through all the noise, and when Moody woke him, with the jailer at his side, he thought he was being taken away for execution. Moody released a total of eight prisoners that night, but according to press reports, after a few hours four of them returned to jail. Probably they feared recapture which, as members of Moody's party, would inevitably mean execution.

After leaving the jail, Cosgave and another man raided the sheriff's house where they tried to release another prisoner, Joseph Lowrie, who also refused to go with them. The party then rejoined forces, raiding an American officer's home, stealing arms for their own use and destroying the remainder. On their way back to New York they captured a Major and Lieutenant with 11 men. Not being able to take them they were given their parole to travel to New York independently, to deliver themselves up. Nothing has been traced to indicate whether they did so. As Moody's party continued on their way, they were continually skirmishing with the Americans, but after dividing into smaller groups, they all managed to get back into New York.[329]

Maxwell, a man of good education, stayed with Moody for sometime, but the story has an unhappy ending. Later in the war, he was recaptured, taken back to Newton, placed in the same dungeon and then hanged under the same sentence on which he had been before convicted. He was offered a reprieve if he would tell them who the Loyalists were that assisted Moody. He replied,

> I love life and there is nothing which a man of honour can do, that I would not do to save it; but I cannot pay this price for it. The men you wish me to betray must be good men, because they have assisted a good man in a good cause. Innocent as I am, I feel this an awful

moment: how far it becomes you to tempt me to make it terrible, by overwhelming me in the bases (t) guilt, yourselves must judge. My life is in your power; my conscience, I thank God, is still my own.

He died with the most solemn statement of his innocence and his unshaken allegiance to his Sovereign. His death was not easy. Though he was a small and light man, the rope on the first attempt broke. Before being hanged for the second time he is reported as saying,

Gentlemen, I cannot but hope that this very extraordinary event will convince you, of what I again solemnly protest to you that I am innocent of the crime for which you have adjudged me to die.

So died one of the Convention Prisoners.

Moody was bitter about Maxwell's death. He had arranged to have Maxwell transported back to New York by the earliest means, but Maxwell had refused to go saying,

To you I owe my life; to you, and in your service, let me devote it. You have found me in circumstances of ignominy; I wish for an opportunity to convince you, that you have not been mistaken in thinking me innocent. I am, and you shall find me, a good soldier.

Subsequently, Moody found a Loyalist who admitted that it was he who had burgled the house.[330]

CHAPTER 10

The March North

C ONGRESS had resolved that the remaining prisoners, on leaving
Charlottesville, should be taken to Maryland, to be accommodated
in barracks at Fort Frederick. They decided that fifty percent of the
the food supplies needed for the prisoners and their guards, should be
provided by Maryland. The remaining fifty percent should still come
from Virginia. Maryland was also instructed to provide the necessary
guards to take over from the Virginians at the border, but they protested
they did not want the prisoners. The barracks at Fort Frederick were
in a tumbledown condition and quite insufficient to house the remaining
British soldiers. The Governor of Maryland had not only informed
Jefferson of this before the prisoners left Charlottesville, but at the same
time he had expressed his fears that accepting the prisoners would
increase the likelihood of making Maryland a target for a British attack.
To a large extent, the colony had escaped the devastation caused by
the war.[331]

By the time the Convention Prisoners reached Winchester in Northern Virginia, Wood found the Maryland militia waiting across the
Potomac River. But for what? According to Anburey they were not
there to escort the prisoners into Maryland, but were there to use force
to stop prisoners and guards crossing the river. Whether Anburey
exaggerated the situation by stating they would go that far is not known,
but it is clear that Wood was not prepared to risk a breach with the
Maryland militia. He gave orders for the prisoners to halt in Winchester,
while he went to the Maryland state capital, Annapolis, to sort out the
situation. There, he seems to have been successful in getting the
Marylanders to accept the prisoners, but at the same time they convinced
him of their inability to provide their share of the food supplies needed.
Wood wrote to Jefferson from Annapolis, implying that Virginia was
better able to provide all the provisions, because their government had
armed militia, enabling it to use force to extract the supplies from its

citizens. Jefferson was incensed with Wood's viewpoint and replied in no uncertain terms,

> I cannot conceive but that the legislature of Maryland, if they find that their quota of specifics cannot be produced by money, will think it right to introduce force into their state also. At any rate I cannot believe it will be thought equal to impress our citizens for the deficiences of any other state.[332]

A month later, Jefferson was still expressing frustration with Maryland saying,

> We can order them [the prisoners] to the banks of the Potomac but our authority will not land them on the opposite side.[333]

Both on the way to, and at Winchester, the escape attempts again escalated. Private Joseph Cload (20th) was one who escaped and was caught. After a period in Philadelphia jail, he worked his way to Elizabeth Town. There he stole a boat and reached the British in Staten Island. Loyalists in Winchester were very active in assisting the prisoners to disappear. One letter Washington received complained,

> Tory sympathisers who lived near Winchester were only too willing to assist the British in escape attempts.

Some months later, a junior American officer went further. Exaggerating the attitude of the people in the area, claiming they had revolted, he said they were refusing to lend any assistance, and it is to be feared they will arm the prisoners against us. According to Madison, as soon as the inhabitants of Winchester and the counties in its neighbourhood heard that their grain and meat, might in future, be purchased rather than impressed, they reversed their position and petitioned the Governor and the Secretary at War, to let the prisoners remain. They tried their best to keep the prisoners within the town, recognising the long term benefit, if the food supplies could be found. One American officer estimated that nine tenths of the inhabitants were sutlers, anxious to retain the prisoners on any terms.[334]

Maryland was not the only state to object to accommodating and feeding the Convention Prisoners. When in March 1781 it was proposed they be sent on to Pennsylvania, that state ordered their agent to contribute no further supplies of flour to the American army. This made Washington indignant, saying he could not bring himself to believe that the state was so devoid of patriotism and perspective, as to ignore the needs of the army because the support of 1,500 prisoners was added to its burdens.[335]

After a delay of several weeks at Winchester and Martinsburg, the British prisoners did move into Maryland, only to suffer far worse conditions than anything they had experienced to date. Lieutenant Colonel Moses Rawlings, the commissary of prisoners at Fort Frederick had already written to the Maryland Council to say the tumbledown barracks could not house all the prisoners and that provisions were unobtainable. He also pointed out that he had had to stop a mass break-out by the prisoners. The Convention Prisoners, anxious for accommodation, offered to build barracks, if the state would purchase the timber required. The War Office in Philadelphia tried to help by writing to the Maryland Governor saying there was a distressed situation at the post for want of provisions. Rawlings recommended the prisoners be split up, with many to go to Frederick Town a few miles to the east. This was done and were housed in the County poorhouse. The remainder, once more, had to build huts to accommodate themselves.[336]

It was from Fort Frederick that the only known escape of a Convention officer took place. He was Captain John Bailis (9th) who, presumably for some transgression, was without parole and was incarcerated in conditions similar to the men. This relieved him of being on his honour not to escape and together with an officer prisoner of war, they took off, reaching New York in three months. Because the eighteenth-century parole system, often followed by exchange, officer escapes were extremely rare during the War of American Independence. The most notable was that of Ensign Clarke of the 43rd Foot, not a Convention officer, who had refused to give his parole. He made three attempts to reach the British lines. When a British intelligence officer learned he had been retaken for the third time, he commented he, "probably will meet with rough usage." Clarke finally signed his parole. The Americans, were probably pleased to be rid of him, since they then allowed him to reside on the British side of the lines until he was exchanged.[337]

Those fortunate enough to be allocated to Frederick Town enjoyed a short period of good conditions. They received adequate food and comparatively comfortable quarters in the poorhouse. Some were allowed to go into the countryside to purchase vegetables. Sergeant Barry (9th) left behind ill at Winchester, escaped and surreptitiously overtook the column, spending a day with the prisoners in the town. When he arrived in New York, he reported the provisions were better than for some considerable time. However, this did not stop the men from leaving and they were going off by "threes, fours, sixes and sevens every night." He said the idea prevailing amongst them was to make a push to join General Arnold, who they understood had taken a post at Portsmouth in Virginia. No record survives as to the degree of success experienced by these men, but as mentioned in Chapter 8, with Phillips by this time in overall command at Portsmouth, any prisoner arriving would have proved very useful to him in one way or another.[338]

The shortage of guards caused Rawlings to recommend that all the prisoners be moved into Frederick Town. This was done, with the married men being allowed to settle in the town. Even then, this did not resolve his problem. The county lieutenants were not producing sufficient militia to provide the estimated 200 guards needed. On one occasion the number available was only 29. The guards who did muster, refused to cut wood even for their own use. The conduct of the prisoners did not help. Rawlings complained to Washington that British prisoners were the most difficult to handle. There were continuous incidents occurring which were often started by the prisoners being abusive to the guards.[339]

The good conditions at Frederick Town did not last long. Supplies once more ran precariously short. On New Year's Day 1781, the commissariat stated that while on the march, the troops had been well supplied, but there were now "only a small stock of provisions on hand." At one point the men were eleven days' rations in arrears, forcing Brigadier General Hamilton to protest to the Governor of Maryland.[340]

Conditions were deteriorating to such a level that by the end of February, Congress was forced to act. On 26th February 1781 the Board of War reported to Congress "we find ourselves embarassed for want of means," and then carried on,

Our accounts from those of the Convention Troops now in Maryland are very disagreeable. They are so precariously supplied that the soldiers are sent thro the country to collect provisions and being unguarded great numbers daily desert. These evils will be increased by a junction of the whole and therefore we submit to congress the propriety on fixing on some stationary place for these prisoners where they can be supplied and proper magazines and guards provided that this business may at once be put in a proper train and the embarassments of temporarly measures be thereby prevented.[341]

Congress answered this plea on 2nd March, when they resolved that the British prisoners, should be moved to York, Pennsylvania. The Germans, who were now following them and had by this time reached Winchester, were to go to Lancaster, Pennsylvania. This resolution was passed, despite the strong opposition of the Pennsylvania delegates who did not want the problem of the prisoners laid at their door.[342]

American patience with the repeated desertion attempts by the British Convention Prisoners began to wear thin. On 24th March 1781, the American War Office in Philadelphia issued instructions to Colonel Wood,

The very considerable desertions . . . among the Convention Troops and the repeated neglects on the part of the British Generals to pay for their support furnish undeniable proofs that the present system requires immediate remedy; from now on the non-commissioned officers and soldiers of the British Convention Troops are to be closely guarded to prevent them from escaping; if any of the officers are discovered to be conniving to promote the escape of the troops, they shall be deemed to have broken their paroles . . . until payment is made as stipulated in Article 5 of the Convention, they are to receive no more provisions than are usually issued to prisoners of war; the officers are to be put on parole and sent to Simsbury in Connecticut; the soldiers to remain at Frederick Town in Maryland but can be moved to another part of the state.[343]

The action of the War Office emanated from a resolution proposed in Congress during the previous week by Colonel Theodorick Bland. The American officer, formerly responsible for the Convention Prisoners at Charlottesville, and now a delegate to Congress from Virginia, had entered the picture once more. Frustrated at the amount of time Congress had to spend on their affairs, he had introduced the following resolution,

Resolved the troops under the Convention of Saratoga be declared and treated as prisoners of war the stipulations on the part of Lieutenant General Burgoyne in behalf of that army not having been complied with, and the capitulation of Charlestown having been infringed on the part of Great Britain.

This resolution failed to pass on the 17th March but with slightly modified wording was accepted on the 23rd March 1781. It finally erased any remaining fiction on the part of the Americans that the Convention of Saratoga was a valid treaty. The accusations against Burgoyne still rested on the very weak grounds discussed in chapter 5. The new Charleston complaint had nothing to do with the Convention Prisoners. It was probably introduced because of the weakness of the original arguments.[344]

The immediate effect of this resolution meant the rations supplied to the Convention Prisoners, instead of being at the level of serving American soldiers, were now reduced. Officially, they should have still received 10 ounces of bread and meat daily. The failure to supply the former ration entitlement meant the resolution made no practical difference to the amount of food actually received by each prisoner. The lower level of ration supply required still did not help the Americans. By 24th May, Moses Rawlings was growing despondent. Without supplies, he stated that he had no money and was,

> at a loss how to act . . . what will become with the guard and prisoners God only knows.[345]

Having abrogated the Convention of Saratoga, six days later Congress had also passed another resolution, separating the officers from the men, the former to go to Connecticut. The farewell took place while the prisoners were at Lancaster on their way to York. Anburey has left a description of what happened and the emotions felt by both officers and men. Once again it provides evidence that despite the savage eighteenth-century discipline that ruled the British Army, close ties existed between officers and men. Anburey wrote,

> Distressing and humiliating as the scene was, when we commanded our men to pile up their arms and abandon them on the plain of Saratoga, still much greater was the separation of the officers from the men at Lancaster. On the morning it took place the regiments were paraded

near the barracks, which are picketed in, and converted into a prison. At a small distance was drawn up a regiment of continental troops, the Colonel of which behave extremely polite, saying, he should not march the British troops to the barracks, till their officers informed him they were ready. When the Colonel was informed he might march the men, the American troops, forming a square around the British soldiers, conducted them to the prison.

The sight was too deeply affecting, and we hastened from the spot. Could you have seen the faces of duty, respect, love and despair, you would carry the remembrance to the grave. It was the parting of child and parent, the separation of soul and body—it effected that which the united force of the inclement seasons, hunger and thirst, incessant barbarity, adverse fortune, and American insults heaped together, could never have effected—it drew tears from the eyes of veterans, who would rather have shed their blood. As far as sounds could convey, we heard a reiteration of 'God bless your honors'. It was such a scene as must leave an everlasting impression on the mind. To behold so many men, who had bravely fought by our side—who in all their sufferings looked up to us for protection, forced from us into a prison, where experiencing every severity, perhaps famishing for want of food, and ready to perish with cold, they had no one to look up to for redress, and little to expect from the humanity of Americans.[346]

The senior British officer, Brigadier General Hamilton was no Phillips. While he expressed "great displeasure" at the separation which was directly against the terms of the Convention, he added any protest, even if made, would be in vain. He strongly recommended the soldiers to behave in every respect the same as if their officers were present. Though separated, they should remember that subordination was due to the non-commissioned officers, who still had authority over them. The General expressed his regret he was unable to furnish supplies of clothing and provisions and therefore directed the paymasters to give the men their arrears of pay before leaving. Anburey thought this would enable them to provide for themselves and stated that most received twenty or thirty pounds. He mentions one man had forty five pounds due. Fox, expressing the amount in gold, says he received half a guinea.[347]

Not all the money was spent on food and clothing. While rations remained in short supply, there were plenty of stills around the country and Anburey says soldiers had been in a continued state of intoxication. He commented, "I need not tell you of the inordinate passion that soldiers in general have for liquor, and what a difficult matter it is to restrain them from it; but where it is continually before them, next to an impossibility." This led to some deaths. He records the case of two men who drank the liquor hot out of the pipe, and the next morning were found dead in their beds.[348]

Although the Americans now classed the Convention Prisoners as ordinary prisoners of war, they still would not allow them to take part in the general exchange. They continued to be hostages to Congress's political aims. They stayed as an identifiable group, although due to overcrowded accommodation often alongside other prisoners of war. The officers were more fortunate and continued to be exchanged at a steady pace. When they were separated, they had, in conformity with eighteenth-century practice, taken their servants with them to Connecticut. It seems the maximum advantage was taken of this to release as many men as possible. From available evidence, an average of two servants were exchanged with each officer. When Burgoyne and other officers entered New York on parole, they were allowed to take with them twenty men as servants. While waiting at Windsor, Connecticut, a memorandum from an American sutler shows that between 23rd July and 6th October 1781 food and quarters were provided for "near 400" of the Convention Prisoners. At that time the number of officers remaining could not have exceeded 150. The number of other ranks taking advantage of exchange in this way is supported from other records. These show that when a group of 19 officers left Windsor, they took with them 43 servants. Later, another 200 men arrived in New York on the 10th September 1781 with their officers. In this manner, the number of prisoners were reduced still further. There is also evidence that some NCOs were quietly included as servants and exchanged.[349]

Apart from the Convention Prisoners who managed to get to New York either as officers' servants or as invalids, no others, except officers, were ever exchanged. Early histories of the Royal Artillery, the 29th and 31st Foot all mention the exchange of their men during the last months of 1780. This was not so. More than one strength return show the men of these regiments continuing as prisoners until the end of the war. Further, in May of 1781, General Haldimand, commanding in Canada, also wrote that, "the long talked of exchange of the Convention Army has in part taken place." Nothing appears in the records of the negotiations that any partial exchange was finally agreed or ever took place. Nor is any exchange of other ranks mentioned in contemporary memoirs. The references can only refer to officers, invalids, officers servants or escapees repatriated back to their regiments.[350]

Rescue of the remaining prisoners was still not out of everyone's mind. A Loyalist in Winchester, Dr. Henry Norris, had proposed a plan to enable the prisoners to break-out. He stated all it would require was 100 arms and 100 pounds of powder. Nothing was done about his proposal, probably because it was considered impossible to achieve. Clinton sent a man to Cornwallis in the south, bearing a proposal to liberate the Convention Troops. His plan would require a minimum of force. Nothing came of this. The closest to a mass rescue attempt was the mounted incursion made by Colonel Banastre Tarleton, who raided Charlottesville after the prisoners had left. With 250 mounted men, and knowing the prisoners had been marched north, he missed capturing Thomas Jefferson at Monticello by minutes, but secured several members of the Virginia assembly. They found twenty or so Convention Prisoners, probably German, working in the area. They informed him many more were close by, but he could not afford the time to stay and made no search for them.[351]

Food shortages continued to be the biggest problem faced by the remaining prisoners and on 23rd May, the Board of War recommended to Congress that the Convention Prisoners be moved back to Massachusetts. Led by the delegates from that state, who had seen enough of them, Congress refused to approve the resolution. Theodorick Bland entered the fray once again by proposing that the Board of War move the prisoners, "in such manner and to such place as they think most conducive to the good of the union in general." This resolution passed, but it still did not allay the suspicions of one delegate from Massachusetts that his state would have to feed the prisoners and he voted against it. His suspicions were justified. In a letter from Washington to Congress, it appears that Rutland in Massachusetts had once more been selected and a march to that place by some of the prisoners had started. As a guard for the route through Easton, Pennsylvania to Rutland could not be found, he advised halting them in Pennsylvania, which was done.[352]

The Convention Prisoners continued to be considered a security risk. A letter to the Maryland Governor from Frederick Town wanted them taken out of town and put in a prison.

> Public Safety is eventually in danger wherever these troops are kept.
> When prisoners move out of Fort Frederick conventioners could move in.

Congress was already searching for a permanent place to keep the prisoners and had established a sub-committee to consider the problem.[353]

In a vain effort to resolve accommodation and supply problems, Congress now had to order a series of confusing movements. For several weeks men were on the march to and from different places. In order to make room for them, recaptured prisoners also had to be shuffled around. By mid-June the British prisoners were at Lancaster, Pennsylvania. With them were about 100 recaptured escapees for whom there was no room at Philadelphia where most, by now, had been concentrated. Excluding recaptured escapees, the number of British Convention Prisoners had now dwindled to about 600.[354]

The men stayed nine weeks at Lancaster, then the largest inland town in the thirteen colonies. In August, the British Convention Prisoners were ordered to move to York, Pennsylvania, which had been selected as their permanent holding place. With an eye to any rescue attempt, their long suffering escort commander, Colonel James Wood, was able to report that he had fixed them on good ground, very convenient to "throw them" back across the river in any emergency. As usual, they had to start work on further barracks and they cleared a hundred acres of woodland. One comment made was that the plantation on which they stayed had considerably reduced in value, with the guards destroying almost all the fence rails. Fox recalled,

> they turn'd us into the woods and put a chain of Centinels round us.
> there we had to build huts, the ground was mark'd out for building
> regular streets . . . After the huts were builded we sunk wells and made
> a grave yard ¼ m from the camp rail'd and fenc'd ¼ acre.[355]

The men, once more, were without clothing. They had, "parted even from their shirts," and most of them were without blankets. Their condition, added to the years of starvation rations, lack of shelter when moving, and overcrowding in the limited accommodation available, now took their toll. Hundreds of the prisoners, their wives and children went down with "Camp" and "Jail" fevers. George Fox expressed the theory that the "yellow fever" came from refugees who had been turned out of the Philadelphia jail and were in the Lancaster stockade when the prisoners marched in. He recalled, "our men . . . died like rotten sheep". Surgeon's Mate Benjamin Shield (21st), left a harrowing description of what he had to face when some of the prisoners had reached York, while those too sick to move remained at Lancaster. In a letter to Brigadier General Hamilton, Shield described how at Lancaster, he ordered all who were able to sit up into wagons. He had intended to stay behind to care for the worst cases, but on hearing what was going on in York, he decided to move there with the wagons. He found lying there the corpses of 40 men, women and children and had to make his first task their burial. He had laid the foundation for a hospital but the men were falling sick so fast, there were not enough men to attend them and to proceed with the construction. After acknowledging the assistance of Sergeants Bush (RA) and Nunworthy (20th), he added,

> I assure you it is a distressing situation and I have often been at a loss to distinguish which most deserv'd to be lamented by their country in whose cause they have and are still hourly suffering, the sickening, the dying or the dead; . . . (those) now here who have been at the very jaws of death, and yet live in hourly dread of falling a sacrafice to this infernal distemper, after having escaped perhaps three or four times, through a most escrusiating, and lingering sickness; there is now in camp a shocking instance of the distracted state of mind accompanying these poor men in their sickness of a man who in his delerium cut of the head of his own child with an axe He belongs to the Canada Companies, is now recovered, and is thoroughly sensible of his own wretchedness there is much more distress these poor men apprehend from the severity of a long winter without your interposition in their favor for many of them have parted even from their shirts to support themselves in their sickness, and most of them are without blankets . . . need clothing, money & medecine.
> PS There is now on the sick list 196 exclusive of those still at Lancaster.

No record has been traced giving either the total numbers or the names of those who died at this time. Nor have their graves been found.[356]

Despite their weakened state, Convention Prisoner escapes were still taking place. Privates John Moore and Mathew Ashert, (both 62nd) had escaped from Lancaster on the 24th July 1781 and they got into New York by the 13th August. There is no record of how they managed the journey in such a short period of time. A clue might be that after their escape they were not drafted into a regular British regiment, but served in a Loyalist regiment, the American Legion.

Private Charles Hawley (47th) also escaped from Lancaster about the same time and made a very fast journey into New York, in company with a party of no less than 39 captured British soldiers of Cornwallis's army. Privates George Sutherland and James Garrett (both of the 21st), succeeded in reaching safety although on the way Sutherland had to spend two months in Lancaster jail. Sutherland finished the war with the Black Watch and Garrett in the 17th Dragoons. Private Cornelius O'Brien (24th) after escaping from Lancaster on 26th June 1781, was forced to take the long way round to New York. He was recaptured by the crew of a privateer when he was trying to hire a boat at Egg Harbor to take him into New York. They took him to New London in Connecticut, but he was able to escape from there by passing himself off as a civilian. He arrived in New York on 19th August 1781.[357]

Those who used the Pennsylvania militia to escape included William Miller (34th) who spent eight days with the 9th Pennsylvania before reaching his own lines; Peter Thompson (20th) used the 5th Pennsylvania; two others used the 3rd York, they were John Frederick Ginlink (one of Lieutenant Nutt's recruits for the 33rd Foot) and John Fish (62nd). Samuel Gake (also 62nd) spent some time with the 1st Pennsylvania Brigade.[358]

For nearly two years, the remaining prisoners now stayed in one place. Food and clothing was never plentiful. In November 1782, George Washington issued a passport for the relief ship Amazon with a cargo of clothing and necessities for the prisoners. After unloading at Wilmington, the sheriff and other officials of Chester County, Pennsylvania, impounded the cargo without authority and used the supplies locally. While Congress held an enquiry into what had happened, no penalties were levied, and the prisoners once more went without.

If a move of the prisoners had been ordered there could now have been little response. The war for all intents and purposes was over, for on the fourth anniversary of the Convention of Saratoga, Cornwallis at Yorktown, Virginia, his supply line cut-off by the French navy, had sent a drummer across the lines to Washington, in a prelude to negotiating a surrender. The remaining prisoners who had declined to escape, for the most part settled down to await repatriation.

The British soldier in America had never found any difficulty in attracting American girls, perhaps due to the number of their own menfolk being away serving in their armies. Those who associated with the prisoners were described by Americans as suffering from "scarlet fever." Such liaisons inevitably led to marriage and children, and this in turn led to a greater desire on the part of the men to find work to enable them to feed their families. To facilitate this, the soldiers were divided into two groups. The single men who were more likely to escape, were placed in "Camp Security," which was a regular prison complete with stockade; the "men of good character" and the married men, with their wives and children, were camped outside the stockade, in an area called "Camp Indulgence." In April of 1782, 470 soldiers were living in the camp, which probably consisted of huts without foundations.[359]

Congress had tried to stop the men from working in return for food and clothing. Under pressure from their citizens who needed the prisoners to produce food, they finally gave in and subject to certain conditions, authorised the men's employment. They required a bond of £1,000 to be given by the employer as security against a man escaping while employed. In addition a payment of $4 per month had to be paid to government.[360]

A few of the men who went to work became very successful and later owned their own farms. Very often they worked off the money the American farmers had paid as bail. These men were called "Redemptioners," their contracts being made legal and binding by having the arrangement made public at church. Those married men working in this manner, probably constituted the largest number of the prisoners who eventually became absorbed into the American population.[361]

Fox records that an Irish farmer paid a bond of 30 pounds for him to work on his plantation 27 miles from the camp. Fox received $2 per month and board for his efforts. When some clothing came in from New York he decided to go back to camp and he refused an offer of $3 monthly to stay. At a subsequent job he was paid by a Dutchman $3 per month to cook, cut wood and look after a horse and cow. Those prisoners remaining in the camp with their wives and children, followed a variety of trades, including making lace, buckles, spoons and other "mechanical trades" which they had learnt during their captivity. Lamb, who had been captured for the second time at Yorktown, visited them during one of his attempts at freedom, and was very critical towards men of his former regiment.

> I perceived that they had lost that animation which ought to possess the breast of the soldier, I strove, by every argument, to rouse them from their lethargy. I offered to head any number of them, and make a noble effort to escape into New York, and join our comrades in arms; but all my efforts proved ineffectual.[362]

In considering his criticism, it must be remembered that inveterate escaper Lamb, who in World War II terminology was a real "Colditz" man. Just as in World War II the large majority of prisoners of war sat out their time in prison camps without censure, so the remaining Convention Prisoners are entitled to the same consideration. This is particularly so, in view of the fact that at that time, the official British army policy frowned on escaping. It should also be remembered that a number of the remaining prisoners had married American women and now, in addition to themselves, they had the welfare of their wives and children to consider.

The British defeat at Yorktown had brought most of the fighting to an end, except for some skirmishing and clandestine warfare. The cessation of fighting did not bring liberty to the prisoners and their problems. Escaped men were also still on the run trying to gain their freedom, and those recaptured still languished in jails, prison ships and dungeons. With the surrender of Cornwallis, the towns of Winchester in Virginia, Frederick Town in Maryland, and Lancaster, York and Reading in Pennsylvania, became the home for thousands of new prisoners of war. While the Convention Prisoners who did not escape continued as an identifiable community in their two camps some four miles east of York; those that did escape and were recaptured, found themselves in prisons and camps, inextricably mixed up with prisoners other than from the Convention Army. Those captured at Yorktown were also causing headaches for the Americans. Lincoln, now Secretary for War, reported to Washington that he estimated there were "perhaps" 900 prisoners from Yorktown who had escaped on their march northwards and were "strolling through Virginia."[363]

While in Lancaster the prisoners' guards included Moses Hazen's 2nd Canadian regiment. Hazen, an American who had settled in St John's, Canada, had been trained in Roberts' Rangers during the previous war. He was rabidly anti-British, and had formed his regiment from disgruntled Canadians soon after the commencement of hostilities. His regiment became known as Congress's Own, which as related, had been used by Convention Prisoners making their escape. This made him even less sympathetic to the prisoners' plight. From his base in Lancaster, Hazen became very active in the pursuit of escaped prisoners. He not only accused his guards of assisting escapes. Under his leadership, several hundred Pennsylvanian residents were charged with crimes for helping the British in various ways. These included aiding prisoners while on the run. In this connection, Hazen concocted a scheme whereby, not only could he carry out his duties in an efficient manner, but at the same time make money for himself. He needed cash to purchase land to replace that which he had lost in Canada when he threw his lot in with the Americans. Since the start of the war Pennsylvania had passed a series of laws imposing penalties for assisting escaped prisoners. These included a fine of £50 or 39 lashes. Half the fine was to go to the person giving information leading to the conviction of the perpetrator. Hazen recruited one or more British deserters to go out into the surrounding areas posing as escaped prisoners. They would then report to Hazen the names of the people who had helped them; in this way 50 inhabitants were caught and charged with helping escapees. 35 of them were found guilty and of these, 25 were fined, with Hazen registered as the informant. In this manner he was awarded £1,425, a very substantial sum in those days. Unexpectedly, those charged put up a spirited defence. Firstly, they claimed that so many prisoners were being allowed out to work or to find provisions, they could not tell if the man was an escaper or not. Secondly, having discovered Hazen's plan to obtain payment for himself, they accused him of entrapment by deliberately sending out prisoners in this manner. The court was obviously not happy with Hazen's conduct and remitted the fines for all except 5 of those charged. Hazen went without most of his devious earnings.[364]

Because of the number of escaped prisoners at large, Congress considered a resolution recommending the states, "grant a reward of $8 at Continental expense for the recapture of each enemy prisoner and that they provide for the punishment of any person harboring, secreting, assisting, abetting, or comforting, any prisoner of war." Although it seems that eventually Congress declined to pay the rewards, in Pennsylvania the state government decided that something had to be done. Their system of fines and lashes was not working so they changed their tactics. Emulating the British, who paid £5 for the recovery of American prisoners who escaped in England, they passed a law granting a bounty of eight dollars for each escaped prisoner who was apprehended and brought before a justice of the peace. Overnight the justices found themselves swamped with recaptured prisoners turned in for the bounty. In the new Philadelphia jail housing recaptured escaped British soldiers, the number of prisoners rose from 485 in October 1781 to 908 in July 1782. It was quite apparent that many Pennsylvanians had known of prisoners in their midst, but had previously done nothing about them. The state would be made bankrupt if bounty payments continued at the same level. Subsequently, a measure forced on them by lack of money, the state council decided to exclude payments for Convention Prisoners.[365]

Except by commando elements such as Butlers' Rangers, (which had escaped Convention Prisoners serving in its ranks), little fighting was taking place. Regardless of the generally quiet situation, Congress remained uninterested in changing the no-exchange status of the Convention men. They were uncertain as to what the British intended and holding the prisoners still gave them a trump card. Even as late as October 1782, Madison thought that Carleton, in a letter to Washington, used such language as, "portending a revival of the war against the United States." Carleton was in effect giving a lecture, and an indictment of the conduct of the Americans with regard to the exchange of prisoners of war. The British Commander-in-Chief, referring to American statements that prisoners should be punished unless their maintenance had been paid for, said it was contrary to "the practice of nations at war ever since the barbarous ages." Carleton added that Congress could easily and honourably remove the burden of caring for the prisoners, by agreeing to the proposal of exchanging British soldiers for American seamen. In this way, "Congress at long last would carry out the terms of the Convention of Saratoga by liberating soldiers who should have been restored to their country five years ago."[366]

The Americans need not have worried about the future. The defeat at Yorktown brought big political changes in England. Germaine was removed as the minister responsible for the war, and he went into the House of Lords as Viscount Sackville. A motion in Parliament on 22nd February 1782 to cease the prosecution of the war was opposed by Lord North's ministry and defeated by one vote. North's attempt to adjourn the debate five days later was defeated by 19 votes, and the original motion was adopted without a division taking place. Soon after, negotiations for a peace treaty opened with the Americans.[367]

After months of haggling, the Treaty of Paris was finally made recognising the independence of the United States and the news reached New York on 5th April 1783. On 21st April Washington sent Carleton a copy of a Proclamation from the "Sovereign Power of the United States", ordering a cessation of hostilities. Washington wanted it made known and publicly proclaimed at all the outposts of the American army as soon as possible. Carleton, issued notices expressed in similar sentiments. At last the way was clear for the release of the prisoners. When the news reached some of them on 22nd April, they cheered for King George. At one place, this so annoyed a French officer, he attacked and killed four German prisoners.[368]

In his letter to Carleton, Washington gave him the choice of marching the prisoners overland to New York, or marching to the coast to be transported by British vessels to New York. Carleton rejected the latter, probably due to the shortage of shipping caused by evacuating Loyalists to Nova Scotia. The marching destination was to be Elizabeth Town in New Jersey where they could cross to British occupied Staten Island and on into New York. Those in Reading would go to the coast and then by ship to New York. An escort would be provided for the prisoners because of "the tenor in the country." Washington asked that Carleton appoint an officer to work with War Secretary

Lincoln in Philadelphia. In response, Carleton appointed Brigadier General Alured Clarke with several officers assisting him, to superintend the march "and to prevent any irregularities which disorderly persons may be disposed to commit."[369]

Security for the prisoners was no small problem. Despite the signing of the peace treaty there were still wide-spread suspicions throughout the thirteen states, that the British would start hostilities again. An American officer who expected to be involved in escorting the prisoners commented that there were rumours that General Carleton would not leave New York and was collecting all the British troops to be available if the United States did not comply with parts of the peace treaty. He said that circumstances,

> must convince the weakest minds, that it would be inconsistent with sound policy to disband our army while so many of those who have been our open, and now are our secret enemies, remain in arms on the continent.[370]

Clarke travelled immediately to Philadelphia. On 5th May, Lincoln set out in detail his proposed arrangements, which included sending all the sick and invalids to Philadelphia where they could be accommodated until ships arrived for them. He also instructed "your officers to attend each division as you may think proper to maintain order and discipline among the troops." He added, "To render the exertions of your officers efficient by enabling them to arrest and punish delinquents I have ordered an escort of American troops to march with each division." In the event, there were no incidents and Corporal Fox recalled, "the American guard being only a matter of form."[371]

The following day, Clarke wrote to Carleton saying the Americans are facilitating the move and there were no difficulties; boats for crossing to Staten Island should be prepared to start on 9th May. Clearly worried the American attitude might change, he added,

> You will see how little time I have to methodise the business in the manner I could wish, and that I know would be satisfactory to you Sir; but I thought it better to avail myself of the temper in which I found them here, on my arrival; and by scrambling through a few difficulties, leave something to chance; . . . I do not mean to create difficulties by demanding an account of the deficient men at present;

but shall defer all enquiries into that business till those they seem so well inclined to give us, are in your possession.[372]

Clarke's fear of a change of heart was well-founded. Last minute obstacles for the return of the prisoners were raised. Theodorick Bland, that nemesis of the Convention Prisoners ever since he commanded the escort on the march out of Cambridge over four years previously, tried to stop them leaving. On 8th May, he proposed in Congress that the prisoners should be detained until a British answer be given, regarding the delivery of slaves, who, after the signing of the peace treaty, had taken refuge with the British. The British would not return them because of the failure of the Americans to fulfil a part of the treaty. The situation was considered sufficiently serious for Washington to meet with Carleton. This took place on 13th May, the only time the Commander-in-Chiefs of both sides met. Although Washington described the British attitude as, "a palpable and scandalous misconstruction of the Treaty," he was not prepared to stop the prisoners, who by that date were already on the move. Madison summed it up saying, "the progress already made in the discharge of the prisoners . . . makes it probable that no remedy will be applied to the evil."[373]

Several routes for the march were used. Fox found himself in the notorious jail in Philadelphia, just evacuated by recaptured escapees moving one day ahead of his group. Fortunately it was for only one night. He described it as "a nasty place."[374]

On 27th May, Clarke reported from Philadelphia that most of the men had been moved and commented,

> The number of men sent in falls very short of what is specified in the lowest return given me by the adjutant general and yet I much fear there will not be many more of them forthcoming.

He was wrong. Both the Americans and British, in their haste to move the prisoners, had concentrated on those in Virginia, Pennsylvania and Maryland. Everyone had forgotten about those prisoners still languishing at Rutland in Massachusetts and other northern jails. In a letter of apology from the American War Office, Lincoln's aide stated "their detention has been accidental altogether—I hope it has not produced any material inconvenience."[375]

In the haste to move the prisoners, and in the midst of the larger problem of evacuating New York, very few records have survived as to who returned and what happened to them. It seems that some were kept in boats waiting for shipping and did not go into New York, but were immediately placed on vessels in the harbour destined for Europe or Canada. Fox says his ship was in New York Harbour for five weeks before sailing.

It is unlikely that any separate accounting was made of the hundreds of recaptured escapees now released. Likewise, no record has been traced of the number of Rutland survivors who came in late. Nor were the invalids or those troops who travelled to New York by ship from Philadelphia counted. Those of the ten British infantry regiments involved in the Convention of Saratoga, who marched into New York under Brigadier General Clarke's command, totalled 511 men.[376]

Some of those who had escaped still had problems. There was the matter of their pay while they had been prisoners or on the run. As early as October 1781, Clinton had appointed a Board of Enquiry to examine the claims of the prisoners. He had established a precedent in introducing a bounty for escaped prisoners reaching New York. He now made another innovation by paying an allowance to cover the clothing the men should have received while they were incarcerated or on the way back to British lines. Under the King's regulations each man should have received his uniforms from his Colonel. The prisoners, since Saratoga, had seen very little of these. Clinton set a value for the clothing not provided, at one guinea per year. This was to be paid with each man's arrear of pay. The annual amount due to a private was then calculated:

	£	s.	d.
Pay for one year	9	2	6
Uniform allowance	1	1	0
Poundage (allowances)		12	2
Total for year	£ 10	15	8

To cover broken periods this sum was reduced to a daily amount, which came to $7^{33}/_{365}$ pence per day. Once again Clinton came down on the side of the prisoners. With a long explanation of why it was done, he authorised the daily amount to be rounded upwards to

8 pence per day as compensation for the hardships they had gone through.[377]

When Carleton assumed command, he constituted a similar Board which had commenced work on 20th January 1783. Only 118 escapees and exchanged men went before it, probably all borderline cases. Many of the men had already been transferred from New York; some claims had been settled by their new regiments; others had been paid by Clinton's 1781 board; no details of pay adjustments have been traced concerning those who returned to places other than New York. Two further boards were constituted in New York in October 1783 but again details of the cases examined have not been traced.[378]

Carleton's board laid down very stringent, harsh and somewhat unfair rules as to who was entitled to receive payment. They refused settlement to any man who had spent time with the American forces, or who had worked at their trade while escaping. They made the observation that these had received wages, rations and clothing for those services; further, that some men had not taken the first opportunity to reach British posts. In taking that position the Board appeared to ignore the difficulty in doing what, several years after the event, may have appeared easy to accomplish. Even more unfair was their rejecting the claims of men who had escaped prior to 31st March 1778. They fixed on that date as being the day of the suspension of the Convention by the Americans. Until then, they were of the opinion the men should have stayed put. The date fixed, was quite wrong. Congress suspended the Convention on the 8th January 1778 and the British were certainly aware of it by 3rd February. They also rejected applications from those captured before the Convention was signed. The Board ruled they were prisoners of war and they should not have escaped at all, but waited for exchange,

. . . for had they waited the event they would have been regularly exchanged, as the generality of them were.

The Board never explained how these men could have known that years later an exchange would eventually be agreed upon. Clinton, with his efforts to encourage escape, would have taken a much different view.

At the hearings the men were examined at length by the Deputy

Advocate General. Approximately one half of the applications were rejected on the grounds listed above.[379]

Throughout 1783, until the city was abandoned, escaped British prisoners continued to dribble into New York in ones and twos, often to receive a much colder reception than had greeted those who arrived earlier. Carleton had little feeling or consideration of what the men had gone through during the past six years. He upheld Clinton's offers of pardon, and was prepared to provide transportation to Europe or Canada, but he did not countenance any excuse from soldiers who had spent too long in enemy territory. On the 13th May he published an order to all his regiments:

> The Commander in Chief has so far pardoned several English deserters, as to allow them to return within the lines, and to send them home, but their dishonor is not done away. No regiments here shall receive them nor shall they again serve in this army. Tis recommended to the soldiers of every British, and the soldiers of every British American Corps to kick all such rascals out of the quarters should they have the impudence to come in among them.

His final word was expressed a week later,

> All deserters who come within the lines are to report themselves within 24 hours to the Officer Commanding the next post. Those who do not comply with this order will be sent to the provost and be deprived of the benefit of pardon. Certificates to be given to those deserters who surrender themselves in the above manner.

He was serious! From this time on, two or three names of men charged with desertion appear in the Provost's reports.[380]

The terms of the peace treaty required Britain to give up those places in the thirteen states which they still occupied. New York City, with Staten Island, were the last, and they planned to evacuate them by the fall of 1783. This left very little time to move the remaining thousands of Loyalists who opted to go to either Canada or Britain. In addition to those who left in earlier years, during 1783 up to 25th November when the last vessel sailed, some 29,244 civilians were carried away. Only when the last of these had boarded their ships did Carleton move his remaining forces. These totalled 17,200 soldiers and exprisoners, and the numbers involved meant every ship being filled to capacity.

Great credit is due to Carleton and his staff in ensuring no one was left behind. Anyone who wanted to leave was found a place, and Carleton received a well-deserved peerage in recognition of his efforts.[381]

In Britain and Ireland, recruiting parties of the captured regiments had continued with their work in keeping the absent regiments alive. As those prisoners who had declined to escape returned, some were drafted in groups to other corps, but many mingled with the new recruits who had joined their regiments. In this manner, a nucleus was formed on which the rebuilding of the regiments took place. Traces of the Convention Prisoners' names can be found on the regimental muster rolls for several years after the war. Promotion of ex-prisoners appear to have been common; others are shown discharged as "worn out", and still other names appear on applications for admission to the Chelsea Hospital. Two ex-prisoners still had not had enough suffering. Samuel Howarth, an escaper, and James Dent, probably also an escaper, (both 9th) asked to be drafted to a regiment about to go to Jamaica. At that time, a posting to the West Indies was considered to be a death sentence![382]

CHAPTER II

The Numbers Game

MOST books published about the Convention of Saratoga have avoided detailed information about what happened to the prisoners after the suspension of the Convention. Where opinions have been expressed they often assume that most deserted. This uncertainty is not the fault of the historians. Unless additional muster rolls, strength returns, jail and court records are found in substantial quantity, which is unlikely, we will never know accurately what happened to all the prisoners. In the absence of additional information, only reasonable assumptions can be made.

On the question of desertion, we have seen that incarcerated in York, Pennsylvania, there remained in 1782, 470 British Convention Prisoners. By that time, some of these, perhaps as many as a third, were married with children, and were living in "Camp Indulgence." It is unlikely any of these left their families to return to the army. They probably "disappeared" very quickly, when the British officers came to march them off to New York in the spring of 1783. In addition to these, there were those, living in rural Pennsylvania, who had escaped being handed over to the justices of peace when the reward offered for their arrest was withdrawn. We know that several became successful farmers. There were probably others in similar circumstances, at the places where the prisoners were previously held for long periods of time, such as Cambridge and Rutland in Massachusetts and in Western Virginia. Some of those in Massachusetts may have regretted the position they had got themselves into. Sergeant Thomas Taylor, who we last met starting on a clandestine journey from St. Johns, had contacts with several deserters, made during his secret journeys. In 1784, he informed the Commanding General in Canada, that deserted soldiers living in Massachusetts would return if assured pardon. Taylor offered his services to contact them. This offer was not taken up, because with the war ended, the army was being reduced, and it was cheaper not to bother with them.[383]

Traces of individual British Convention Prisoners who did desert and became Americans are rare. Evidence of German and Loyalist deserters are much more numerous, and some false trails have been laid when these have been described as British deserters. They were deserters, but they were not British soldiers! We do know of some cases of British desertion, a few of whom we met in Chapter 4. In addition, Lamb recorded that in a house in Virginia, he met some 40 British deserters who had determined to remain in the country and had taken up farming in the locality. Lamb was invited to join them but he refused. Other deserters identified include, Privates Thomas Thomson and John Howes, who deserted on the first march to Cambridge. They both married American women in July of 1779. A third Convention Prisoner bearing the name James Robinson, married in Simsbury, Connecticut, in June of the same year. By the following November he had deserted his wife. He disappeared in the direction of New York and may have even arrived there. He could have been one of the two James Robinson's listed in Appendix 5. His wife, Deborah, realising she would not see him again, divorced him in 1784. A grenadier, Charles Stevens, deserted and settled in Turkey Hills, Connecticut. He became adept at digging ditches and was known as "The Ditcher." Years later, when two girls addressed him as Mr. Ditcher, he retorted, "I am a grenadier of General Burgoyne's army and was a big man before you were born." In another case, two British soldiers who deserted on the march to Virginia, applied for American citizenship. Congress refused to grant the applications because they felt if they did so and the two were not returned at the end of the war, Britain would refuse to return American prisoners.[384]

There was a great shortage of labour in the northern colonies during the war. None of the prisoners appear to have found difficulty in finding employment while on the run. This was due, not only to the number of Americans who had joined the Continental Army, or were serving in the militia for long periods of time, but also to the effect of the general expansion taking place in agriculture. Undoubtedly, there were cases of men who, escaping with the best of intentions, tired of being hunted and spending months and years in jail, finally gave up the effort and settled down to work. The conditions of employment, were in many respects, superior to those they could expect at home.

Turning to the records of those that made home runs back to the British army, throughout the references listed in this work, large numbers of escapees are mentioned, but with names omitted. Records cast little light on who these might have been. We have seen how Brigadier General Clarke at the end of the war, reported the number of men recovered fell short of what had been indicated in the lowest of the returns provided by the Adjutant General. The word "lowest" suggests that British Headquarters were themselves confused as to how many they thought were still prisoners. They clearly did not know the number of men who had been prisoners in the first place. Burgoyne's and Kingston's returns differ by more than 750 men. Phillips's return contains at least one adding error and the figures shown may have been contrived. Appendix 3 highlights the differences in the starting figures.

To add to the confusion, British Headquarters did not know how many had escaped and were already back with British or Loyalist regiments. Over a period of more than five years the escapees had succeeded in reaching British units in no less than five army commands, many hundreds of miles apart, i.e. Canada, Rhode Island, New York, Portsmouth and in the Carolinas. It is unlikely whether any effort was made to compile a central record of what was going on, and the figures given to Clarke would have consisted of one of the starting figures less those known by Headquarters to have reached New York. Even some of the escapees reaching New York may not have been included in their figures. Certain regiments appear to have quickly welcomed escapers who stumbled into their part of the line and they may not have informed the army command of their arrival. World War II, in an age of more detailed records, has numerous examples where allied army units added, without authority, all sorts of people to their strengths. Appendix 5 lists by name those now identified as escaped, or who attempted to escape.

In summary, the overwhelming amount of evidence uncovered indicates that most of the prisoners not traced did escape, and that only a minority deserted. It seems that Fortescue was quite correct when he summed up that,

> . . . although there were a few men who purchased comfort at the price of desertion, the majority stuck faithfully to their officers, or escaped and made their way to the British Army at New York.[385]

Articles of Convention Between Lieutenant-General Burgoyne and Major-General Gates

I

The troops under Lieutenant-general Burgoyne, to march out of their camp with the honours of war, and the artillery of the entrenchments, to the verge of the river where the old fort stood, where the arms and artillery are to be left; the arms to be piled by word of command from their own officers.

II

A free passage to be granted to the army under Lieutenant-general Burgoyne to Great Britain, on condition of not serving again in North America during the present contest; and the port of Boston is assigned for the entry of transports to receive the troops, whenever General Howe shall so order.

III

Should any cartel take place, by which the army under General Burgoyne, or any part of it, may be exchanged, the foregoing article to be void as far as such exchange shall be made.

IV

The army under Lieutenant-general Burgoyne, to march to Massachusetts Bay, by the easiest, most expeditious, and convenient route; and to be quartered in, near, or as convenient as possible to Boston, that the march of the troops may not be delayed, when transports arrive to receive them.

V

The troops to be supplied on their march, and during their being in quarters, with provisions, by General Gates's orders, at the same rate of rations as the troops of his own army; and if possible the officers'horses and cattle are to be supplied with forage at the usual rates.

VI

All officers to retain their carriages, batt-horses and other cattle, and no baggage to be molested or searched; Lieutenant-general Burgoyne giving his honour that there are no public stores secreted therein. Major-general Gates will of course take the necessary measures for the due performance of this article. Should any carriages be wanted during the march for the transportation of officers' baggage, they are if possible, to be supplied by the country at the usual rates.

VII

Upon the march, and during the time the army shall remain in quarters in Massachusetts Bay, the officers are not, as far as circumstances will admit, to be seperated from their men. The officers are to be quartered according to rank, and are not to be hindered from assembling their men for roll call, and other necessary purposes of regularity.

VIII

All corps whatever, of General Burgoyne's army, whether composed of sailors, batteaumen, artificers, drivers, independent companies, and followers of the army, of whatever country, shall be included in the fullest sense and utmost extent of the above articles, and comprehended in every respect as British subjects.

IX

All Canadians, and persons belonging to the Canadian establishment, consisting of sailors, batteaumen, artificers, drivers, independent companies, and many other followers of the army, who come under no particular description, are to be permitted to return there; they are to be conducted immediately by the shortest route to the first British post on Lake George, are to be supplied with provisions in the same manner as other troops, and are to be bound by the same condition of not serving during the present contest in North America.

X

Passports to be immediately greanted for three officers, not exceeding the rank of captains, who shall be appointed by Lieutenant-general Burgoyne, to carry despatches to Sir William Howe, Sir Guy Carleton, and to Great Britain, by the way of New York; and Major-general Gates engages the public faith, that these despatches shall not be opened. These officers are to set out immediately after receiving their despatches, and are to travel the shortest route and in the most expeditious manner.

XI

During the stay of the troops in Massachusetts Bay, the officers are to be admitted on parole, and are to be allowed to wear their side arms.

XII

Should the army under Lieutenant-general Burgoyne find it necessary to send for their clothing and other baggage to Canada, they are to be permitted to do it in the most convenient manner, and the necessary passports granted for that purpose.

XIII

These articles are to be mutually signed and exchanged to-morrow morning at 9 o'clock, and the troops under Lieutenant-general Burgoyne are to march out of their entrenchments at three o'clock in the afternoon.

[signed]   Horatio Gates, Major-general.

[signed]   J. Burgoyne, Lieutenant-general.

Saratoga, Oct. 16th, 1777.

To prevent any doubts that might arise from Lieutenant-general Burgoyne's name not being mentioned in the above treaty, Major-general Gates hereby declares, that he is understood to be comprehended in it, as fully as if his name had been specifically mentioned.

Horatio Gates.

The British Convention Regiments

Regiment	*Regiment Subsequently Named*
Royal Artillery (1 Battalion)	Royal Regiment of Artillery
9th Foot (10 companies)	Royal Norfolk Regiment now part of the Royal Anglian Regiment
20th Foot (10 companies)	Lancashire Fusiliers now part of the Royal Regiment of Fusiliers
21st Foot (10 companies)	Royal Scots Fusiliers now part of the Royal Highland Fusiliers
24th Foot (10 companies)	South Wales Borderers now part of the Royal Regiment of Wales
29th Foot (2 companies)	Worcestershire Regiment now part of the Worcestershire & Sherwood Foresters Regiment
31st Foot (2 companies)	East Surrey Regiment now part of the Princess of Wales's Royal Regiment
34th Foot (2 companies)	Border Regiment now part of the King's Own Royal Border Regiment
47th Foot (8 companies)	Loyal North Lancashire Regiment now part of the Queens Lancashire Regiment
53rd Foot (2 companies)	King's Own Shropshire Light Infantry now part of The Light Infantry
62nd Foot (10 companies)	The Wiltshire Regiment now part of the Royal Gloucestershire, Berkshire and Wiltshire Regiment

and
Lieutenant Nutt with 154 recruits mostly for the 33rd Foot
now The Duke of Wellington's Regiment

The British Convention Prisoners
on 17th October 1777

The number of British other ranks, who, on 17th October 1777, became Convention Prisoners under the terms of the treaty, can only be estimated. Of the four strength returns prepared, no two completely agree, and two differ considerably. One, signed by Burgoyne, was subsequently used by those British junior officers who left memoirs of the occasion. Phillips, used very similar figures in a return he prepared on 1st August 1779. This was when he was about to be paroled, prior to exchange. It endeavoured to reconcile the 17th October 1777 figures with those of 1st August 1779. This document, by month and by regiment, is very detailed and covers promotions. In footnotes to the figures, Phillips indicated occurrences in Canada which caused differences in the opening numbers. From these, it seems possible that several men counted in both his and Burgoyne's returns, never left Canada.

Colonel Wilkinson, the American Adjutant General, reported much lower figures. Part of the difference between his and the British returns may have been due to confusion on his part, over who were to be allowed to march to Canada. He shows no figures for the "Canadian Companies" and if when making the return, they were described as such, he may have thought they were entitled to be treated as Canadians. Burgoyne and Phillips on the other hand, would have known they were British soldiers, to be repatriated to Europe. This is pure speculation, and in any case does not explain all the differences. It could be, that certain staff positions were not treated by Wilkinson as soldiers. These would have been the musicians, bat men and others who, although in uniform, received little or no military training. Likewise, Burgoyne and Phillips may have included in their rank and file figures, the so-called contingency men. These were the three fictitious men per company, allowed for in regulations to cover recruiting expenses. All explanations for the differences between the records can only be based on conjecture.

A major element contributing to the confusion, is the return prepared on 14th November 1777 by Major Kingston, Burgoyne's Deputy Adjutant General. His paper was prepared nearly a month after the event, with very little detail. He does not distinguish between officers and men, nor does he separate the figures for British sick and wounded from the German. He shows a figure of 300 for deserters, but he provides no information on the numbers before or after the date of the Convention. Even after making allowances to remedy these factors, his figure for other ranks is still by far the lowest of the four returns. By the date he prepared the document, British soldiers had already begun to disappear in large numbers and it is just possible, low figures were given to hide the true facts from the Americans. George Washington quoted Kingston's figure on at least one occasion and other American officers have also used them. Copies of the returns used by Burgoyne, Phillips and Kingston can be found in the Clinton papers at the William L. Clements library in Ann Arbor. The Wilkinson figures can be seen in his memoirs.

The following table sets out the details shown on each of the returns, together with adjustments introduced reflecting the above comments.

AS SHOWN BY THE OFFICERS CONCERNED

	Burgoyne	Phillips	Wilkinson	Kingston
Sergeants	162	165	158	
Drummers & Fifers	135	141	114	
Rank & File fit for duty	2365			
Sick in Hospital & Camp	361	2883	2409	2442
Musicians	36			
Bat men	139			
Total other ranks	3198	3189	2681	2442

Possible Causes of Differences

Canadian companies not shown on Wilkinson Return (flank companies of 29th, 31st, 34th & 53rd)			387	
Approximate number of officers included in Kingston total				(180)
British sick and wounded using Burgoyne's figures				361
Deserters indicated on Kingston return				300
Possible total other ranks on 17th Oct. 1777	3198	3189	3068	2923

Jails and Barracks in Which the British Convention Prisoners Were Incarcerated

CONNECTICUT
Guilford
Hartford
New London

MARYLAND
Fort Frederick
Frederick Town

MASSACHUSETTS
Boston (including prison ships)
Cambridge
Rutland
Taunton
Worcester

VERMONT
Bennington

NEW JERSEY
Elizabeth Town
Morristown
Sussex County

NEW YORK
Albany
Fishkill
Poughkeepsie
West Point

PENNSYLVANIA
Carlisle
Easton
Fort Pitt (Pittsburg)
Lancaster
Philadelphia
Reading
York

RHODE ISLAND
Providence

VIRGINIA
Charlottesville
Richmond
Staunton
Winchester

Soldiers Identified as Escaped
or Attempted to Escape

Many on this incomplete roll can be found on more than the one record shown. All the sources listed should be searched for additional information. Many names have been omitted where no confirmation has been found that they were soldiers of Burgoyne's army.

Abbreviations

BHP	British Headquarters Papers
CL Intel	Clements Library—André Intelligence Book
Fryer	King's Men, Mary Beacock Fryer, 1980.
Hald	Canadian Archives, Ottawa, Haldimand Papers
HSP	Hist Soc of Pennsylvania—Bradford Collection
MSA	Massachusetts State Archives—Revolutionary Rolls Vol 8 Kingston Prison Ship 5.2.1778
NYL Intel	New York Public Library—Clinton Intelligence Books

★ Indicates escapee was originally captured before signing of Convention but not before 16th August 1777.

	Reference		*Reference*
REGIMENT NOT IDENTIFIED			
Carnegie, Christian	CL Intel	Purnell, Thomas	CL Intel
Edwards, Thomas	NY Intel	Stone, William ★	Fryer
Maxwell, Robert	Chapter 9	Temple, Cpl Andrews ★	Fryer
Mayne, John	NYL Intel	Vickers, Robert	HSP 2.4.80
McCoy, Angus	HSP 2.4.80	Walker, John	HSP 2.4.80
McCoy, John	Chapter 9	Watson, Samuel	HSP 15.4.80
Murphy, Corporal	BHP 38,319		

Reference   *Reference*

ROYAL ARTILLERY

Byrn, Edward	NYL Intel	Webster, John	Chapter 9

9th FOOT

	Captain John Bailis	Chapter 9	
Alcock, Samuel	HSP 2.3.82	Keen, Charles	BHP 51, 177
Barnes, Thomas	NYL Intel	Lamb, Sgt Roger	Chapter 7
Barry, Sgt —	Chapter 10	Leaklighter, Philip	Chapter 4
Borch, Patrick	HSP 12.5.82	McCarty, —	HSP – – –
Brown, C	HSP 2.3.82	Moon, Thomas	HSP 2.3.82
Brown, Michael	HSP 30.4.81	Moore, Andrew	HSP 30.4.81
Brown, Will	BHP 37, 78	Murphy, Loughlin	Chapter 7
Casters, Morris	HSP 5.2.82	Purvis, William	HSP 7.4.82
Clemens, John	HSP 2.3.82	Robinson, James	Chapter 8
Coppock, Peter	BHP 51.177	Sanders, Robert	Chapter 4
Coving, William	HSP 30.4.81	Smith, Andrew	Chapter 4
Davey, Sgt —	HSP 2.3.82	Smith, Charles	HSP 2.3.82
Dougherty, James	HSP 2.3.82	Smith, John	HSP 2.3.82
Dyers, William *	Chapter 1	Tasswell, John	HSP 17.6.80
Ennsle, James	BHP 37, 78	Turner, James	HSP 2.3.82
Fiddiam, John	BHP 29, 320	Turpin, Thomas	HSP 5.2.82
Finn, Henry	BHP 51, 75	Webber, Robert	HSP –.5.79
Flynn, John	HSP 5.2.82	Wheatley, William	HSP 2.3.82
Gray, James	Hald A690, 18.5.80	Wilkinson, Thomas	HSP 2.3.82
Holt, Henry	HSP 2.3.82		
Howarth, Samuel	HSP 5.2.82		

20th FOOT

Baker, Cpl John	BHP 37, 78	Innis, Patrick	Chapter 4
Beatty, William	Chapter 4	Jackson, Sgt John	Chapter 7
Bishop, Henry	HSP 2.3.82	Jones, Timothy	BHP 26, 34
Brophy, Michael	BHP 51, 177	Kennedy, William	HSP 2.3.82

	Reference		*Reference*
Clayton, John	Chapter 8	McDonald, Francis	HSP 2.3.82
Cload, Joseph	Chapter 10	McLoughlin, Henry	HSP 2.3.82
Clog, James	HSP –.12.78	McNamara, Thomas	Chapter 4
Conway, Francis	BHP 26, 34	Miller, Edward	Chapter 8
Dewhurst, John	Chapter 4	Mitchell, Thomas	BHP 51, 177
Edwards, John	Chapter 9	Molton, George	Chapter 4
Flanagan, John	BHP 38, 320	Morris, John	NYL Intel
Floyd, Francis	HSP 30.4.81	Mullen, John	BHP 51, 177
Fox, James	BHP 38, 320	O'Brien, Arthur	NYL Intel
Fulston, James	HSP 2.3.82	Rhoads, John	Chapter 8
Gaskill, William	HSP 2.3.82	Saddler, John ★	Chapter 2
Hall, Thomas	BHP 26, 34	Seals, William	Chapter 4
Hannagan, John	Chapter 8	Slub, Martin	NYL Intel
Hardgrove, William	BHP 51, 177	Stockdale, John	HSP 30.4.81
Hayes, Edward	Chapter 4	Terry, Cpl William	Chapter 4
Howey, William	BHP 51, 177	Thomson, Peter	Chapter 10
		Walker, John	HSP 2.3.82

21st FOOT

Adams, Cpl	HSP 2.3.82	McDonell, Thomas	HSP 8.9.81
Bain, David	HSP 2.3.82	McKay, Alexander	BHP 26, 34
Berry, James	HSP 2.3.82	McLeod, James	HSP 2.3.82
Black, Ian	BHP 51, 177	Mills, Peter	BHP 38, 320
Campbell, Alexander	HSP 5.2.82	Park, James	HSP 5.2.82
Campbell, John	BHP 38, 320	Picard, James	BHP 39, 211
Cockburn, Alexander	BHP 38, 319	Porteus, John	BHP 38, 320
Crookshanks, William	NYL Intel	Robeson, John	HSP 2.3.82
Donaldson, Ian	BHP 51, 177	Robinson, James	HSP 2.3.82
Donavon, Thomas	BHP 38, 320	Shannon, James	HSP 2.3.82
Duke, James	BHP 45, 41	Shannon, Joseph	BHP 26, 34
Ennis, John	BHP 39, 210	Skirvin, Alexander	Chapter 8
Fenton, James	Chapter 7	Smith, Alexander	HSP 2.3.82
Fraser, Alexander	BHP 45, 41	Smith, Alexander	HSP 2.3.82
Fraser, Donald	BHP 51, 177	Sutherland, George	Chapter 10

	Reference		Reference
Fraser, John	HSP 2.3.82	Sutherland, William	HSP 2.3.81
Garrett, James	Chapter 10	Taggart, Drum Maj Robert	BHP 51, 177
Gordon, Peter	Chapter 7	Tark, James	HSP 30.4.81
Hewart, Robert	Chapter 7	Taylor, Theo	HSP 2.3.82
Jameson, David	BHP 51, 177	Thompson, Paul	Chapter 4
Kennedy, Alexander	Hald 21873, 45	Thomson, Daniel	BHP 38, 228
Kerr, Sgt Andrew	BHP 26, 34	Thomson, Donald	BHP 38, 41
Kinnear, James	HSP 2.3.82	Troth, Samuel	Chapter 9
McCormick, David	HSP 2.3.82	Trousdale, Thomas	BHP 8.9.82
McDonald, Rundle	HSP 2.3.82	Young, Thomas	HSP 2.3.82

24th FOOT

	Reference		Reference
Alcock, Joseph	Chapter 8	Major, John	Chapter 4
Annetts, James	BHP 38, 320	Martin, Hugh	BHP 38, 320
Barker, Richard	Chapter 4	McManus, William	Hald 21873
Barrete, Auguste	Chapter 4	Morgan, James	HSP 5.2.82
Bond, James	Chapter 7	Murphy, Sgt Tim	BHP 26, 34
Bush, Will	BHP 45, 33	O'Brien, Cornelius	Chapter 10
Clarkson, Sgt Robert	HSP 5.2.82	O'Brien, Robert	BHP 26, 34
Clews, Jonathon	Chapter 2	Osborne, Alexander	HSP 5.2.82
Driskill, Daniel ★	Chapter 1	Page, Richard	BHP 26, 34
Fox, Ambrose ★	Chapter 7	Page, Robert	HSP 2.3.82
Fox, John Christian ★	Chapter 4	Pocock, Charles	Chapter 7
Fox, Lawrence	BHP 38, 320	Price, William ★	Hald 21876
Hackett, John	BHP 320	Richards, John	HSP 5.2.82
Hale, Benjamin	BHP 38, 320	Saunders, Henry MSA	
		Shaw, John	HSP 2.3.82
Honor, Samuel	HSP 2.3.82	Sherdon, Edward	MSA
		Stephens, Charles	Chapter 7
Hughes, John	Chapter 4	Sylvester, Robert	HSP 2.3.82
Ivery, John	HSP 2.3.82	Trudget, Thomas	Chapter 6
Jones, Daniel	MSA		
Judd, Lawrence	BHP 38, 319	Wilkins, Daniel	BHP 39, 212

	Reference		*Reference*
King, John	HSP 2.3.82	Witterson, Joseph	HSP 2.3.82
Lockhart, John	HSP 2.3.82	Woodwick, Thomas	HSP 2.3.82

29th FOOT

Bishop, William	HSP 2.3.82	McCartney, Sgt Alex	BHP 37, 78
Cameron, John	Chapter 8	Middleton, John	HSP 2.3.82
Davis, James	HSP 2.3.82	Miller, Thomas	HSP 2.3.82
Findlay, Andrew	BHP 37, 38	Munds, William	HSP 2.3.82
Johnson, Isaac	Chapter 8	Quick, Philip	Chapter 7
MacDonald, Sgt John	Chapter 8	Taylor, David	Chapter 4
		Woodrow, Joseph	HSP 2.3.82

31st FOOT

Cameron, Sgt —	BHP 26, 34	Reed, Cpl —	HSP 2.3.82
Donaldson, Charles	HSP 2.3.82	Reeves, Robert	BHP 51, 177
Kelly, Patrick	Chapter 7	Riley, James	Chapter 8
Main, George	BHP 39, 213	Ward, John	Chapter 7
McLaurin, John	BHP 51, 177	Webb, Paschal	HSP 2.3.82
Rann, John	BHP 37, 78	Winters, John	BHP 26, 34

34th FOOT

Bradshaw, James	BHP 51, 177	Keddyswedaw, William	BHP 38, 320
Gallegher, —	BHP 26, 34	Miller, William	Chapter 10
Hopkins, Jeremiah	NYL Intel	Morris, Richard	Chapter 8
		Renshaw, Henry	BHP 37, 78

47th FOOT

Barnsley, Thomas	Chapter 4	Maguire, James	Chapter 3
Clansey, Robert	Chapter 9	Mahon, Andrew	NYL Intel
Cooney, Drummer John	BHP 26, 34	Maloney, Patrick	Chapter 4
Crow, Cpl Joseph	HSP 5.2.82	Mansfield, Robert	Chapter 4
Deering, John	Chapter 4	Mason, William	Chapter 4
Dowling, John	HSP 10.4.81	Moiss, John	NYL Intel
Duffey, Joseph	HSP 2.3.82	Molton, Thomas	HSP 5.2.82

	Reference		*Reference*
Fee, Thomas	Chapter 4	Nagan, John	HSP 2.3.82
Fletcher, Ian	HSP 2.3.82	Nicholson, Sgt Richard	Chapter 9
Fogerty, Cpl William	Chapter 8	Piersall, Thomas	Chapter 4
Forster, Samuel	HSP (undated)	Quarternon, Sgt Thomas	HAS 2.5.82
		Rainsford, Henry	HSP 2.3.82
Frazerly, Thomas	HSP 2.3.82	Robinson, James	Chapter 7
Gault, Crosby	HSP 2.3.82	Shanley, Patrick	Chapter 4
Golding, John	BHP 51, 177	Smith, Bryan	BHP 45, 33
Griffith, Thomas	HSP 2.3.82	Sudders, John	Chapter 4
Halfpenny, John	HSP 5.2.82	Sutherland, John	Chapter 4
Hawley, Charles	Chapter 10	Swindle, Thomas	Chapter 4
Haysworth, Henry	BHP 51, 177	Symester, Thomas ★	Chapter 2
Heslop, William	Chapter 7	Taggart, Sgt W.	BHP 26, 34
Hester, Michael	HSP 2.3.82	Taylor, Thomas	Hald 21873
Hinsworth, Henry	BHP 37, 78	Tiffin, Michael	Chapter 7
Jackson, Thomas	Chapter 4	Warren, William	Chapter 7
Lamb, Drummer Joseph	BHP 37, 78	Watson, John	HSP 2.3.82
Lane, George	Chapter 4	Willington, Samuel	BHP 26, 34
Lynch, Michael	HSP 5.2.82	Woodsides, William	Chapter 8

53rd FOOT

	Reference		*Reference*
Armstrong, Alexander	HSP 2.3.82	McContree, John	BHP 51, 177
Brooks, James	BHP 37, 78	McGann, John	HSP 8.9.81
Carmichael, John	HSP 30.4.81	McGill, William	Chapter 4
Cosgrave, Richard	Chapter 9	O'Brien, John	HSP 2.3.82
Crooks, William	BHP 38, 320	Owens, Joseph	HSP 2.3.82
Dixon, Joseph	Chapter 8	Pew, Richard	BHP 37, 78
Drury, John ★	Chapter 1	Rawlinson, Richard	HSP 2.3.82
Duncan, John ★	Chapter 1	Rogers, George	HSP 19.4.81
Head, William	BHP 38, 320	Smith, John ★	Chapter 1
Holmes, George	Chapter 7	Storer, John	BHP 37, 78
Keyser, Johan	Chapter 4	Strod, Will	BHP 38, 321
Lee, George	BHP 37, 78	Wishart, John ★	Chapter 1
Lipkin, Henry	HSP 5.2.80		

Reference   *Reference*

62nd FOOT

Adams, John	Chapter 4		
Ashurst, Mathew	Chapter 10	Patten, John	Chapter 4
Carr, Volunteer Daniel	Hald 21873	Rivers, John	BHP 38, 320
Craven, —	Hald 21873	Senior, Bart	BHP 37,,78
Cuff, James	Chapter 4	Sims, James	BHP 37, 78
Fish, John	Chapter 10	Spencer, Richard	HSP – – –
Frell, Edward	Chapter 4	Stanton, William	BHP 38, 320
Gake, Samuel	Chapter 10	Stephens, Alexander	BHP 52, 128
Griffin, James	BHP 38, 325	Stradford, Will	BHP 37, 78
Jewell, Edward	Hald A690	Stoddart, John	Chapter 4
Montgomery, Edward	NYL Intel	Stubbs, Cpl John	Chapter 8
Moore, John	Chapter 10	Taylor, Sgt —	HSP 21.12.80
Newinstead, Frederick	BHP 39, 210	Thornton, William	Chapter 4

LIEUTENANT NUTT'S PARTY OF RECRUITS

Allen, William	Chapter 4	Hubbard, Edward	Chapter 4
Fowkes, Samuel	Chapter 8	Pepper, Will	BHP 51, 177
Ginlink, John Frederick	Chapter 10	Weir, Christopher	Chapter 7

Abbreviations Used in Notes, References and Bibliography

AAS	Proceedings of the American Antiquarian Society
ADD MSS	Additional Manuscripts (The Haldimand Papers) Archives,, Ottawa, Canada (originals in BL)
AHM	American Heritage Magazine
AHR	American Historical Review
BHP	British Headquarters Papers (The Sir Guy Carleton Papers) NYPL (originals in PRO 30/55)
BL	British Library, London
CL	William L Clements Library, University of Michigan, Ann Arbor
CMSP	Calendar of Maryland State Papers (The Red Books)
ETHS	East Tennessee Historical Society
HALD	Haldimand Papers
HSP	Historical Society of Pennsylvania, Philadelphia
JCC	Journals of the Continental Congress
JCSV	Journals of the Council of the State of Virginia
JSAHR	Journal of the Society for Army Historical Research
LOC	Library of Congress
MAH	Magazine of American History
MHSJ	Massachusetts Historical Society Journal
MSA	Massachusetts State Archives, Boston
NEQ	New England Quarterly
NYHS	New York Historical Society
NYPL	New York Public Library
PCC	Papers of The Continental Congress, National Archives, Washington DC
PMHB	Pennsylvania Magazine of History & Biography
PRO	Public Records Office, London
RHNJ	Documents relating to the Revolutionary History of the State of New Jersey

SCHS   Sussex County Historical Society, Newton, New Jersey
SECP   Minutes of the Supreme Executive Council of Pennsylvania
VFNHP   Valley Forge National Historical Park
VHM   Virginia Historical Magazine
WMQ   William & Mary Quarterly

References

1. Du Roi 10th Jul 1777: Trevelyan 3, P118/9 quoting Betting Book at Brooks's 29th Jun 1777, London Evening Post 14th Aug 1777 and The Last Journals of Horace Walpole 22nd Aug 1777.
2. Burgoyne (iv): also summarised at Nickerson I, P83 *et seq.*: Anburey 2, P4.
3. Mackesy P224.
4. Nickerson 1, P52/3 says the strategy would have worked: Channing P260/P268 (note): Knepper P4: Anburey 2, P211: Moore 1, P30 quoting New Jersey Gazette 27th May 1778: Nickerson 1, P103: Lamb P144: Burgoyne (iii) P26: Glover P130: Fryer P52/3; JSAHR XVI.
5. Graydon P215.
6. Brandow P103.
7. Sosin P281 *et seq.*: Sexagenery P66: Brandow P95: Lamb P146 records cases where the Indians acted humanely towards enemy.
8. Lamb P145/8 quoting Saunders's News Letter of August 14th 1777: Digby P261/2, Nickerson 2, P183: Lossing P96/101: Channing P266.
9. Burgoyne (ii) P112: Burgoyne (i) 10th, 11th, 24th, 31st Aug 1777: Du Roi P119/127: Nickerson I, P112/3.
10. Burgoyne (i) 18th Jul 1777: Pausch P108.
11. Burgoyne (i) 6th, 16th Aug 1777.
12. MHSJ 1, P352/3: Du Roi P125: Channing P267: Stone (ii) 1, P239.
13. Nickerson 1, P277: Lamb P217 (note): Hudlestone P184: Van Doren P12: Trevelyan 3, P210: Fryer P192.
14. Dabney P7: AHR XXXV, (1930) P542/559: Wilkinson 1, P264. Fryer P79/80: Stone (ii) 1P187 *et seq.*.
15. Pope 16th Aug 1777: Channing P263, MHSJ 1, P357.
16. Du Roi P122: Digby P250/P260/3.
17. Du Roi P122: Burgoyne (i) 17th Aug 1777: Anburey 2, P234/6: Brandow P120.
18. Du Roi P120/7.
19. Burgoyne (i) Aug 21 1777: Du Roi P127: JSAHR P160.
20. Du Roi P126/7: Channing P265: Burgoyne (ii) P21.

21. Pope 13th Sept 1777: Digby P256/267: Brandow P120/1: Stone (i) P40/1, Anburey 1, P240.
22. Brandow P123/6: Digby P266: Nickerson II, P287: Wilkinson 1, P248.
23. Brandow P124: Channing P267.
24. Digby P269: Brandow P138: Stone (i) P42: Hughes P12.
25. BL Addl Mss 21699 19th Jul 1777. PRO CO 42/36 11th Aug/15th Oct 1777. In a later strength return JSAHR XIX, P165/6 shows 153 men of 47th and 135 men of 62nd were captured.
26. BHP V 39, P319/V 29, P244/253.
27. Anburey I, P242: Burgoyne (i) 18th Sep 1777.
28. Ward P505: Brandow P127: MAH II, P692: Wilkinson 1, P236.
29. Burgoyne (i) Sep 19 1777: Tuchman P5.
30. Lamb P158.
31. Brandow P128/P506.
32. Ward P508: Brandow P129: Stone (ii) 1, P240/2 states Wilkinson averred that Arnold did not go on to the battlefield until near the very end..
33. Ward P510: Brandow P129.
34. Hadden 1, PLXXI: Ward P508/511: Brandow P129/131: Lamb159/160: Pausch P135/140: Anburey 1, P242/7.
35. Ward P512,
36. Pettengill P102: Moore 1, P497/8: Anburey I, P251.
37. Ward P512.
38. Pope 20th Sep 1777.
39. Burgoyne (i) 20th Sep 1777: Stone P50: Wilkinson 1, P252/3.
40. Anburey I, P248: Pausch P143: Pope 20th Sep 1777: JSAHR P159. Wilkinson I, P246.
41. Burgoyne (ii) P25: Burgoyne (i) 21st Sep 1777: Stone (i) P50/1: Channing P269: Pausch P150.
42. Lamb P162: Thacher P106: Anburey 2, P21/30.
43. Pausch P149: Digby P277: Burgoyne (i) 23rd Sep 1777: Strach.
44. Stone (i) P52: Pausch P156/8.
45. Burgoyne (i) 3rd Oct 1777: Stanley P158: Lamb P163: Riedesel (ii) P100: Channing P270.
46. Digby P304: Riedesel (ii) P100.
47. Riedesel (ii) P101.
48. JSAHR P160: Burgoyne (i) 6th Oct 1777: Riedesel (ii) P102.
49. Wilkinson 1, P267: Pausch P160: Channing P271.
50. Wilkinson 1, P268: Ward 2, P523.
51. Furneaux P225: Riedesel (ii) P102: Wilkinson 1, P268/9: Lamb P163/4.

Pausch P166: JSAHR P160: Anburey 1, P257: Stanley P161: Hudleston P229: Ward 2, P530/1

52. Mackenzie (ii) Return of Casualties: Pettengill P105: Wilkinson 1, P270: Deering P109.

53. Fortescue 13, P243.

54. Sexegenary P88: Wilkinson 1, P273 claimed Arnold had been drinking freely and exposed himself rashly.

55. Riedesel (i) P53: Thacher P112: Wilkinson 1, P282: Ward P533: Potts 3, P68/P72/3 9th Oct 1777/return dated 14th Nov 1777.

56. BHP V 38P319/V· 29P244/253.

57. Digby P302: Strach: Pettengill P107: Riedesel (i) P54: Lamb P165.

58. Wilkinson 1, P281/2.

59. Wilkinson 1, P285/6: JSAHR LXVIII, P160: Sexagenary P90: Ward P534.

60. Riedesel (ii) P103: JSAHR LXVIII, P161: Stanley P164.

61. Stanley P164: Ward P534: JSAHR LXVIII, P161: BHP V38, P319/V29, P244/253: Anburey 1, P271.

62. Riedesel (ii) P103: Clinton (i) Phillips to Clinton 25th Oct 1777: Anburey II, P272/P347/P513/4.

63. Stanley P167: Channing P272.

64. PRO WO 36/4P10: Riedesel (ii) P104: Clinton (i) from Phillips 25th Oct 1777.

65. Riedesel (ii) P105: Anburey 1, P273/4: Stanley P166.

66. Fraser P54: Wilkinson 1, P298/300.

67. Wilkinson 1, P300/1.

68. Wilkinson 1, P301.

69. Wilkinson 1, P302.

70. Wilkinson 1, P302/3.

71. Riedesel (ii) P107.

72. Hadden 2, P480: Fryer P223.

73. Wilkinson 1, P310/1: Riedesel (ii) P107.

74. Lamb P193/4: Stone (ii) 1P213/P306/7.

75. Burgoyne (iii).

76. Riedesel (ii) P107.

77. Wilkinson 1, P312/4: Sexagenary P114.

78. Wilkinson 1, 314/7.

79. Dabney P12.

80. Clinton Papers 25th Oct 1777.

81. Wilkinson 1, P333.

82. Burgoyne (ii) P56: Burnett P281: Adams 2, P358.

83. Wilkinson 1, P321/2: Sexegenery P115/8: Coleman P279/280: Digby P319/320: Clinton Papers 25th Oct 1777.

84. Sexegenary P119: Anburey 2, P32.

85. Sexegenary P119/121.

86. Sexegenary P122/3: Anburey 2, P2.

87. JSAHR LXVIII, P162: Riedesel (i) P64/6: Sexegenary P124: Anburey 2, P20: Gates 18, P1025: Etting V17.

88. Sexegenary P124/5.

89. Anburey 2, P24/5: Wright P344/5, Stanley P185.

90. Phillips Return 1st August 1779: BHP V38, P319/V29P244/253.

91. Clinton (i) Tryon to Clinton Oct 26 1777: Knepper P19/20.

92. Burgoyne (ii) Second Appendix #X.

93. Washington IX, P378/440/465/469: Sparks 2, P13/4.

94. Adams 2, P357 (note): Knepper P16 quoting JCC IX, P851/P18: Burnett P259/261.

95. Mackenzie (i) 1, P194: Hudleston P220/1.

96. Knepper P26: Hudleston P220/2.

97. Knepper P23/4 quoting The Hessians P181.

98. Knepper P24.

99. PRO CO 42/38 Powell to Germaine 8th Nov 1778: The level of Carleton's relations with Germaine can be judged from correspondence in CO 42/37, see particularly Carleton's two letters to Germaine written 15th and 16th Oct 1778.

100. Ellet 1, P97/8.

101. Knepper P32/3: Dabney P35.

102. Batchelder P18: JSAHR LXVIII, P162.

103. Batchelder P32/3: Lamb P195/6.

104. Anburey 2, P36.

105. Batchelder P33.

106. Ellet 1, P99: Wall P71: Batchelder P17/8.

107. Hadden 2, P329.

108. NEQ XIX, P453.

109. Heath P448: Batchelder P30/P37/9/P41/3/P55/6: Anburey 2, P40: Knepper P31.

110. Potts P115/6.

111. Heath P19.

112. Hadden 2, P337/8.

113. Heath P175: Hadden 2, P337/8: Batchelder P64: Wall P80: Knepper P33: Dixon P212: BHP V9, P49 letter Vallancy to Phillips 21st Jul 1778:

BHP V9, P41 letter Phillips to Heath 12th Sep 1778: Mackenzie (i), P416.

114. Dabney P38.
115. Batchelder P60.
116. Batchelder P62/3.
117. Batchelder P62/3: BHP letter 21st Aug 1778.
118. Knepper P75/6: Phillips Return 1 Aug 1779. Hadden 2, P328/330. Houlding P15.
119. Hughes P79.
120. BHP V38, P319/V29, P244/253.
121. Lamb P253: Hutchinson P206/7.
122. Mackenzie (i) 1, P282.
123. Lamb P388/P396: Anburey 2, P254.
124. Hadden 2, P331.
125. BL Add Mss 21807 Howe to Haldimand May 3 1778: Anburey 2, P254: Lamb P262: BHP See many pay warrants drawn by Captain Handfield paymaster for the absent Convention Prisoners: Mackenzie (i) P702. Mackenzie (ii).
126. Bland 1, P141 from Phillips 3rd Jul 1779: Clinton (i) 25, 25th Oct 1777.
127. Clinton Papers, André Intelligence book: Knepper P77 quoting Burgoyne to Howe 18th Nov 1777, and Howe to Burgoyne 21st Nov 1777.
128. Hadden 2, P331.
129. Washington XI, P73 (note).
130. Washington XI, P73 12th March 1778.
131. Washington XI, P98/9.
132. Washington XI, P180.
133. Haddon 2, P348/9.
134. Washington XI, P320/1.
135. Washington XI, P337.
136. Webb 2, P73/5.
137. Washington XI, P424.
138. Jefferson 4, P193.
139. Washington XXII, P1.
140. Ballantine P12/3.
141. BHP V38, P319/V29, P244/253.
142. Ibid.
143. Ibid.
144. Clinton (iii).
145. BHP V38, P319/V29, P244/253.
146. Fowler P280/1: Maurer P61: Lincoln 6th Nov 1780.

147. Fowler P246.
148. Paullin P238/9. BHP V 38, P319/V 29, P244/253: The British were
    not the only ones to act in this way. Lincoln 5th Feb 1779 describes
    case where 8 American seaman took over a British ship.
149. Ibid: Fowler P87.
150. BHP V 38, P319/V 29, P244/253.
151. PRO WO 1/11, P216: NEQ XVII, P427.
152. Wall P94 quoting The New Jersey Gazette 28th Nov 1781.
153. Anburey 2, P132/3: Curtis P8: Jameson P97.
154. Ballantine P31/2.
155. Clinton (ii) 27th Aug 1779.
156. Clinton (i) 14th Jun 1779.
157. See references to escaped prisoners arriving at St. John's in BL Addl Mss
    21793, 21794 and 21795: Stone (ii), although biased on one side, gives
    details of many of the fights which took place.
158. BHP V 38, P319/V 29, P244/253.
159. Ibid.
160. Ibid: BHP V 39, P210.
161. BHP V 38, P319/V 29, P244/253.
162. Mackenzie (i) 2, P422.
163. Clinton (ii) 8th, 11th, 24th Jul 1778.
164. Clinton (ii) 3rd, 5th Sep 1778.
165. Clinton (ii) 5th Sep, 3rd Oct 1778.
166. Clinton (ii) 4th Nov 1778.
167. BHP P257 Item 1201 Phillips to Clinton 14 Jun 1778.
168. Washington X, P10/13.
169. Webb II, P50/1.
170. Knepper P58/9.
171. Knepper P61/2. Burnett 2, P568.
172. JCC X, P30/5: Heath P130 et seq..
173. Fraser P5 et seq..
174. Knepper P63.
175. Knepper P66: Dabney P18: Burgoyne (ii).
176. Riedesel (i) P143. Knepper P67 (note): Dabney P18.
177. Burnett 2, P596: Knepper P64: Dabney P20.
178. Knepper P65: Trevelyan P220/1. Burnett P262.
179. Sparks 2, P329/30.
180. Howe's letter can be seen in CL. A complete reprint with other notes
    appears in AHR XXXVII, 1932, P721/3.
181. AHR XIII, 1908, P876: Mackenzie (ii).

182. Batchelder P73/4.
183. Batchelder P74/5: Exchange of sailors was approved – see Lincoln 12th Aug 1778.
184. BHP V 9, P20.
185. Batchelder P59/60.
186. Hudleston P270: Pettengill P131: Knepper P74.
187. Hudlestone P270.
188. Dabney P38: Heath P164 letter from Heath to Burgoyne 10th Jan 1778: Hadden 2, P338/9: Pettengill P131: Knepper P155/6.
189. Unless otherwise noted, statements and incidents described are from Henley. This version was taken down in shorthand by a British officer who was present and published by Burgoyne on his return to England. A copy is in LOC. An American version indicates that much stronger language was used by Reeves and others. This version can be found in ETHS Publication #18, 1946, P3 *et seq.*.
190. Heath P171: Washington XI, P320/1.
191. BHP V 38, P319/V 29, P244/253.
192. ETHS Publicatiosn #18, 1945.
193. Burgoyne (v): Heath P171/5: JCC 10, 3rd Mar 1778: Washington XI, P320/1: Glover P131/2.
194. Batchelder P67/9.
195. Heath P177/8.
196. Heath P180/1.
197. Heath P206/9, Washington XII, P517.
198. Heath P170/1/P209.
199. Metzger P262: Clinton (i) 18th Jan 1778: Knepper P119/120.
200. JCC 10, P184: Anburey 2, P124: Wall P83 quoting Heath papers, MHS Collection 7th Series Vol 4, P228: AAS Oct1914, P292.
201. Clinton (i) 18th Jan 1778: Knepper P119/121.
202. Anburey 2, P124: Dann P56.
203. Dabney P45: Anburey 2, P125.
204. Washington XI, P424.
205. BHP V 38, P319/V 29, P244/253.
206. Ibid.
207. Ibid.
208. Ibid.
209. Ibid.
210. Ibid.
211. Ibid.
212. Dann P56.

213. Knepper P137/8. Clinton Papers Germaine to Clinton 2nd Dec 1778.
214. Friends: Graydon P306: Jefferson 2, P31.
215. Anburey 2, P184, 212, 271: Jefferson 2, P125/212 from Harvie 29th Dec 1777/15th Sept 1778.
216. Washington XIII, P119.
217. BHP V 9, P154/6: BHP V 38, P319/V 29, P244/253: Gates 19, P20/2.
218. BHP V 38, P319/V 29, P244/253.
219. Ibid.
220. BL Addl Mss 21793, 18th May 1780.
221. Dixon P217: Knepper P139 quoting Riedesel and Hamilton to Heath 26th Oct 1778: Washington XIII, P208: Metzger P205: Webb 2, P132: Clinton (i) Oct 1777.
222. JSAHR P163: King P13 book 6: BHP V 9, P54.
223. LOC Clinton Intelligence Book: Valley Forge National Historical Park Publication.
224. Bland (ii) from Phillips 30th Sep 1779.
225. Washington XIII, P218/P274/8.
226. Washington XIII, P278/9.
227. Washington XIII, P279/280.
228. Hughes P53/6.
229. CL, Phillips Return 1st August 1779.
230. Coker P2: Jefferson 2, P31 from John Harvie 29th Dec 1777.
231. Lee P40/3: Metzger P161.
232. Lamb P254 *et seq.*.
233. Lamb P288 *et seq.*.
234. BHP V 38, P319/V 29, P244/253.
235. Ibid.
236. Bland (i) I, P108.
237. SECP 11, P626/7, 635/9, 643. Dixon P221/2.
238. Anburey 2, P181.
239. Anburey 2, P183: Dixon P222/3: Washington XIV, P63.
240. Anburey 2, P183: Du Roi P151/2, P157.
241. Anburey 2, P183/4, P 211: PRO WO 1/11 P799.
242. Anburey 2, P184: Jefferson 2, P237 to Patrick Henry 27th Mar 1779.
243. JSAHR P163: Pettengill P150/1: Dabney P62 quoting Virginia Gazette 26th Feb 1780.
244. Madison 1, P279: Dann P238, P345.
245. Jefferson 2, P237 to Patrick Henry 27th Mar 1779: PRO 30/55 P2021 letter 21st May 1779.
246. JCSV II, P250: Washington XIV, P57/8, P164: Anburey 2, P219.

247. Jefferson 2, P486 to President of Congress: JCSV 2, P254: Anburey 2, P186: Bland (i) 1, P158.

248. Anburey 2, P185, P211.

249. PRO CO 42/37 6th Nov 1778: BL Addl Mss 21697 letter to Germaine 10th Jun 1778.

250. Washington 19, P258: Bland (i) 1, P141 letter from Phillips 3rd Jul 1779.

251. Clinton (i) letters Phillips/Gates 1st/ 3rd Dec 1778, Gates/Phillips 3rd Dec 1778, Phillips/Clinton 8th Dec 1778. Gates is defended in VHM 63, P357 article by Bernard Kollenberg.

252. Washington XV, P8/10.

253. Bland (i) 2, P19.

254. VHM 9, P166.

255. Flexner P290.

256. Madison 2, P169: Jefferson 4, P110. PRO WO1/11, P743.

257. Gratz Case 4 Box 10 Phillips to Bland 12th May 1779.

258. VHM 9, P164/5.

259. VHM 9, P166.

260. CL, Phillips Return 1st August 1779: Bland (i) 1, P141.

261. Bland (i) 2, P19.

262. Anburey 2, P211 and 252/3: JSAHR P164.

263. Anburey 2, P253/4: BL Addl Mss 21507 17th May 1780: PRO WO 30/55, P2025.

264. CL Phillips Return 1st August 1779.

265. BHP V 38, P319/V 29, P244/253.

266. Ibid.

267. Ibid.

268. Ibid.

269. Ibid.

270. Ibid.

271. CL André Intelligence Book.

272. Fryer P129/131: BL Addl Mss 21797 letter to Major General Haldimand 26th Apr 1782: NYPL Clinton Intelligence Book 31 July 1778.

273. BHP V 38, P319/V 29, P244/253: See also several mentions by Captain Handfield in BHP.

274. Ibid: Clinton (iii).

275. Sparks 2, P324.letter from Jefferson 17th July 1779.

276. Ibid: Washington XIV, P63/P134.

277. NEQ XXIII, P400: Madison 7, P323 and 408: CL André Intelligence Book 24th Jun 1779: Bradford 4, letter 29th Mar 1781 from David Sproat.

278. Bradford, 18th Jan 1780 from Tim Pickering, War Office, and 29th Aug 1780 from Abraham Skinner.

279. Washington XV, P90/P339: Bland (i) 2, Letter Phillips to Jefferson 3rd Sep 1779.

280. Dixon P228: Lincoln 26th May 1779.

281. Washington 17, P163/4.

282. CL Phillips Return 1st August 1779.

283. PRO 30/55, P2021 Phillips to Clinton 27th May 1779: Bland (i) letter from Phillips dated 25th Apr 1781: VHM 9, P163.

284. Dixon P229.

285. Madison 3, P118 (note) 29th Apr 1781: Jefferson 5, P227/8, P632/3.

286. Sparks 3, P369: Bland (i) 2, P29/31: Gratz Case 4 Box 30 Letter Phillips to Oswald 1st Sep 1780: Hamilton 2, P215 letter from Washington to Jefferson: Ibid P228.

287. Hamilton 2, P268/P275.

288. Jefferson 3, P423: Dabney P69.

289. Hamilton 2, P289/292, P295/301, P308/9, P346, and 26, P382. Much of this correspondence can be found in PRO CO 5/99.

290. Jefferson 3, P449.

291. Jefferson 3, P453/P533.

292. Jefferson 3, P436/P567. Dabney P69.

293. Dixon P230 quoting Lt. Gov Dudley Diggs to Robert Forsythe 17th Aug 1780 Official Letters of Virginia 2, P168/9: Jefferson 3, P581.

294. Sparkes 2, P97.

295. PRO WO/11, P739/767/843/

296. PRO WO/11, P847.

297. JCC XVIII, P842/3: Dabney P71: Jefferson IV, P95/6.

298. Sparks III, P93: Jefferson IV, P72/5, P88, P92, P100/1, P120.

299. Wood says there were 804 other ranks. They probably marched in two groups as Hamilton Vol XXVI, P382 lists 1072 excluding those of the 9th and 47th Foot.

300. Houlding P135.

301. Fryer P168. Some have expressed the view that if the British had ceased regular military offensive operations which finally resulted in the disaster at Yorktown and relied on internal dissension and guerilla war, they would have won the war.

302. Clinton (ii) 18th Jul 1780: CL André Intelligence Book 10th Aug 1779: NYPL Clinton Intelligence Memorandum Book 21st July-10th Nov 1778.

303. Hatch P71: Bakeless P266.

304. Fryer P26/7: Clinton (i) Letter John André to Joseph Stanbury 10th May 1778.

305. Hatch P153/6, P159: PMHB 7, 1883, P389: Bakeless P261.

306. Mackenzie (i) I, P275: Hughes P55.

307. Lamb P254 *et seq.*, P388 *et seq.*.

308. Mackenzie (i) 2, P430.

309. Clinton (iii).

310. Mackenzie (i) 2, P586/7.

311. BHP V 45, P92.

312. BHP V 25, P144.

313. Bakeless P262 *et seq.*.

314. See many references to accused persons in SECP 12/13.

315. Bakeless P163.

316. BHP V 38, P319/V 29, P244/253.

317. BL Addl Mss 21793/21796/21841.

318. Mackenzie (i) 2, P407.

319. Bradford 3, P42 Letter dated 8th Sep 1780..

320. Bradford 4, Letter dated 20th Mar 1781.

321. JCC 27th Feb 1778: Hatch P151: Hazel quoting Memoirs of General John Stark.

322. Moore P30 quoting New Jersey Gazetter 25th Mar 1778: Bakeless P261.

323. Moody: Sussex P58: SCHS, affidavit by Daniel Coxe London 17th Jan 1784: A distorted version of Moody's adventures, written in 1844 appears under Sussex County in Historical Collections of the State of New Jersey by John W. Barber and Henry Howe.

324. NYPL Clinton Intelligence book 13th Sept 1778.

325. PRO 30/55, 1853 (i) /2205.

326. BHP V 38, P319/V 29, P244/253: RHNJ V, P283.

327. Clinton (iii).

328. RHNJ IV, P380/1.

329. Moody: RHNJ IV, P476: Clinton (iii).

330. Moody.

331. Jefferson IV, P95/6. Dabney P71.

332. Anburey 2, P269/270: Jefferson 4, P210/1.

333. Dixon P236.

334. BHP V 38, P319/V 29, P244/253: Madison 3, P320 (note): Dixon P182/6: Gilbert 8th Jun 1781.

335. Washington XXI, P371.

336. CMSP #4 Part 1 #1048: Knepper P210: Dabney P73: Eelking P215: JSAHR P165: Dixon P235.

337. Metzger P122: Mackenzie (i) 1, P222.
338. Wood, from Joseph Crockett dated New Years 1781: Anburey P286: Clinton (i) Wm. Campbell to Phillips 7th Feb 1781.
339. Wood, letter from Joseph Crocket: Dixon P189/191.
340. Etting P71: Wood, letter from Joseph Crocket.
341. JCC 26th Feb 1781 P195/6.
342. JCC XIX, P229/230/P259/263.
343. CMSP #4 Part 1 #1088.
344. JCC 17th March 1781 P274.
345. JSAHR P166: Wood, letter from Colonel Rawlings 24th May 1781.
346. Anburey P294/5.
347. Anburey P291/2: JSAHR P165.
348. Anburey P292.
349. Sparks 2, P122: Stiles: Mackenzie (i) 2, P659: BHP V 38, P319/V 29, P244/253: Eelking P151: Connecticut P191.
350. Laws: Egle 4th series, 2, P301/2: BL Addl Mss 21764, Haldimand to Brigadier General Powell 9th May 1781: PCC, RG360 item 59, vol 2, P355.
351. Tarleton P297: Knepper P 254.
352. Dixon P178: Dabney P76: Wall P95 quoting Washington to Congress 12th Jun 1781.
353. CMSP #4 Part 1, P1068/1094.
354. Egle HBGP 4th Series, 2, Notes and Queries: JSAHR P165.
355. Madison 6, P444 (note) ; Prowell P233. Egle HBGP 3rd series II, P132: JSAHR P165/6.
356. PMHB XIX, P116/8, 1895, letter from Surgeons Mate Benjamin Shield to Brigadier-General James Hamilton 30th Aug 1781: JSAHR P165.
357. BHP V 38, P319/V 29, P244/253.
358. Clinton (iii).
359. Madison 6, P123 (note): Bowie P197: JSAHR P166: Stayer P24: PCC, RG360 item 59 vol 2, P355.
360. Metzger P146/7.
361. Eelking P216/7.
362. JSAHR P166, Lamb P398.
363. Dixon P181.
364. JCC 22, P372: Ousterhout P291/2.
365. NEQ XVII, P299: Madison 4, P130 (note): Dixon P192/3 quoting Secretary Lincoln to President of Congress 3rd Jul 1782 PCC item 149, 1, P481/2.
366. Madison 5, P255/7.

367. Canadian Archive report 1888 Ottawa P575/6.

368. BHP V 42, P280: Eelking P218.

369. BHP V 42, P96.

370. Gilbert 16th May 1783.

371. BHP V 41, P13: JSAHR P167.

372. BHP V 41, P13.

373. Madison 7, P28, P40.

374. JSAHR P167.

375. BHP V 38, P188/P173.

376. BHP V 52, P103, Return from Brigadier General Clarke to General Carleton: BHP V 50, P323, Paymaster Handfield's return 3rd Jun 1783 shows 540, which may have included other invalids or escapees.

377. Mackenzie (ii) undated, (probably late 1781), paper prepared by the paymaster for escaped prisoners.

378. Boards headed by Major Graham (37th) and Lt. Col Gordon (80th) are mentioned without detail in BHP October 1783.

379. BHP V38 #319/V29 #244/253.

380. Mackenzie (ii) Guy Carleton Orderly Book: BHP Provost reports.

381. It is estimated that in all, 45, 000 went to Nova Scotia and 8, 000 overland to Upper Canada. Others went to Great Britain. See various references in Fryer.

382. BHP V38 #25.

383. Addl Mss 21, 873 #230.

384. Belcher 1, P267 makes clear that General Greene referred to German deserters when mentioning British deserters: Lamb P390. Wright P345: Nason: Guinan: Dabney quoting JCC XVI, #913.

385. Fortescue P243.

Bibliography

ADAMS *The Adams Papers,* ed L.H.Butterfield, Series 11, Adams Family Correspondence. 1963.

ANBUREY *Travels Through the Interior Parts of America,* Thomas Anburey. 1923 edn.

BAKELESS *Turncoats, Traitors and Heroes,* John Edwin Bakeless. 1959.

BALLANTINE *Autobiography of an English Soldier in the United States Army,* George Ballantine. 1986 edn

BATCHELDER Paper read January 22 1918 Samuel F Batchelder MHSJ Jan 1918. See also his *Bits of Cambridge History,* Harvard University Press. 1930.

BELCHER *The First American Civil War,* Henry Belcher. 1911.

BLAND—

(i) *The Bland Papers: Being a Selection from the Manuscripts of Colonel Theodoric Bland, Jr.* ed Charles Campbell. 1840.

(ii) Bland Letters (Ms in LOC).

BOWIE 'German Prisoners in the Revolution', Lucy Leigh Bowie, *Maryland Historical Magazine.* 1945.

BRADFORD The Thomas Bradford Papers, HSP.

BRANDOW *The Story of Old Saratoga,* John Henry Brandow. 1919.

BURGOYNE—

(i) *Burgoyne's Orderly Book* ed E. B. O'Callaghan. 1860.

(ii) A State of the Expedition from Canada as laid before the House of Commons by Lieutenant-General Burgoyne. 1780. CL.

(iii) The Substance of General Burgoyne's speeches on Mr. Vyner's motion, on 26th May and Mr. Hartley's motion on 28th May. Printed for J. Almon. 4th ed 1783. LOC.

(iv) Thoughts for Conducting the War from the Side of Canada together with King George III memorandum and Germaine's letter dated 26 March 1777 to General Carleton. CL.

(v) Letter to his constituents from Burgoyne. September 24 1779. LOC.

BURNETT   *The Continental Congress*, Edmund Cody Burnett. MacMillan. 1941

CHANNING   *A History of the United States*, Vol III, Edward Channing. 1912.

CLINTON—

   (i)   Sir Henry Clinton Papers. CL.

   (ii)   Clinton Orderly Book. CL.

   (iii)   Information on Deserters 1780–1781. NYPL.

COKER   Kathy Roe Coker quoting The American Loyalists; Notes on their Organisation and Numerical Strengths by Paul Smith, WMQ 3rd series, 25 April 1968, P 260.

COLEMAN   Eyewitness to Burgoyne's Surrender, Dudley Coleman. MAH Vol 29, 1883.

CONNECTICUT Records of the State of Connecticut Vol 5 (1783/84).

CURTIS   *The Organisation of the British Army in the American Revolution*, Edward E. Curtis. 1926.

DABNEY   *After Saratoga: The Story of the Convention Army,* William M. Dabney, unpublished dissertation University of New Mexico. 1954.

DANN   *The Revolution Remembered*, John C. Dann, VHM Vol 21 P 345. 1980.

DEERING   'How an Irishman turned the tide at Saratoga', James A. Deering, *American Irish Historical Association*, Vol. 10, 1911.

DIGBY   *The British Invasion of North America, Lieutenant Digby's Journal,* ed James Phinney Baxter. 1887 edn, 1970.

DIXON   'Divided Authority; The American Management of Prisoners in the Revolutionary War', Martha Williamson Dixon, unpublished dissertation, University of Utah. 1977.

DU ROI   *Journal of Du Roi the Elder*, ed Charlotte S. J. Epping. 1911.

EELKING   *The German Allied Troops in the North American War of Independence 1776–1783*, Max von Eelking, translated by G. Rosegarten. 1893.

EGLE   *Notes & Queries: Historical, Biographical & Genealogical: Relating Chiefly to the Interior of Pennsylvania*, ed William Henry Egle.

ELLET   *The Women of the American Revolution*, Elizabeth F. Ellet. 1969 edn.

ETTING   Etting Collection, HSP.

FLEXNER   *The Traitor and the Spy*, James Thomas Flexner 1953.

FORTESCUE   *History of the British Army*, John W. Fortescue, Vol. 3.

FOWLER   *Rebels Under Sail: The American Navy During the Revolution*, William M. Fowler Jr. 1976.

FOX   'Corporal Fox's Memoir of Service, 1776–1783', Article by J. A. Houlding and G. Kenneth Yates, JSAHR Vol. LXVIII.

FRASER   *Skulking for the King*, J. Fraser. Boston Mills Press, Erin, Ontario. 1945.

FRIENDS   '*Exiles in Virginia during the Revolutionary War*', Society of Friends, Philadelphia. 1848.

FURNEAUX   *Saratoga: The Decisive Battle*, Rupert Furneaux. 1971.

GATES   Horatio Gates Papers. NYHS.

GILBERT   *Winding Down. The Revolutionary War Letters of Lieutenant Benjamin Gilbert of Massachusetts, 1780–1791*, from original manuscripts in CL.

GLASRUD   'The Use of Indians in the War of the American Revolution; A Re-Assessment of Responsibility', an article by Jack M. Sosin in *Race Relations in British North America, 1607–1783*, ed. Bruce A. Glasrud & Alan M. Smith. 1982.

GLOVER   *General Burgoyne in Canada & America*, Michael Glover. 1976.

GRATZ   Gratz Collection., HSP.

GRAYDON   *Memoirs of a Life Chiefly Passed in Pennsylvania within the Last Sixty Years*, Alexander Graydon. 1822.

GUINAN   *East Granby; the Evolution of a Connecticut Town*, Betty Finn Guinan and Mary Jane Springman. 1983.

HADDEN   *A Journal kept in Canada and upon Burgoyne's Campaign in 1776 and 1777* by Lieutenant James M. Hadden, Royal Artillery; also orders kept by him and issued by Sir Guy Carleton, Lieutenant General John Burgoyne, and Major General William Phillips in 1776, 1777 and 1778. ed by Horatio Rogers. 1884.

HAMILTON   *The Papers of Alexander Hamilton*, ed. Harold C. Syrett, Columbia University Press. 1961.

HATCH   *Major John André; A Gallant in a Spy's Clothing*, Robert McConnell Hatch. 1986.

HAZEL   *Frontier Spies. The British Secret Service, Northern Department during the Revolutionary War*, Hazel & Matthews. 1971.

HEATH   *Memoirs of Major General William Heath, by Himself.* 1798. New edition edited William Abbatt 1901.

HENLEY — Proceedings of a Court Martial, Held at Cambridge, by order of Major General Heath Commanding the American Troops for the Northern District, for the trial of Colonel David Henley, accused by General Burgoyne of Ill Treatment of the British Soldiers, etc. 1778. LOC.

HOULDING — *Fit For Service. The Training of the British Army*, J. A. Houlding. Oxford University Press, Oxford, 1981.

HUDLESTON — *Gentleman Johnny Burgoyne*, F. J. Hudleston. 1927.

HUGHES — *A Journal by Thomas Hughes* (1778–1789), Cambridge University Press. 1947.

HUTCHINSON *The Diary and Letters of His Excellency Thomas Hutchinson, Esq.* Vol. II, ed Peter Orlando Hutchinson. 1886.

JAMESON — 'Musicians at War', Henry Jameson, *Band International*, Vol. 15, November 1993, P97, International Military Music Society.

JEFFERSON — *The Papers of Thomas Jefferson*, ed. Paul Leicester Ford. 1904.

KING — Diary of Alexander King. CMSP Book 4.

KNEPPER — 'The Convention Army 1777–1783', George W. Knepper, unpublished dissertation, University of Michigan. 1954.

LAMB — *An Original and Authentic Journal of Occurrences during the late American War from Its Commencement to the Year 1783*, Roger Lamb. 1809, reprinted 1968 from a copy in NYPL, Arno Press.

LAWS — *Battery Records of the Royal Artillery 1716–1859*, Lt. Col M.E.S. Laws, R.A. Institute, Woolwich.

LEE — 'Stone Walls Do Not a Prison Make', W. Storrs Lee, AHM Vol. 18, 18 Feb 1967.

LINCOLN — *Naval Records of the American Revolution*, Charles Henry, Lincoln. 1906. LOC.

LOSSING — *Field Book of the Revolution*, Vol. 1, B. J. Lossing. 1969 edn.

MACKENZIE—

(i) *Diary of Frederick Mackenzie Giving a Daily Narrative of His Military Service as an Officer of Royal Welch Fusiliers 1775–1781* in Massachusetts, Rhode Island and New York. 2 vols. 1930.

(ii) Frederick Mackenzie Papers 1775–1783, CL.

MACKESY — *The Coward of Minden*, Piers Mackesy. 1979.

MAURER   'Military Justice', article by Maurer Maurer in *Military Analysis of the Revolutionary War*, KTO Press, Millward, New Jersey.

MADISON   *The Papers of James Madison*, ed. Wm. T. Hutchinson & Wm. M. E. Rachal. 1962 edn.

METZGER   'The Prisoner in the American Revolution', Charles H. Metzger, Dissertation, Loyola University. 1971.

MOODY   *Lieutenant James Moody's Narrative of his exertions and suffering in the cause of Government since the year 1776*. 2nd edn, 1783. LOC.

MOORE   *Diary of the Revolution From Newspapers and Original Documents*, Frank Moore, 2 vols. 1860.

NASON   'The Goodwives of Simsbury quoting Superior Court File Papers, Hartford District Divorce Records 1740–1795', Mary L. Nason, unpublished dissertation, Trinity College, Hartford. 1985.

NICKERSON   *The Turning Point of the Revolution or Burgoyne in America*, Hoffman Nickerson, 2 vols. 1928.

OUSTERHOUT   *A State Divided: Opposition in Pennsylvania to the American Revolution*, Anne M Ousterhout. 1987.

PAULLIN   *Navy of the American Revolution*, Charles Oscar Paullin. 1906.

PETTENGILL   *Letters from America 1776–1779*, ed R. W. Pettengill. Houghton Miflin Company. 1924.

PHILLIPS   General Return of the British Troops under the Command of Major General Phillips as they stood on 17th October 1777, at Saratoga, with a return of the present state in Virginia on the 1st August 1779 etc. etc. CL.

POPE   Richard Pope's Book, written by Lieutenant Richard Pope, Ms in Huntington Library, San Marino, California.

POTTS   Papers of Jonathon Potts, HSP.

PROWELL   *History of York County, Pennsylvania*, George R. Prowell. 1907.

RIEDESEL—

    (i)   *Letters and Journals Relating to the War of the American Revolution*, Baroness Frederika Charlotte Luise von Riedesel, translated by William L. Stone. 1867.

    (ii)   *The Memoirs & Military Journals of Major General Riedesel*. ed J. Munsell.

SEXAGENARY *The Sexagenary or Reminiscences of the American Revolution,*
            Anonymous but believed to be by John P. Becker. 1866.
SPARKS   *Correspondence of the American Revolution: Being Letters of*
            Eminent Men to George Washington, 4 vols, ed. Jared
            Sparks. 1853.
STANLEY   *For Want of a Horse: being a Journal of the Campaign against*
            the Americans in 1776 & 1777, Anonymous. ed George
            F. B. Stanley. 1961.
STAYER   'Camp Security: Prisoners of War in York County,
            1781–1783', Jonathan R. Stayer, unpublished honors
            project submitted to the faculty of the History and
            Political Science Department of Messiah College.
STILES   *History of Ancient Windsor.* Stiles.
STONE—
    (i)   *The Campaign of Lt Gen John Burgoyne and the Expedition*
            of Lt Col Barry St Leger, William L Stone. 1970 edn.
    (ii)   *Border Wars of the American Revolution,* William L Stone.
            2 vols. 1843
STRACH   'A Report on the Identity of the Type and Composition
            of the Three Bridges Built on the Hudson River
            between August and September 1777 by the British
            Forces under Lieutenant-General John Burgoyne',
            Stephen G. Strach, 1980. Unpublished paper Saratoga
            National Park.
SUSSEX   *History of Sussex & Warren Counties,* New Jersey. SCHS.
TARLETON   *History of the Campaigns of 1780-81 in the Southern Provinces*
            of North America, Banastre Tarleton. 1787.
THACHER   *Military Journal During the American Revolutionary War,*
            James. A. Thacher, 1862 ed.
TREVELYAN   *The American Revolution,* Part III, Sir George Otto
            Trevelyan. 1907.
TUCHMAN   *The First Salute,* Barbara W. Tuchman. 1990 edn.
VAN DOREN   *Secret History of the American Revolution,* C. Van Doren. 1941.
VIRGINIA   *Journals of the Council of the State of Virginia.*
WALL   'The story of the Convention Army', Alexander J. Wall
            NYHS Quarterly Bulletin Vol, XI, Oct. 1927.
WARD   *War of the Revolution,* Christopher Ward, 2 vols, ed. John
            A. Alden. 1952.
WASHINGTON *The Writings of George Washington,* 39 vols, ed. J. C.
            Fitzpatrick.

WEBB | *Correspondence and Journals of Samuel Blachley Webb*, ed. Worthington C. Ford. 3 vols. 1893 reprinted 1969 from a copy in the Columbia University Libraries, Arno Press, Inc.

WILKINSON . | *Memoirs of My Own Times*, General James Wilkinson. 3 vols. 1816 reprinted 1973 AMS Press Inc.

WOOD | Papers of Colonel James Wood, HSP.

WRIGHT | *The Story of Western Massachusetts*, Harry Andrew Wright, Vol 1.

Index

(An index of escaped Convention Prisoners
can be found in Appendix 5)